BE FREE OR NOT BE FREE

SOCIALIST FREEDOM

A. Y. Ph.D. and S. Y. Ph.D.

WESTBOW
PRESS®
A DIVISION OF THOMAS NELSON
& ZONDERVAN

WestBow Press books may be ordered through booksellers or by contacting:

WestBow Press
A Division of Thomas Nelson & Zondervan
1663 Liberty Drive
Bloomington, IN 47403
www.westbowpress.com
844-714-3454

Scripture quotations taken from The Holy Bible, New International Version® NIV® Copyright © 1973 1978 1984 2011 by Biblica, Inc. TM. Used by permission. All rights reserved worldwide.

ISBN: 978-1-6642-0918-3 (sc)
ISBN: 978-1-6642-0917-6 (hc)
ISBN: 978-1-6642-0919-0 (e)

Library of Congress Control Number: 2020920289

Print information available on the last page.

WestBow Press rev. date: 10/31/2020

CONTENTS

GREAT THOUGHTS FROM GLOBAL LEADERS

Dr. A.Y provides a unique viewpoint on issues of importance to the current political discourse in America, especially as it relates to the issue of socialism from a Christian and Biblical perspective. He was raised in an authoritarian socialist country, and, after completing his theological training in a free country, served for several years as a pastor, evangelist and Bible school leader in another major socialist country before being expelled and coming to America. His first-hand account of his experiences and those of his extended family, friends and ministry colleagues living in a socialist context, and his reflections on the current American political environment, are both provocative and compelling. His insights and analyses provide a valuable contribution to the current American debate about the role of socialism in our nation.

John F. Carter, Ph.D.

Dr. A.Y and Dr. S.Y. have written a very excellent and compelling message to America! The book is written with passion and God given genius! I am stirred to pray like never before for the heart and the soul of this land I love so much and to also sound an alarm that the lion of Socialism is crouching at the door of America! This work is a brilliant expose of the horrors of full-grown socialism from people who have suffered so much at the hands of socialistic government. Every lover of God, America and Democracy, must read this powerful book!

Rev. Tom Anglin

I want to congratulate Dr. A.Y. and Dr. S.Y. on this wonderful work about socialism and detailed analyses of real life in some socialist countries. I could not agree with them more about the limited freedom and many serious violations of human rights in many socialist countries. My family and I also experienced so many of those "socialist commandments" when I was put in various jails for a total period of 10 years and I was under 20 years of strict surveillances in a socialist country until my family and I were deported from that socialist country. This book provides much valuable information to readers about the choice of socialism and the great republic.

Rev. Dr. Paul A.

"Freedom is the heart cry of humanity and should be available to all people regardless of race of color. You will find this book to be a bright light shining through the darkness of false promise of socialism. The writers, Dr. A.Y. and Dr. S.Y., pulls the mask off those with hate and disdain for America. We know the profound phrase, "Know the truth and the truth will set you free." Not only are those words spoken by Jesus Christ, but they are the driving purpose in the writing of this book. Read and know the truth."

Rev. Dr. J. W. Sloan

Please Make Your Decision To Read This Book Until The End!

The Many Victims Need You To Hear Them Out
The Victims Do Not Want You To Fall Into The Same Deceptive Path.
Kindly Help Others Know The Truth By
Making This Book Available to Them.

Many Heartfelt Thanks and Gratitude To the Millions of
Americans and People of The Nations For Receiving and
Embracing the Millions of Victims From Many Socialist Nations
and Regimes and Tyrannies To Your Lands Of Freedom.

Please Note That
Your freedom to read this book is at the expense of the
loss of freedoms and sufferings by millions of people
in socialist regimes, including the writers.

We hope that you would treasure the great freedoms
and the great protection of many human rights
that America and Americans do have.

**Please Send Us Your Stories So We Could
Learn From Your Experiences**
And We Would Share Your Stories In Our Next
Books If You Are Willing To Do So.
nationsrevivals@yahoo.com

SPECIAL APPRECIATION

This book could not be possible without the prayers, encouragements, patience, sacrifices, insights and wonderful support of our parents, spouses, children, brothers and sisters and many family and church members. This is their book, their experiences and their stories and we had the honor to put their stories together. We regret that many of their names could not be listed here now for security purposes.

We are indebted to the many supports, spiritual guidance, love, prayers and blessings of great spiritual leaders around the world and throughout the tough and great years that we do not often express our heartfelt gratitude publicly: Rev. Dr. Paul A. and Rev. Ruth A., Rev. Dr. Nate S. and Rev. Dr. Chris S., Rev. Dr. Richard S. and Rev. Jewel S., Rev. Lawrence K. and Rev. Nettie Y. and our former board members: Rev. Dr. Richard S., Joe T., Mark M., Peter. B., Joshua D., Mary F., and their wonderful families.

We would like to say many appreciations to Dr. John F. Carter, our former excellent professor and President of Asia Pacific Theological Seminary and the Chairman of the Board of Asia Pacific Theological Association for his many academic, intellectual and spiritual investments in our lives. Without his precious critical thoughts, suggestions, advices and insights, the coherence of this book could not be possible. Thanks a lot also to Ma'am Bea Carter for your love, cares, supports and many prayers.

We would also appreciate Dr. David S. Lim, the President of the Asian School for Development and Cross-cultural Studies and the President of China Ministries International-Philippines, for his great academic insights on the subject matter of socialism that greatly challenged the writers to develop greater thoughts and discussions on socialism and the current situations.

We would like to express our many gratitude to special people and their family members for their wonderful fellowship, generous support, great encouragement, bountiful care and love, and constant prayers: Rev. Dr. Mark D. and Dinh N., Joseph F. and Mary Y., John D. and Kitty D., John, Matthew and Mary, Rev. David K. and Tram U., Bang T. and Loc D., Mindy N., Henry T. and Moon T., Rev. Jessie C., Stephanie P., Don N. and Phuong N., Thomas L. and Jenny L., Kathryn and Steve G., George L. and Orchid H., Tiffany D., Tan H. and Hannah Mom, Alex H. and Megan Mom, Rina B., Lisa L., Vinnie T., Hally T., Chau P., Chi H., Christine N., Vicky N. and Steve H., and many others.

This book could not be better and more beautiful without the many diligent and creative works of WestBow Press, a division of Thomas Nelson and Zondervan and staffs in their design, editing, marketing and distribution of this book and to make this book available readers worldwide. Thanks a lot to Eric Schroeder, the Senior Publishing Consultant, Joe Anderson, the coordinator of WestBow Press, Tim Fitch, Publishing Services Associate and Lucas Biery for content evaluation and many other staffs.

Most of all we would like to give thanks to our Loving and Almighty God for all of His wisdom, blessings, protections and providences. Thank You, Lord, for Your many strengths, inspirations, thoughts and guidance throughout the process. Thank You, Lord, for the many healings, deliverances, renewals, reflections, and powerful touches. Lord, may You also bless every reader and their family members abundantly and may You bring healings, miracles and peace to every home.

BE FREE OR NOT BE FREE: AN INTRODUCTION

Pastor Bill came and visited Christians in a socialist country and he was arranged to preach at an underground church on a Sunday morning. I went to pick him up at the hotel and we went to the meeting place. As normal, we just drove around first to see if there was any "tail" following us before we headed to the meeting place. Then Pastor Bill and I entered the house church as believers were worshiping.

He was about to preach and suddenly the policemen rushed into the room. The policemen were so happy to "catch such a big fish" because they would make a great report and they would have a great record for promotion due to the arrest of a counter-revolutionary group of people and their connection with a Westerner. Pastor Bill was a Westerner and the great thing was they caught him on spot.

In the early day, due to the political issues, the ideological differences, the wars and the tense diplomatic relationship between the Soviet-type socialist nations and the Western world, foreigners and especially Americans were not welcome here. Westerners were often suspected as the agent of CIA who came to manipulate the local people and indoctrinate people with corrupted ideology of capitalism.

Capitalism and capitalists were not really welcome to the socialist nations, which were not very opened to Westerners particularly in the early day. This was simply because capitalism and capitalists were seen as the enemies and rivals of socialism and socialists and they were considered the exploiters of the poor and the causes of the poor's sufferings, unstable jobs, social inequalities and wealth gap.

The capitalists and the socialists were also the enemies and rival in real wars. The capitalists wanted to overthrow the socialist leadership in the name of freedom and human rights while the socialists wanted to overthrow the capitalists for the sake of equality and prosperity. Due to the war experiences and different ideologies, the socialists were skeptical about the activities of Westerners in the socialist lands.

Westerners were also closely watched by the authorities because the Soviet-type socialists often suspected that the ultimate purpose of many Westerners in coming to the socialist nations was to connect to their allies and to stir up the political revolution against the socialist government. So the secret connection with Western people was also considered as dangerous and suspicious activities.

Sometimes, the abbreviation of the word "C.I.A" by Christians and interpreters also pose some troubles because the socialist authorities did not take "CIA" as Christian International Association or Churches In Actions but Central Intelligent Agency. The wrong use of words by the speakers and the suspicious interpretation of the words by the authority also caused persecutions due to misunderstanding.

Foreigners are now welcome to the socialist countries for businesses, investments, trades, cultural, technological and educational exchanges, but Western influences are still strictly monitored in social, educational and religious settings. Western thoughts, news, politics, educations and religions are not really welcome in socialist countries because socialism does not welcome capitalism and other ideologies.

Many foreigners may not feel the restrictions in modern socialist countries, as they are free to do businesses, to communicate, to travel, to marry local people. Most foreigners are treated differently from the local people due to trade, cultural and diplomatic relationships. Foreigners may be forgiven for the "mistakes" they made but that is not so with local people whose freedom and rights are restricted.

Foreigners could have international church services and they could do charity works in local communities. They may attend religious services at places of worship approved by the government. Local people are not allowed to join these international services, a government officer will be there during church services to check someone's passport if he or she suspects the attendant is a local citizen.

When foreigners get closer to local people and their activities they would feel much the presence of the authorities and the monitoring of the government. How many foreigners could safely stay in the soviet-type socialist countries when they publicly defend the human rights, the political right or the religious right of local people or criticize the government, leaders and policies? Maybe this is once in a blue moon.

Foreigners are not allowed to join places of worship that are not approved by the government. They are forbidden to conduct Bible study group or a prayer group with local people. If they do, that is illegal. In fact, most foreigners who work in some socialist countries know that they are not allowed to do so because those guidelines on religious practices are written in their working contract when they signed it.

As the policemen rushed to the balcony of this unregistered service to call more policemen to come up, I saw an opportunity to escape. So I grabbed the hand of Pastor Bill, he understood and responded quickly as we rushed out of the door and running down the staircases. Pastor Bill and I made the move so fast and we could get out of the apartment building before other policemen entered the building.

Pastor Bill and I quickly got on the motorcycle and we rode away. The policemen on the third floor of the apartment where we were at, saw us riding the motorcycle away, so they shouted and called other policemen on the ground to chase after us. We rode so fast on that day but the policemen were also very fast. We need to cut the "tail" as soon as possible or else they would get us soon.

So we quickly rode into an area where there were many small roads and shortcuts so we could easily cut them off. As usual, we made it and I took Pastor Bill back to the hotel safely. I still could not imagine how was it possible for Pastor Bill to sit well and tight in that small motorbike. I did not remember if he grabbed hard my shoulders or if he squeezed my neck during that fun and unforgettable escape.

For security we had to say goodbye quickly so I did not have a chance to ask him how did he feel when he saw the policemen came in? How did we jump the stairs from the third floor to the ground floor that quick and it must be a miracle then that our legs were not twisted? I wondered how was it possible for him to sit well in the motorbike when I made so many swerves through the corners to cut the tails?

We were among the blessed people who were free from the many pursuits, arrests and persecutions of the socialist authorities then but millions of people did not and still do not have many opportunities to free themselves from the tight grips and the merciless hands of the Soviet-type socialists. People's thought, communications, speeches, behaviors, travels and lives were and are still under socialist control.

Of course, no one likes to be monitored and no one likes his or her freedoms and rights to be limited and censored but how many people could avoid the monitoring of a socialist regime? The autonomy, monopoly and the sovereignty of socialism lead to the scrutiny of ideas that are not supporting or against the socialist ideology, the brutal suppressions of demonstrations for peace, justices, and human rights.

Before the socialists came into power, the socialists propagandized that common people had no freedom, properties and wealth under the former government so people could never change their future, destiny and social status because they were under the control of the greedy and rich people. The socialists called for a political revolution to abolish the social classes and the inequalities among the people.

The socialists promoted that the strength of socialism was in the collective and shared power of the people but that power was in the hands of the capitalistic elites or the bourgeoisies. The elites manipulated the powers and thus the proletariats were oppressed and were the victims of the elites' abuses of power, and people had no freedom. So people must fight against the elites to get their power back.

In addition, the private ownership of lands, properties, businesses or corporations were to be abolished or monitored because private ownership led to the exploitations of workers by the owners, the gap between the rich and the poor, and the social classes. This led to inequalities, unhappiness and oppressions. Only social ownership could make the shared wealth and shared power available to people.

The idea sounded fabulous to many common people as no one wanted to be exploited and it really hurt when other people had better living conditions, more wealth, and greater opportunities than the others did. The socialist idea touched the human needs of being equal and the desires of sharing wealth. The socialist idea seemed to release human burdens from poverties, debts and many pressures.

At those fabulous ideas and sound promises of socialism, people in millions across 40 former socialist nations responded to the call for political revolution and they succeeded to overturn the power of the capitalistic elites and to establish the new socialist countries. The people fought hard for the ideology that called for freedoms, shared power and shared wealth, did they or do they receive what they fought for?

Unfortunately, what the socialists promoted in those countries and what they have been praising in the U.S. is just one side of a coin. They painted great pictures and beautiful prospects of a socialist utopia that was unrealistic and has never been realized. Sweet honey really kills flies and hundred millions of people across the continents were really bound, destroyed and killed by socialism and the socialists.

The American socialists only talk about and promise the appealing benefits of free education, healthcare, stable jobs, free of debts, and great social benefits. Do they reveal the rampant failures, injustices, corruptions, and abuses of power in the socialist countries? Do they talk about the costly prices or the devastating consequences or the chronic nightmares of that ideology? Of course they don't.

Just like Prof. Richard Wolff and liberal professors who believed and were indoctrinated with the thought that the economic system of socialism really promotes freedom, equality, prosperity, justice and democracy, many Americans are now indoctrinated with the beautiful and glorious vision of the U.S. as a powerful democratic socialist country with wealth that common people may enjoy equally.

Americans and nations have been taught that capitalism has many flaws and issues in creating an egalitarian society. The people are told that capitalism has led to corruption, unstable jobs, the gap between the rich and the poor, and restriction of freedoms. The news repeatedly confirms that capitalism fails and is already dead. And American socialists are now calling for new political revolution and changes.

Americans and nations are indoctrinated and challenged by mainstream media and the leftist politicians to believe that socialism is a higher form of government than that of capitalism and thus socialism must be a better government to fix the many issues that capitalism cannot do. The socialists cannot wait to apply the socialist ideology and agenda at the curiosity of millions of people who are also eager for it.

Sen. and Socialist Bernie Sanders spoke at Georgetown University in 2015 that, "And in my view, the billionaire class, must be told loudly and clearly that they cannot have it all, that our government belongs to all of us, not just a handful of billionaires. But this goes beyond politics. We need to create a culture, an entire culture which, as Pope Frances has reminded us, cannot just be based on the worship of money."

"We must not accept a nation in which billionaires compete as to the size of their super yatches while children in America go hungry and veterans, men and women will put their lives on the line to defend us sleep out on the streets. Today, in America, we are the wealthiest nation in the history of the world. But few Americans know that because so much of the new income and wealth is going to the people on top."

He emphasized, "In fact, in the last 30 years, there has been a massive redistribution of wealth. Problem is, it has gone in the wrong direction. In the last 30 years, we have seen trillions of dollars flow from the hands of working families in the middle class to the top 1/10 of 1%. A handful of people, top 1/10 of 1% who have seen a doubling of the percentage of the wealth that they own during that period."

Sen. Bernie Sanders and the socialists successfully convinced millions of Americans that America could not accept the fact and cannot be the country that the 1/10 of 1% of the top rich owned as much wealth as the bottom 90%. This fact is strong enough to persuade people that there is a real economic inequality and that the rich Americans are greedy and are not willing to share their wealth to the poor.

So Sen. Bernie Sanders called Americans to create a new socialist culture to replace and eliminate the failed capitalism and the wealthy, corrupted capitalists that only worship money and profits, with socialism and the great socialists for equality and freedom. He called for a socialist culture with social ownership and big government where wealth and social benefits are going to be equally distributed to the people.

He called for a socialist government that would belong to the people and protect the people but not a group of the elites or billionaires. He called for a socialist country that would care for the poor and the underprivileged people so that there would be no one to go hungry, homeless and to be exploited. The call of the socialists seemed to be great and people responded as it met the desires of the people.

Yet, the call of Sen. Bernie Sanders and the American socialists failed and was not realized at the end of his 2020 presidential campaign. But that call for equality, caring government, wealth distribution, prosperity, replacement of the failed capitalism and the greedy capitalists, and freedom is now turning into actions with nationwide demonstrations, protests and riots, and extreme violence in the U.S.

What is the truthfulness of that call of the socialists? The reality proved the socialist culture is always short-lived, disastrous and it has never been sustainable even in the current socialist countries and the former ones in more than one-century of the socialist existence. The longer the socialist culture lasts in a country, the more the people experience the limited freedom, oppressions and losses of human rights.

American socialists call Americans to establish a socialist government that does belong to the people and not the handful of billionaires. Is it true that the socialist government does belong to the people or does it belong to corrupted, greedy and wicked socialist elites? Why do the socialist countries are always listed among the top countries with oppressions, injustices and violations of human rights?

American socialists call Americans to create a socialist culture that is not based on the worship of money. It is interesting to note that the socialists call Americans to fight for wealth distribution and economic equality and this call is obviously profit and material oriented, so how is it possible for the socialists to not worship money or material things when this is their real intention? They indeed yearn for wealth.

American socialists call for a new socialist culture where children would not go hungry. The truth is hundred thousands of children died in the socialist nations due to poverty and are still struggling for daily foods while American children throw foods away. American children are offered with free foods if needed while millions of poor children are struggling to pay for meal fees at schools in socialist countries.

American socialists call for a new socialist culture to replace the greedy capitalists who do not share their wealth to the poor and needy people. How many socialist millionaires and billionaires are sharing wealth in the socialist countries and around the world? They only corrupt and exploit people's wealth and national wealth. The truth is the capitalist philanthropists could be found everywhere around the world.

American socialists call for a new socialist culture to change the situations where capitalism and the capitalists are the causes of the homelessness and the sufferings of the veterans, men and women who put their lives on the line to defend America and Americans to sleep out on the streets. Why is this not the failures of the democratic leaders, the leftists, their inability and corruption in their own states?

American socialists call for a new socialist culture to replace the failed capitalism in creating wealth and equalities. This is one of the biggest lies of the socialists as there is no socialist country that is able to survive and sustain with the socialist economic system. The current socialist countries must apply the capitalistic economic system to revive their economy and their counties while putting blames on capitalism.

American socialists call for a new socialist culture to make people happy with many free social benefits. Is it true that the socialist culture would offer better benefits and happiness than the capitalistic culture? That is just a beautiful dream and it is forever a great dream of people in the socialist countries. Why do millions of people from the socialist countries are still finding way to go to the U.S. and free countries?

American socialist call for a new socialist culture to offer great wealth and economic equality. Is it true that the socialist culture could offer better economic equality than the U.S. does? Or is there any socialist country that could do that better than the U.S. does? Why do the nations always send relief packages and financial help to many socialist countries if the socialist countries are really wealthy?

Americans would find out that wealth gap is obvious in Sen. Bernie Sanders' perfect countries of the Scandinavia and it is even more obvious in all socialist nations. Millions of workers in the U.S. could afford to purchase their houses at the "greed" of the capitalist billionaires while millions of workers in the socialist countries could hardly pay the rent at the "equality" of the socialist billionaires, leaders and elites.

Americans would soon re-realize that thanking to the Christian teachings, practices and influences, American culture and Western cultures that have been strongly influenced by Christianity, offer better cultures of economic opportunities, wealth distribution, benevolences, social welfares, appreciation of human values, respect of human rights, and exercise of freedoms than any socialist nations could do.

Americans would soon find out that the American government does belong to Americans more than it does to the people in socialist countries. In the socialist countries, the government did and does belong to the political party and the socialist leaders. The socialist government does protect the political party, the ideology and the socialist leaders more than the will of the common people.

Americans would see that social justices are hundreds of times better done to Americans in the U.S. than it is done to the citizens of the Soviet-type socialist nations. Annual reports of international humanitarian agencies and justice agencies always prove the fact that injustices, oppressions, violations of human rights, and limited freedom are now rampant in all the Soviet-type socialist countries still.

Americans would soon conclude that Americans share more wealth than people in the socialist nations. Americans bless nations of the world more than people in the socialist countries could do. Majority of Americans are above the poverty lines while the majority of people in socialist countries are still under poverty lines. The wealth gap in the socialist countries is even wider than the wealth gap in America.

Americans would soon realize that the rich in the capitalist country like America make million lives in America and around the world to be stable, rich, equal and comfortable while in socialist countries, the small groups of socialist leaders control and corrupt the wealth of the nation. The socialist leaders are filthy rich but leaving millions of people in unemployment, poverty, miseries and gloomy future.

Americans would soon know that the wealth of the socialist leaders, their children and family members in socialist countries are corrupted and transferred into the hands of the greedy socialist leaders at the sufferings and injustices of millions of people. The sharing of wealth in socialist countries is a familiar concept but still a distant reality, yet the exploitation of people's wealth is a common practice.

At the current, American socialists did not tell Americans the truth that, "Socialism and its twin partner communism cannot be separated, and in fact socialism has its modern roots in the *Communist Manifesto*. It was there that Karl Marx and Friedrich Engels laid the blueprint for a type of socialism that called for total social change and class warfare" according to Michael E. Telzrow on New American.

American socialists did not tell Americans the truth that socialism failed in all countries where socialism was applied. It failed in former Soviet Union. It failed in Eastern Europe. It failed in East Germany. It failed in Asia. It failed in Africa. It failed in South American. Is there any logical reason that socialism would be successful in America when it only created inequalities, sufferings, injustices and wealth gap?

American socialists did not tell Americans that the people in socialist countries and former socialist countries also received those nice and similar promises before. Unlike Americans, those people not only experienced those empty promises but they also experienced the painful truths of socialism and the oppressions of greedy and cruel socialists who promised glory and equality, but tragedies are the endings.

American socialists did not tell Americans that the persecution, oppressions and the losses of many freedoms were the main reasons why so many people were and are willing to run away from socialist countries. The escapes were not fun and easy but were risky and dangerous and the people must face with many deadly situations and horrible consequences but they risked their lives for the freedom call.

Their freedom of speech is speechless and is forbidden to say anything about the failures and bad policies of socialism. Their freedom of press is the oppression and pressures toward people who raised their voices against the cruelty and impossibility of socialism. Their freedom of peaceful gathering is the suppression and tortures of peacemakers, politically freedom fighters, and human right activists.

Their freedom of trials by the jury is to be trialed according to the will and the dictates of the socialist leaders. Their freedom to pursue happiness is only confined in the prospect of the socialist ideology and the political party. Their freedom of religions is limited and persecuted at the will of the socialist leadership. Their freedom for life is to obey the commands of the socialist regime.

The nations have seen the great and massive exodus of millions of people from socialist countries in decades. Whether these people were running from Europe, Asia, Europe or Latin America nations such as Cuba, El Salvador, former Soviet Union or Venezuela, they all run for life. The people of the socialist countries were and are still running away from the socialist countries due to the tyrannies.

These were the reasons why people of the free worlds witnessed the great exodus of millions of the socialist victims to run for their lives from the socialist regimes and tyrannies to American and many free nations. These reasons were the real struggles for millions of people in the past and it is still the struggles of millions of people today to make such a decision to flee from the current socialist nations.

Though the economic situations in some socialist countries are getting better now but freedoms will never be possible to people. If the government and the socialist leaders loose their power, they could not control people any longer and they could not enjoy their excessive power and corrupted wealth. The people would execute the leaders because of the many crimes against humanity that the leaders did.

Even the young generations who were born and grew up in the socialist countries and they were indoctrinated so well with the socialist ideology that they used to be very obedient and submissive to the party and the socialist leaders. Now, they were enlightened by the recent oppressions of the peaceful gatherings. They fought against the socialist powers but they failed because they are still weak then.

The people long to take over the country as soon as possible because they now understand what is the meaning of real freedoms after so many years of being manipulated, indoctrinated, dreamed, deceived, oppressed and coerced. How long do the struggles of powers last? History showed that no socialist country could last more than a century. So, it still takes a few more decades for people to suffer then.

Ironically, millions of Americans now want to start that vicious-decades-cycle of socialism when so many countries already got rid of it and million people in the few remaining socialist countries are now fighting hard to get out of the oppressive regime of socialism and the brutal socialists. Ironically, million Americans still choose to follow the socialist deception that killed and trapped millions of people.

You may react, "Wait, that is not the socialism that the Democratic Socialists of America and American socialists are proposing to America and Americans." It is the Soviet type of socialism that the DSA and American socialists are working hard to make it to happen but they purposely do not want to make it clear to Americans and people of nations yet. However, their agendas and actions speak louder about that.

Most people only pay attention to the great promises and the free offers of the socialists. They may be excited at the call for the political revolution and even cultural revolution to carry out socialist agenda but they may not realize the ultimate goals that most socialists want to accomplish through their half-truth disclosed agendas: big government, social ownerships and elimination of capitalism.

Sen. Bernie Sanders did not explain much about the type of the socialism that he wanted to achieve except stating that he is a democratic socialist. He explained his socialism more through his freebies, better wages and wealth distribution. The DSA makes it clearer that they want to carry out social ownership and to replace capitalism and the capitalists or the wealthy people and their corporations.

The Green New Deal would require big government to make it to happen and it requires central planning, social ownerships of corporations and major industries. It would not be difficult to conclude that the type of socialism that American socialists are aiming for is the Soviet type of socialism with strong emphasis on big government, social ownership of businesses and equal wealth distribution.

The socialists would argue that even American socialism shares the major characteristics of the Soviet socialism but it is a democratic one and not a repressive socialism. History proves that, "For most of its history, the USSR was a highly centralized state" stated Wikipedia on Republics of the Soviet Union. Americans now witness this repressive socialism in their own land through their recent riots.

The Union of Soviet Socialist Republics marked its characteristics of Soviet-type socialism with its oppressive leadership, big government, social ownership, violation of human rights and limited freedom. It was once the nightmare of the nations and millions of its hopeless citizens in the former socialist republics. Its history was tainted with countless stream of blood of million innocent people.

Whether it is the Soviet socialism, green socialism, democratic socialism or whatever socialism, when the socialists are in power, oppression would surely take place. Our books, "**The 12 Commandments of Socialism**" and "**The Boat of Destiny**" explain more experiences and the characteristic of Soviet socialism that American socialists naïvely want to make it to happen to Americans and in America.

The recent riots and violent protests by the leftwing democrats, communist leaders, trained Marxists, socialists and anarchists who looted stores, destroyed businesses, burnt communities, promoted lawlessness and murdered innocent people across the U.S., would prove the truth and the fact that the new socialist culture that American socialists are calling for would not make America a better place to live.

That new socialist culture shows the violent nature, the abuse of power, and the inequality of races. That new socialist culture shows nightmares, fears and the big loss of precious freedom. That new socialist culture shows the ungodly nature, the new ruthless regime, and the deception of wicked government. That new socialist culture shows the greed for power, control and wealth. Those are the real facts.

That new socialist culture shows clearly that when these communists, Marxists, socialists and the radicals were to take over the U.S., more horrible things would take place. That new socialist culture shows the serious violations of human rights. The brutal attacks, shootings and murders of innocent people are now rampant wherever the riots and the protests take place. Do Americans need this culture?

These protests, riots and violence that have been taking place since the death of George Floyd on May 25, 2020 obviously show the many characteristics of the Soviet-type socialism or the repressive socialism. **First of all**, these events reveal the oppressive leadership that is very controlling, coercive and demanding. Many leaders and members of the riots are very brutal, violent and merciless.

Mainstream media always show on the news that the protests are peaceful and the protesters are unarmed and unharmed. The mainstream media are projecting great images and great impressions about these peaceful protests and demonstrations as the great causes for social justice and freedom. Yet when it is an oppressive leadership, the results are always destructive, hurtful, violent and deadly.

Their lootings of stores, car smashing, defund of police, harms to others, violence, raping of ladies, burnings of cars, houses, churches and communities, shootings, hurting and killing of children and murders of policemen and innocent people would be enough to show the oppressive and militant leadership of the Soviet-type socialists and radicals, the anarchists and angry mobs, the Marxists and communists.

Gun shootings, violence and the number of deaths have been increasing significantly in Chicago, Georgia, Minneapolis, New York City, Ohio Seattle and many democratic states and cities as lawlessness takes over the cities when police forces are defunded and disbanded. Local residents are living in fear, yet the leftwing leaders, mayors and governors still side with the rioters and criminals for more tragedies.

Secondly, leaders and members of the riots are now revealed as the trained Marxists and communists through their Black Lives Matter and Antifa organizations. They are not just the democratic socialists but extremists and radicals. They mobilize Americans for political and cultural revolutions. They also call the government to fulfill their demands or else they would destroy America system.

They demand the defunding of police and even the elimination of the police task forces. They demand the eliminations of prisons. They demand the releases of all prostitutes. They demand wealth to be shared to the poor. Their initial demands already show that they want to destroy peace and order of America and create a society that is filled with fears, uncertainties, insecurities, lawlessness and violence.

Chanelle Helm, the leader of Louisville, Kentucky's branch of BLM challenged Americans to fight white supremacy and to fund black and brown people and their work. White people should "give up the home you own to a black or brown family" reported Mark Megahan on Right Wing News. Yet the victimized and murdered white people are considered racists and are being attacked for being white.

They demand socialism to take over the U.S. of course and they thought that socialism could solve the issues of inequalities, wealth gap, guaranteed jobs, happiness and prosperities. Yet, Americans and people of the nations start to see destructive and disastrous things happening. These are the things that Soviet-type socialism and socialists are the experts to provide to people for more than a century.

Thirdly, the riots and violence also show the oppressive nature of the Soviet-type socialism toward freedom of press, of speech, and of religions, and human rights. Once the socialists are in power, they would silence people, threaten people and take the many precious rights away from people. They would torture, imprison or even kill people who are against the socialist ideology, party and leadership.

In recent riots, many people were humiliated, brutally beaten, as they believe and declare, "All Lives Matter" or "White Lives Matter Too." Yet these people were not allowed to show their belief and freedom or they might be threated, beaten, and they were fired from their jobs or even murdered. The mobs freely destroyed monuments, statutes, places, people and history in the name of Black Lives Matter.

The murder of Jessica Doty Whitaker on July 5, 2020 was a case in point of the loss of free speech and loss of life when the U.S. were to be under the reign of the radicals and Soviet-type socialists. Jessica was shot death after saying "all lives matter." She was only 24 year-old and leaving behind an innocent three-year old son and grieving parents and a brokenhearted fiancé reported Fionnuala O'Leary.

Fourthly, the recent riots and violence also prove the sad fact that so many leftwing democratic leaders, politicians and the leftists are working closely with the socialists, trained Marxists and communists at the sacrifices of so many lives. They are betraying Americans and American values for their political games and gains. They are willing to make America a socialist nation, a Soviet-type state at any cost.

Many governors and mayors are willing to let the radicals, the mobs, the anarchists and the violent socialists to take over cities and states. They easily comply with the many ridiculous, illogical and immoral demands of the socialists, Marxists, communists and even terrorists in opposing to the will of the majority of Americans. They even praise the lawlessness and destruction in the name of freedom.

The "far-left Chicago Major Lori Lightfoot has ordered Chicagoans not to use guns to defend themselves even though the city has descended into lawlessness and chaos in recent weeks under her leadership" reported Baxter Dmitry on News Punch. Many leftwing governors and mayors also allow their states and cities to be in great messes with so many burning, riots, lootings, shootings and killings.

Fifthly, the riots also prove the socialist demands for social ownership and big government. The socialists and mainstream media filled the people's mind with the thought that the U.S government is no longer for the people but for the benefits of the few billionaires, so people must take over the current government and the socialist government would protect the benefits and wellbeing of people.

The socialists attract people with the thoughts that when the socialists are in power, the socialist government would take over the modes of production and the means of distribution, the Americans would share wealth equally from the shared profits, which go to the pockets of elites in capitalism. With the socialist government, people would have their shares and their voices in the decision-making process.

Readers would soon discover that the major characteristics of socialism on big government and social ownership are also the major reasons for the rampant oppressions, abuses of power and corruptions that have been taking place for decades. These characteristics also lead to the limited freedoms, serious violations of human rights, injustices and sufferings of millions of people in socialist countries.

Sixthly, the riots also show another major characteristic of Soviet-type socialism and that is elimination of capitalism. The socialists declare their hatred toward capitalism and the capitalists. This is because the capitalists are considered the people who exploit the poor people for their wealth. The capitalists are the main causes of people's poverty, sufferings, unstable lives and economic inequalities.

The mobs, the radicals and the socialists loot many businesses and stores and rob people. Now they also demand white people and rich people to vacant their houses and give their houses to the poor African Americans. They will soon take over the properties, corporations, businesses and even lives of the capitalists and the billionaires as they did so in so many former socialist countries before.

Recently, after the Sunday looting in a business downtown in Chicago, "Black Lives Matter protesters gathered outside the South Loop police station Monday night to show support for more than 100 individuals who were arrested during the looting Sunday night" reported Jessica Chasmar. The logic for looting is that their futures have been looted from them so it is time to loot back as a way of reparations.

Ariel Atkins, a BLM leader stated clear that, "I don't care of someone decides to loot a Gucci or a Macy's or a Nike store, because that makes sure that person. That makes sure that person has clothes. Anything they wanted to take, they can take it because these businesses have insurance." These looters just do not want to go to work but loot to make them happy at the sufferings of others.

Kshama Sawant said, "Because we are coming for you and your rotten system. We are coming to dismantle this deeply oppressive, racist, sexist, violent, utterly bankrupt system of capitalism. This police state. We cannot and will not stop until we overthrow it, and replace it with a world based, instead, on solidarity, genuine democracy, and equality: a socialist world. Thank you" reported Ian Schwartz.

This call also happened in so many former socialist countries and sadly millions of millennials and innocent people believed and responded to that "great" call to loot businesses, to destroy the properties and wealth of the rich, to execute the rich, to imprison them or to send them and their family members to hard labor camps and new develop zones to create a socialist world of oppressions and injustices.

They did well to destroy the capitalist system with freedom, equal opportunities and healthy competitions to create socialist cultures and countries, which are deeply oppressive, ideologically racist, philosophically sexist, rampantly violent, bankrupt system of capitalism and socialism. Unfortunately and ironically, this is so true to what Kshama Sawant said previously about the socialist cultures and countries.

We hope that Kshama Sawant, Seattle City Councilwoman and millions of the socialists would read this book and other books of ours so that they could really understand what is socialism not from a theoretical conception but also from a reality where socialism could never offer a genuine democracy, solidarity or equality but oppressions, violence and bankrupt system of socialism.

Another major evidence of the Soviet-type socialism in America is that it is tainted with the bloods of innocent people. The rioters shot and beat to death more than 100 people in more than just three months since May 26, 2020 when the riots and protests took place. They have been encouraged by the praises and supports of democrat leaders and their mainstream media for political revolution.

There were more than 250 million deaths caused by the Soviet-type socialists. This also begins in the U.S when young and old people were shot to dead." Elle Reynolds reported, "As the Fourth of July weekend saw at least five children shot and killed, many of their grieving families have pleaded with the Black Lives Matter movement to address violence within communities, not just deaths at the hand of police."

Davon McNeal was shot by a group of five males in Washington, D.C. Secoriea Turner was shot by a group of armed individuals at the entrance of Wendy's restaurant in Atlanta. Natalia Wallace was shot in the head by three suspects in Chicago. Royta De's Marco Giles was shot by several fighting men in Alabama Mall and Jace Young was shot in San Francisco reported Elle Reynolds.

The shocking thing is that the mainstream media and news said almost nothing about these deaths and many deaths that have taken place since the riots from May 26, 2020. "I'm a little dismayed that I didn't receive one question on the deaths that we got in this country this weekend" said Kayleigh McEnany, the White House Press Secretary during the briefing on Monday after the killing on the Fourth of July.

Just like thousands of young socialist guards went to the streets to riot and broke into people's homes to attack, to take over people's properties and killed on spot thousands of innocent people who the young socialist guards suspected or believed that these people did not support socialism and socialist party, the mobs and millennials in America are now doing that to innocent people across the U.S.

At the expression of hatred and anger, the trained Marxists, the communists, the socialists, the mobs and the radicals beat and hurt many people including old and young. Most of the time, the whole group of 5 to 10 people beat one person until those people felt on the floors or the streets and they even became unconscious and their faces were filled with many bloods from the violent kicking or hitting.

Los Angeles Police Department released shocking news when 12 white female bodies were found in garage freezer tagged, "Black Lives Matter." "The bodies had several things in common-they were all white women in their mid-20s, blonde hair and all had the writings marked on them which read "Black Lives Matter" and "BLM" according to Now8News.com.

Last but not the least, the recent riots and protests also show another major characteristic of socialism that is anti-God, anti-Christian and anti-churches. Severe persecutions of religious workers are always evident and rampant in the socialist countries. There is no socialist country among 40 former socialist nations that does not show the persecutions, oppressions and the killings of religious leaders.

The recent riots and protests across the states in the U.S. showed that the mobs, the atheists, the radicals and the socialists vandalized churches and church properties. They also looted the church and damaged churches. They also obstructed believers from attending church services and attacking believers. They disrespected and destroyed religious statutes and they even burnt churches, Bibles and the crosses.

Grace Baptist Church in Troy, New York was interrupted "when about 10 or so protestors walked into the church and announced, "black lives matter. One masked protestor walked up to a man inside the church and showed her tattoo, saying, "Look. I'm a Christian preacher, you dumb f***." The protestors repeatedly said it loud; "black lives matter" drowning out the preacher reported Libby Emmons.

Many churches were vandalized, interrupted and were even burned. When the socialist movement took place in Venezuela, the same things happened. Thousands of young people in many socialist countries destroyed, closed churches and religious places. They burned tons of Bibles, the crosses, and Christian literatures. This is also a warning to churches in the U.S. as this is happening and will become worse soon.

The socialists cannot hide anymore their hidden plans and agenda. They failed their golden opportunity to take over the U.S. through the presidential election as Sen. Bernie Sanders dropped his presidential campaigns. Now they are willing to use forces and violence to take over the U.S. How horrible America would be under their reign? How Americans could survive the reigns of the terrorists and Marxists.

These were also the reasons that victims in socialist nations found way to escape the socialist regimes. Others wait for the opportunities to escape and some will continue to fight until they could obtain full freedom. Others may wonder what to do while many people make quick, fast and decisive decisions to leave. Please read more stories of people escaping the socialist countries in our book "**The Boat of Destiny.**"

Linda and almost 400 people got into that destiny ship. Unlike thousands of boats that were small, unfit and unequipped for the open sea, her boat was a lot bigger and better and it was packed with people when it was supposed to carry about 100 people. The sailors led the boat quickly to the international sea after 10 hours. The people were relieved and were so happy to be free from the grips of the socialists.

They were safe they thought and they were hoping that they would soon land at a neighboring country that could welcome them before their transition to the third world or it would be better if the boat of a free nation could take them directly to the free world. Yet, they did not know that they were now entering the most dangerous areas with so many pirates and most cruel and dangerous ones: Thailand pirates.

They were terrified at the groups of pirates surrounding them. The boat leaders quickly negotiated with the pirates that the people would give the pirates gold and jewelries that people brought with them and that the pirates would spare their lives. The pirates agreed and left after getting a good portion of wealth. But the pirates came back again and again for the jewelries and left without harming the people.

You may ask, why didn't the sailors drive the ship away? They could not do that because the pirates already took away the ship's engines and the people could only hope any ship would come to rescue them. Yet for the next three weeks different groups of pirates kept coming and when they could not get any material things anymore, they searched everyone to get what was left and started raping ladies.

The inhumane raping of old and young was repeated every time the pirates came. The people on the ship were horrified and some could not take it any longer and jumped into the cold sea to end their miseries. Sometimes, the pirates came and when the pirates could not get any material thing, they took away young ladies. Their families fought against the pirates and they were killed in front of the people.

Everyday, the people were waiting and hoping in fears and they were exhausted at the same time because there were no foods and waters lefts. The nightmares continued for a month as they were left in the open sea with so many horrible experiences. They were robbed, terrified, humiliated and raped by the pirates for 18 times. Could we imagine their fears, pains and hopelessness in that one month?

We asked Linda, could you forget those experiences? She said, "I cannot forget that. I was haunted by the many nightmares in my sleep before. Many times, when I woke up I wondered if I were still in the socialist country or if I were still on the boat." Without accepting the Lord as her Savior and her King, she could have become crazy or she would at least have disorders in her thinking like many others.

Without the love of God and the peace of God, Linda could hardly live a peaceful life after all of those painful experiences as the Lord Jesus confirmed that, "Peace I leave with you; my peace I give you. I do not give to you as the world gives. Do not let your hearts be troubled and do not be afraid" (John 14:27). "Come to me, all you who are weary and burdened, and I will give you rest" (Matthew 11:28).

Linda also experienced the promises of God that, "Therefore, if anyone is in Christ, the new creation has come: The old had gone, the new is here" (II Corinthians 5:17). Yet for many people who do not experience those promises yet, their lives are still burdened with their pasts and their pains and they could not be freed until their graves as they said, "when they die they could not even close their eyes."

Though these people were saved from the dangers of the sea and the humiliations of the pirates and the terrors of death but they were not free from the horrors of the painful trip. Many ladies were not free from the sufferings because many of them were soon abandoned by their life partners because their partners could not erase from their minds the repeated raping scenes of their partners by many pirates.

Other ladies found themselves pregnant as the result of the raping and of course they could not accept the unwanted babies from the unwanted rapes. They tried to abort the baby as soon as possible. Others gave birth to the babies and throw the babies into the sea. They did so because they wanted to leave behind their humiliations, horrors, shames and pains to start new lives in new countries.

Yet it is quite a surprise that millions of Americans seem do not really know about the miseries that these millions of people went through at the havocs of socialism and the socialist leaders. Millions of Americans do not seem to recall the millions of dangers and deaths caused by the socialist regimes around the world. They seem to be ignorant at horrible abuses, injustices and sufferings in socialist countries.

Just likes the experiences of the former 40 socialist countries at the beginning, millions of Americans now believe that socialism would bring more freedom and economic opportunities to Americans. They believe that socialism is the way to bridge the great gap between the rich and the poor. They believe that socialism would better meet their many needs. How real and true is socialism for America?

Let us begin with the many signatures promises of socialism and how people in the socialist countries experienced those perfect and great promises of freedom, wealth and equality. People in the socialist countries were and are often promised with freedom from exploitations, oppressions, economic deprivations, inequalities, injustices, burdens, unhappiness, nightmares and captivities. Is it for real?

CHAPTER 1

THE PERFECT PROMISES OF
THE SOCIALIST FREEDOMS

My dear Joseph was brought to the stage again. This stage was neither a stage for an art performance nor a concert for him to show his talent and skill. It was not the stage for the recognition of honor or achievement or appreciation. It was either the stage of humiliation, criticism and suffering or the stage of freedom, and happiness against one's conscience and conviction.

It was the stage of humiliation and suffering as it was the place where innocent people like him to be condemned for whatever the reasons the socialists considered as improper. It was the stage where people shouted at him and criticized him. It was the stage where people would spit on him and throw dirty things at him for being a Christian and a rightist who did nothing wrong against the government or anyone.

It might be a stage of happiness and freedom against one's conscience. If one denied his or her faith or beliefs on that stage publicly, he or she could be released from imprisonment and happily go back home and rejoin the family. Who did not want to do that? The only problem was the denial of their beliefs could be a lie and that denial could go against one's conviction in order to be pardoned and to be freed.

It was the stage where innocent people like him must make a decision to follow the direction of socialism and to be pardoned or to follow their beliefs and convictions and continue to suffer with oppressions, hard labors and incarcerations. That stage also had another meaning and the meaning could be scary because it could mean the last day or the execution of one's life depending on his or her decision on that day.

It was Joseph's turn on that day to be brought to that critical stage. As the procedure, he was criticized by the socialist leaders first, and then he was humiliated and mocked by the crowd. Then it came a time of nice words for pardon and possibly freedom that the socialist leaders often promised to people who were persecuted like Joseph. The socialist leaders asked him, "Will you deny your faith?"

He threw a question back to the leaders, "If I say I don't believe in Jesus anymore, will you believe what I say?" The socialist leaders immediately responded, "Of course we do not believe what you say." He replied against, "you always said that socialism teaches us that we must say the truth so why do you want me to say a lie?" The leaders were shocked and speechless at those words and this fact is so true.

The crowd went on crazy at what they heard and they shouted at him and throwing dirty things on him. They were just like the crazy crowd in Jerusalem more than 2000 years ago who shouted, "Kill Jesus or crucify him." Some Christians quietly prayed for his deliverance because his answer was the sure confirmation of his faith and love to God, but that was also the sure confirmation of his last day on earth.

The policemen asked Joseph, "What is your wish?" In this situation of the imminent death and the last chance or the last wish for life, most of the people would ask the authorities that, "I want to see my parents or my family members for the last time," or "I want to see my wife and children." But he said, "I want to recite the Lord's Prayer." The crowd roared in anger but he wanted to be ready to meet his God.

The authorities surprisingly granted him this desire of his. As he prayed, miracle happened and the crowd saw his face was filled with radiance and suddenly he could lift up his head and straighten his back normally and yet supernaturally. Joseph carried a heavy metal block on his neck wherever he went, so straightening his back was not possible due to the weight of that metal block.

His hands was handcuffed and to make sure the "dangerous criminal, rightist and revolutionary" like him would not run away, the prison guards would put a heavy metal block around his neck. The metal block was so heavy that he could not walk straight and his head must bend down. As he wore that heavy metal block for many years so his back was bent and his head always faced down even until this day.

But on that day, he did not feel anything that was placed upon his neck and he felt the freedom and strength when he prayed. Peace filled his heart and he felt no fears at all. At that moment of heavenly encounter and supernatural manifestation, the authorities were afraid and shocked and they shouted, "Joseph, stop, stop and go back to your cell." What did the authorities and the people see?

For sure, they witnessed the immeasurable and incredible peace upon his face. They saw the radiance or the shining of the Holy Spirit upon his face. We do not know if they see the multiple angels surrounding him as he prayed. They could have seen the fire of wall protecting him or they could have seen the army of the Lord standing in front of him. But we know that Joseph was miraculously saved on that day.

Their questions could not stop Joseph from making his faith known and confirmed. Their humiliations toward him could not intimidate him to pray in the public and to be faithful to God. Their threats of death could not stop him from experiencing God's supernatural power and peace. They could not do anything else and all they could do was to stop him from praying, from sharing his faith and from his freedom.

His life was spared then but his imprisonment and hard labors continued to last for a long time. He was incarcerated in prison and labor camp for 20 years because he hurt no one and he harmed no one. He was not freed because he spoke ill of no one and he robbed no one. His freedoms and his rights were limited for a good reason and that is to glorify God's name, God's love and God's faithfulness.

In that situation, Joseph may remember the words and the prayer of king David, the powerful king and the father of king Solomon saying, "In my distress, I called to the Lord; I cried to my God for help. From his temple he heard my voice; my cry came before him, into his ears" (Psalm 18:6). This could also be your prayer if you are going through a tough situation, struggle, sickness, brokenness, or economic crisis.

In your angers and agnostic attitudes, please do not see colleagues and neighbors as your enemies. In your pains and painful pasts, please do no use violence and forces to hurt others. In your desperations and disappointed days of life, please do not follow the radical ideologies to destroy your life and people's lives. Please come to God for His salvation, love and healing power for your life, family and future.

By the way, there were also many prisoners who renounced their faith and their ideology in those days at the socialist promises so that they could have freedom from the horrible incarcerations, freedom from the mistreatments, freedom from humiliations and freedom from hard labors at the promises of the socialist leaders, but the socialists would not release these prisoners immediately as they promised.

These prisoners and victims did not realize that their compromises to the forceful demands and slippery promises of the bloody and heartless socialists led them to even more pains, shames, guilt and sufferings. They had to betray their friends, their neighbors and even their relatives and family members in hope of the fake freedom promised by the cunning and tricky socialists.

They must give up their convictions and beliefs in hope of a shaky future provided by the greedy and cruel socialists. They were looked down both by the deceitful and sly socialists and the common people. They bore that pains and shames until their graves for betraying their consciences, convictions and calls but the great socialist promises never came true but mental tortures, emotional struggles and death.

The prisoners and victims did not know that the tongue-twisted socialists were so good at using appealing concepts of socialism for equality and wealth distribution as the baits to captivate the hearts of innocent people. But now people in the socialist nations would not be surprised at that because they already knew and experienced the many fake promises, deceptions of the socialist leaders for so long.

But earlier, even millions of intellectuals also fell into the trap of the socialist leaders when the intellectuals were encouraged by the socialist leaders to exercise their freedoms of speech, freedom of press, freedom of thought and other freedoms. They were called to provide their talents, their criticism, and their contributions. They were called to make the thoughts, education and arts to be blossomed.

Though the intellectuals were reluctant at the beginning but then they thought that those freedoms were real and they gladly responded to provide their contributions and critics but they never knew that those freedoms were the taboos in socialist countries. Even the socialist leaders also acknowledged that they used this approach to get the snakes out of the hole so that they could smash the heads of the snakes.

The heads of the snakes must be smashed because the thoughts of the intellectuals were dangerous and contradicting to the socialist ideology and the intellectuals were the potential leaders who could overthrown the socialist ideology and the socialist reign. The intellectuals thought that they could exercise freedoms yet they found their freedoms and lives were confined in horrible prisons and labor camps.

Then, millions of the young people were also called to give up their studies and works so that they could carry out the goal of an egalitarian society. They were quick to respond to the call and to make sure that the people would be free from any ideology but socialism. They went around the villages and towns to persecute those they suspected to be against the socialist regime and the socialist ideology.

The similar call for socialist agenda and political revolution is also happening right now in many cities and states across the U.S. The leftwing leaders, the democratic leaders, the socialist leaders, the Marxist trained leaders and the communist leaders, and the betrayals of the country are calling the millennials to make a political revolution to change America from a Republic state to a socialist state.

Thousands of millennials and members of Black Lives Matter and Antifa joined the many peaceful demonstrations and protests to call for social justices over police brutality. Then, they started to attack and hurt people to prove that Black Lives Matter and other lives did not matter. Then they tortured, punished and murdered people to show black supremacy over white supremacy.

They defund, injured and killed the police to justify their lawlessness. They looted businesses and stores to carry out their social ownership. They robbed things from people in their search of wealth redistribution. They destroyed and burnt cars, houses and communities to demand for the reparations that have nothing to do with them. They brought havocs, violence and destructions under the name of freedom.

The peaceful demonstrations for freedom turned into violent protests and riots. The peaceful marches for justices turned into car smashes, beating up people, burning of shops and communities, raping innocent people, and killing precious lives including small children and old people. The peaceful demands turn into hating one another, fighting and shootings including civilians and policemen and policewomen.

Just like the young socialists, American millennials do not know that they are fooled and manipulated by the top leaders in power to purge and to destroy the rival leaders for their political purposes and gains. If the top leaders fought with other leaders there would be a lot of conflicts in the political party and there might be civil wars again because the rival leaders were also powerful in those days.

When the power and the movement of the young people became so strong and so violent, the top leaders dispersed the young people into the countryside and remote areas by calling the young people to volunteer and go to remote areas to serve the political party and people. Millions of youth fell into the trap and the youth ended up their hard lives and suffered their poverty and famines in those poor areas.

Even the socialist comrades were not spared from the purging. They fought the battle together to make the country free from the control of the capitalists, the bourgeoisie. They made commitment to live and die together for socialism and the socialist country. Yet, the comrades were also imprisoned and killed at the political games when they showed their disagreements to their higher-ranking comrades.

In the same way, millennials, members of Black Lives Matter and Antifa are also the victims of the political leaders and the billionaires and their political games. Many rioters are now in prison for the crimes that they committed. Many others are still under investigations. Instead of enjoy their American dream and prosperous life; they are now serving many years in prison while others face death or life sentences.

The politicians and socialists are the ones who sow divisions of races and the millennials listen to these leaders and now the millennials end their lives in divisions of prison and of emotionless cells. The leaders are the ones who sow hatred and the millennials followed their destructive instructions and now the millennials are facing hatred of life, hatred of races, and hatred of themselves.

The socialists and the politicians are the ones who manipulate the millennials to fight for the new socialist government and now many millennials are fighting their lives behind bars. The socialists and the politicians are the ones who inspire the millennials for riots, lootings and social disorder for freedom and now the millennials are losing their freedom in jails for their wrong and evil acts.

Millions of people were promised with great future of powerful socialist nations with classless society, equality, prosperity, no gap between the rich and the poor, no wealth gaps, no exploitations but the people ended up in equal poverty, equal miseries, equal sufferings, equal oppression, and so many inequalities. People realized at the end that their human rights were serious violated by the socialists.

Whether they were the prisoners, the intellectuals, the socialist comrades, the young people or the common people, all people were promised that they would have freedom from inequality. They would have freedom to pursuit their happiness and great future. Unfortunately the promised freedoms could only be seen on the billboards and media, and limited freedoms are certain in practices and in life.

Unfortunately, in more than 100 years and across former 40 socialist nations that embraced socialism, the socialist promises were quickly responded and highly received because common people were so caught with many idealistic concepts and great freedoms that they were willing to do anything. They could only find those things in dreams and they never see the promises to be realized after a century.

Unfortunately, millions of Americans today are also falling into the same vicious trap and disastrous cycle of socialism at the attractive offers and appealing future with socialism. Millions of Americans are dreaming of the days the greedy socialists would set them free from college debts and pressures, and they would be free from the costs of healthcare and education and free from low wages and low incomes.

Unfortunately, millions of Americans were deceived by the leftists, the socialists and the mainstream media in their twisted messages about the great prospects of socialism. These far-left political leaders painted a great future of milk and honey for Americans with socialism. They wanted Americans to vote for them so much that they are willing to offer and promise anything possible to get the people's supports.

Unfortunately, millions of American Christians know about the horrible facts about socialism but they seemed to be so passive and uninterested to the growing threats of socialism. They are so righteous in their choice that they rather let the wicked socialism to take over America and Americans but they are not willing to support the imperfect leaders who are fighting to stop the socialist evils and deception.

Unfortunately, millions of American Christians do not realize that America and Americans are just a step from the great losses of their democracy, and precious freedoms. They do not perceive that serious violations of their human rights and horrible injustices are at their front doors. They do not even believe that they would suffer greatly from religious persecutions and oppressions by the socialists.

Unfortunately, millions of American Christians are so blind by the deception of the mainstream media, philosophies, ideologies and their political parties that they are willing to vote for the ungodly leaders who are openly against God and the Bible. They are willing to stand with the ungodly people to approve the legalization of gay marriage, abortions, polygamy, and unnatural sexes... that are abominations to God.

Unfortunately millions of Americans cannot wait to see the promises of the leftwing leaders and the great sayings of the socialists to be realized. They offered all the things that everyone is looking for from childcare to retirement, from housing to healthcare, from minimal wage to debt free, from stable job to ownership of the economy, from free transportation to free education and many more.

"When it comes to the welfare state, the country should create a national health insurance system, akin to some Democrats' "Medicare for All" proposals, extend new parents paid leave from work, provide young child free child care and pre-K, and give each family a $300 per month allowance per child. The United States should also provide housing stipends to those on low incomes and increase the minimum benefits for those on senior and disability pensions" reported Charles Krupa.

If Americans need a paid leave, it is available. If Americans need a job, jobs are there for them. If Americans need to be debt free, Sen. Bernie Sanders has his way for them to be free. If Americans need high wage, there is no problem because the minimum wage is $15. If Americans need childcare supports, childcare centers are right there for them. If Americans do not go to work, social welfares are available.

If Americans need free education, College for All is offered. If Americans were worried about the cost of the healthcare, the Medicare for All would be available plus daycare for children. If Americans want accommodation, affordable houses are certain. The dream of Democratic Socialism of America (DSA) and the prospect of the DSA are so great, glorious and glamorous and expounded in the following words.

Peter Gowan said, "a democratic socialist America would be a society where wealth and power are far more evenly distributed, and it would be less cruel, less lonely and less alienating. Democratic socialism aims for the liberation of human agency and creativity-not just in America, but in all the countries that capital exploits and invades for the profits of our nation's billionaires" reported Politico.

But the reality of socialism never meets the dream of Peter Gowan because in so many socialist countries so far, wealth and power never distributed evenly to the people, wealth and power are in the hands of the socialist elites and socialist party. The socialist party is one of the cruelest forms of government and thus it never liberates people but keeping people in loneliness, pains and sufferings.

David Duhalde said, "Establishing democratic socialism means democratizing ownership of capital, our jobs and our personal lives. Socialists believe that if you work somewhere, you should have a say in how it's run. Through unions, worker councils and elected boards, this is possible at the company level today. Furthermore, if your labor generates profit, under socialism you would have an ownership stake and a democratic say in how your workplace is run" reported Charles Krupa.

David Duhalde still lives in the ivory tower of socialism because democracy has never been realized in any socialist country in the last one century. Yes, the "socialists believe that if you work somewhere, you should have a say in how it's run" and that is what they believe but when people raise their voice they would be oppressed and imprisoned. Do common people have an ownership stake?

Rashida Tlaib said, "Socialism, to me, means ensuring that our government policy puts human needs before corporate greed and that we build communities where everyone has a chance to thrive… We're trying to create communities where the education you have access to, or the jobs you're able to get, don't depend on your zip code or your race or gender" reported Charles Krupa.

Charles Krupa on Politico Magazine gave a report of the will and dreams of modern American socialists or supporters of socialism beginning with David Duhalde who believes that "Democratic socialism is about expanding democracy." Rashida Tlaib said, "it's about making communities equal." Connie M. Razza believed, "Socialism would remedy the systematic deprivation of people of color."

Maria Svart said, "it's about giving everyone a voice in decision-making... The problem with capitalism is not just that a system fueled by a wealthy, profit-hungry elite is inherently unstable, or that it leaves whole layers of society starting in the streets. It is that it relies on the dictatorship of the rich. The fundamental difference we expect from a socialist society is that we will all have a voice in the decisions that impact our lives. Workplaces will be owned by the workers who run them, rather than an authoritarian boss"

Whether it is Rashida Tlaib, or David Duhalde, or Connie M. Razza, or Maria Svart, these people do not really know the truth about socialism in practices. They may read and understand something about socialism in theory but in reality the political party and the socialist ideology are even more important than human lives. Thus democracy, equality, people's voice and equal communities are not possible.

Thomas Hanna believed that, "A practical form of socialism in the United States in the 21st century would occur when democratic ownership displaces and supersedes the current, dominant extractive corporate model... full state ownership, partial state ownership, local/municipal ownership, multi-stakeholder ownership, worker ownership, consumer cooperative ownership, producer cooperative ownership, community ownership and sustainable local private ownership."

Peter Gowan held that "Democratic socialism means democratic ownership over the economy." The simple answer is because everything is public owned so people have not much left. We hope these people to read our book "The 12 Commandments of Socialism" so that they would see what socialism could provide but only empty promises and devastative consequences of socialist economic system.

Due to the many freebies offered by Sen. Bernie Sanders, million Americans are expecting to be free from the inequalities, free from debt, free from healthcare pressures, free from works and everything is free. Just imagine that if only half of the population of America does not go to work and just enjoyed social benefits and welfares, America would soon become as poor as Venezuela in just a decade or so.

If socialism were in power in America, Americans might be very happy for the first three to four years because they could enjoy so many social benefits within this period because the socialists must convince the hearts of the majority of the Americans that socialism is to be the only choice for the long run. Besides, the socialists also need sometimes to get the majority support from the Congress.

Then, on the second term, they would start to carry out the Green New Deal massively as the socialists could pass any bill from the Congress with the strong support. By the fifth year of the socialist leadership, they would carry out their plan of social ownership by taking over private ownership of businesses and corporations and taking over the wealth of the wealthy and the middle classes.

It would not be difficult for the socialists to mobilize the people to take down the billionaires and the millionaires and their wealth then because they are already in power and they know well how to stir up the hatred of the common people to take the wealth, the corporations, and the businesses of the rich and powerful people through the elimination of social gap, wealth distribution and social ownership.

The socialists had never failed to take down the wealthy people and the leaders who are against them in all former socialist countries. They also know how to use the young people, their guards and their soldiers who are passionate and eager to make America an egalitarian society to search for the elites, to destroy or imprison these elites and to take over their properties and businesses.

Then the socialists also eliminate the government leaders and politicians from the democratic, republican, or any party leaders who are to go against the will of the socialist leaders. The socialists could do this through economic benefits, position offerings, briberies, sex traps or death threats. The leaders and politicians who are not willing to submit to the socialist leadership would be kidnapped or assassinated.

Before the second term, many wealthy, business people intellectuals and even politicians would try to move their families, wealth and business abroad because they know that tragedies may fall upon them anytime. If not, they would have to run for their lives to other countries anyway when the plan of social ownership is to be carried out by the second term as they are the targets to be attacked and destroyed.

By the end of the second term, the socialists already get all the powers and government leaders they need. Their hands control all the military powers, Congress, national industries and government departments. For sure, there will be many demonstrations and riots to go against these many changes, but the socialists know how to stop these demonstrations with their great promises or suppressions.

America and many Americans may seem to be excited about the many political and economic changes and they would be more eager to see the socialist plans to bear fruits. Many Americans could not wait to see the realization of an egalitarian and prosperous America while others are observing or doubting if the socialist economic plans do really work so Americans could forever enjoy wealth and many rights.

Since the socialists are in control of the government sectors so they could easily change the votes if needed to make sure that the next socialist candidate would be officially nominated to be next president of the U.S. for the third term or more. It is no doubt that the socialists would be successful in doing so and those leaders who put the voting fraud into questions would be silenced or executed by the socialists.

The third term would be very critical to the socialists and the people because many economic and social issues would arise during this time when the Green New Deal and the socialist economic reforms are not working well. Then the government would spend more money to keep the system going and moving. The more the funds are spent and higher the national debt would increase.

Then the people would go on strike when the government is no longer able to provide their salaries, welfares and many social benefits. As the result, products and necessity items are not enough to provide the great demands of the people. America and Americans will face an economic crisis when so many people turn to social welfare which the government could also hardly meet the needs of so many people.

The worse thing happens is when the famines to take place. This would lead to hunger and much social unrest. Then the government must print more money to cope up with the economic crisis and welfares. The inflation would become high and the products are in great shortage and are not good in quality. Money value is depreciated and people could not afford to buy many foods and products.

More millions of people would loose jobs and America would face an economic recess and then depression, and the great sufferings begin with poverty, shortages of foods, poor healthcare services and hunger. Then people would go on strike against the socialist government and the socialist agenda. The people would ask for the removal of the socialist leaders and a comeback with capitalist economic system.

But it was too late then as the government was so powerful to suppress and oppress every demonstration and riots. The death toll would arise by mass murder or sicknesses or hunger. People start their exodus or exiles to Canada or Mexico or other countries to experience the life in the refugee camps as illegal immigrants. Tyranny would be the characteristics of American socialist government then.

Many readers may react and say, "that is just your threat and that could not happen in America." Yes, millions of people around the world also thought that way before and they were not willing to listen to the many advise of the socialist victims. Then what happened to their country, their people and themselves? The few paragraphs described above were exactly what happened in the many socialist countries.

That was the painful history of more than 40 former socialist nations in the past. The remaining few socialist countries are also going through those painful paths. Their experiences could not be wrong and the socialist failures could be concluded with sureness because the socialist economic system has never been effective in all socialist nations and their tyrannies would last for many decades.

From the fourth term, what happen next would be the series of suppressions, sufferings and the widespread poverty of the land in the fourth term. Civil war may take place during this period of the socialist reign or it could be earlier depending on how quick the Americans learned the lessons of the past. Within two decades or so under the socialist reign, America would be no different with Venezuela as it is now.

In socialist nations, the wealth for the mass is not real. How many people want to be wealthy? All people want to be wealthy of course. But you cannot be rich or wealthy in socialism in its true sense because people must be equal to one another. Only the socialist government and the socialist leaders could be wealthy then because the people must be equal poor due to failures in economic reforms.

Equally poor in the socialist countries is a fact and a reality. Equally rich in socialist countries is never realized in reality but only in theory. The truth is the socialist leaders would not want the people to be wealthy and powerful unless they are well under their control. If the people are so wealthy and powerful, the socialist power and their positions are to be challenged and their wealth and lives would be gone.

By the way, this is just a small question for you, "Do you know that many socialists are millionaires like Sen. Bernie Sanders?" When are they going to share their wealth to the poor? There are more than half a million of homeless people here, does any homeless receive the wealth shared by the socialists? Many socialists also own many houses, any homeless person live in their extra houses?

That is the nature of socialism. They promised heaven but they deliver hades. They talk very nice but they perform poorly. The socialist leaders would never give people freedom. There is only limited freedom. There is no freedom of speech, no freedom of press, no freedom of peaceful gathering because if the people have those freedoms, the socialist leaders could no longer control people and in power.

This was and still is the wise advise of Joseph who suffered much in prison and hard labor for 20 years, "If a socialist says that your mother is a lady, you better check if that is true." Just like the word of Joseph, millions of socialist victims would say clear and loud that the promises of the socialists cannot be trusted and could not be true. Their promises are to lure people to vote for and support them only.

In saying so, this does not mean that we do not need free education, free healthcare, free childcare, and free benefits. We enjoy those benefits and rights if we want to call it as human rights. Yet, when those benefits are given and promised in order to achieve something dangerous in the end, then we should not be fallen into that trap especially when that trap of socialism is so obvious and proven to be destructive.

Many children were being molested and even raped at the sweet candies. Many young people are addicted to drug at the pain relieving effects. Many people are lured into prostitutions at deceptions. Many people were bankrupted and even committed suicides at the quick way to earn money through gambling. Those great prospects ended their lives in tragedies and so do the great promises of socialism.

"Socialism, the Utopian economic and political system that promises equality, prosperity, and universal peace through the workings of a collectivist state, has repeatedly been exposed as a colossal failure. Its history, marked by failed societies and brutal dictatorships, is quite literally littered with the bodies of millions of innocents," said Michael E. Telzrow on New American.

Michael lamented that, "and yet in the United States we stand on the brink of a socialist abyss, the edge of which looms ever closer as time passes… but despite socialism's historical failures, it remains attractive to those vulnerable to its false promises of egalitarianism and economic equality. Instead of being relegated to its own proverbial "dustbin of history," it continues to entice well after its failures and crimes have been laid bare for all to see."

One also needs to ask if those promises are feasible. The socialists may use so many examples to convince the people about the inventions and the plans that were once thought impossible but those plans work effectively. So they challenge the people to try their plans and if those plans do not work, no one is harm and so there is no big deal. Yes, the freebies are great and so tempting to be applied but are they feasible?

The following nine promises of freedoms would present to the readers the truth about those freedoms and human rights in the many socialist countries. These socialist promises entail the basic and essential human rights that people in the free world really enjoy but those rights and freedoms are not really possible and available where the socialist tyranny is in power and control.

1st Freedom: Freedom From Exploitations:
Social Ownership and Corruptions

In 2017, when the socialist leaders began the crackdowns on corruption again in a socialist country, the Youth Newspaper in the country immediately reported that "Disciplinary actions were taken at over 300 party organizations, while more than 18,600 Party members were sanctioned for various infractions, of whom 700 were penalized for corruption and deliberate violations of state regulations."

A few years earlier, about 40,000 members of the socialist party were disciplined due to briberies and corruptions. Most of these members were not on trials for their briberies or corruptions. They simply received a reminder, a warning, a note for the relocation of their works or positions, or a charge for them to pay fines. The big leaders are always clean when they are the real criminals behind the operations.

In a nearby socialist country, GAN Integrity reported that, "In the first half of 2017, the Central Commission for Discipline Inspection (CCDA) received 131 million complaints and opened 260,000 cases. More than 210,000 officials were punished for corruption with the above disciplines. The real number of the complaints and officials were caught with briberies and corruptions must be a lot higher.

If 131 million complaints were received within only six months, how many more complaints to be filed and received in the coming months? This initial number is already enough to show the fact that briberies and corruptions are rampant in the socialist country. This initial number shows that it is hardly and it is really a miracle if any socialist member and official is not involved in briberies and corruptions.

Growing up and living in socialist countries, just like millions of the people, we were taught and told that, "if people need the authorities to do something for them, emptied hands do not work." The socialists' motto says the government's existence and the political party are for the people and to serve the people. The socialists call themselves as servants of the people but the people are the real servants in reality.

To make the authorities to feel better and to avoid the term "corruption, people call briberies and corruptions as relationship building or gift culture or appreciation for the fast and kind assistances from the local authorities. Many public services are no longer the public services but the exchanged services for mutual benefits. The people must satisfy the needs and the greedy demands of the public servants.

In fact, these exchanged services are always beneficial to the socialist members and business people or investors who gain from these exchanged services, but the public services are always at the expenses of the common people whose lives are already poor, painful and pitiful and yet the common people are still being exploited financially for the public services they supposedly deserve without any payments.

In 2012, our organization purchased a piece of land as we planned to build up a vocational school. The local authorities and the leaders of education ministry seemed to be very happy and supportive to this project and our organization. The place for the project was six to seven hour drives from where I lived. My coworkers and I made countless trips to that city to meet the leaders for the project.

It saved us many troubles to look for a new land for the project because the land was purchased and transferred to our organization by a friend who made everything possible to get that land before. Yet the proposal for the project took a long time as we went against the "normal procedures" of the gift culture here. We talked to the local authorities that we were Christians and we can't bribe them for favors.

But our organization would appreciate them with some gifts later when the project was completed so we would not violate our conscience and belief. Every time we met, the authorities kept on smiling and thanking us for putting investments in their communities, helping their communities with the training projects and creating the many potential jobs available for the local people from the project.

The meetings with the local authorities went from one lunch to more lunches and from one dinner to the numerous dinners but our project went nowhere and there was no clear response to the feasibility proposal that we sent them. All we were told was to wait for the approval of the higher leaders from the central government. I told the local authorities that I wanted to meet the leaders in charge to no avail.

The local leaders kept praising highly the feasibility, the logistics, the potentials of the project and the contributions to their local people from the training. This was because, our projects partners from automobile and high-tech companies would provide on-job trainings and the companies would pick the workers of their choice for the jobs after the training. But our project was not approved still.

We knew the gift culture and we knew that they wanted money or gift but we could not go against our conscience and our belief, and we must set a good example for many of our believers. If we were to compromise one time, then this would open to countless times of compromises to their demands. As time passed, we also doubted if "this righteous path" would work in this corrupted culture, leaders and society.

The irony was that the socialist leaders always talked very nice. Their talks were holy and inspiring as they always told us that they were the model public servants and they were willing to do anything for the people and their well beings. They would love to assist us in any possible ways so that the local people would be blessed and be beneficial from the project as soon as possible.

But those were just the empty words and the project did not make any progress as time passed when their greed and wants were not satisfied. My coworkers and I went to different leaders of various departments as we were told to do so yet we were just like a ball that was being kicked from one professional player to another rising star. Unfortunately the players were not allowed to make any score.

Since our organization already got the land legally so my coworkers and I discussed that we should do some basic constructions first while waiting for the approval of the project proposal. We asked the professional company to make the layout for the basic constructions. The layout was ready but it must be approved by many different departments in the city before we could begin the basic construction.

It took my coworkers and I again a long, long time to go to various departments for the environment-protection permit, safety permit, building permit, occupancy permit, development permit, construction permit, contractor permit and many permits that we had never heard of in our life. Then my coworkers and I had to wait again for their approvals without knowing when could we get those permits.

Then we were told to go from one office to other offices to get the many permits. The land officials would say that we needed to have the permit from the construction office first before they could take the building layout into considerations. The environment department required the safety department to issue first the permit while the latter needed the permit from the former first.

The construction officials would say that there needed to have a permit first from the environmental office before they could do anything. Then the environmental officials said the design must be approved first by the council members. Then, the list of the offices and the officials were added and plus the list of many new documents that we must submit in various offices and departments.

According to the property or land laws, we were given a specific time for the land to be developed and if the developers were not able to develop the land according to the proposed purposes then the government would take over the land. The endless procedures took so long that the due date of the project were near and yet even the approval for the basic construction was not possible.

At the due date approached, we were under a lot of pressures at the potential loss of the land and debts and the great pressure to compromise. The authorities took the initiatives and gave us many solutions and offers to make the project a reality but there were "prices" to be offered from our side for everything to be done. They knew that we were at the dead end and only their helps could turn the situation around.

If we were to give some "gifts," all the blocks would be removed and the project would be realized without many obstacles. If we were to "pay them gifts," the due date of the project would be extended indefinitely as investors and developers often did and are still doing. The local government could also give us many extra benefits that both parties could enjoy the shares of wealth and great government supports.

At last, my coworkers and I agreed to give up the project to be faithful to our Christian faith but there was a big price of debt and pains that we still had to face for many years then. But one thing for sure was that the decision of giving up the project and not compromising our faith saved us especially from many illegal dealings, briberies and corruptions as many investors were led in that vicious circle.

The conclusion is corruption could never disappear from the socialist countries because the socialist system is to nurture corruption. Corruption is built in the socialist system. Pitiful people must "feed" the bottomless hungers and desires of the socialist members and leaders for wealth and power. The government and the leaders always gain something from the people and the people are always at loss.

As the result the rampant corruption, the socialist elites, leaders, princes and princess own many lots of lands, villas, and properties while the common people are still struggling hard to pay for the rent of their little huts. The wealth socialists enjoy their lives in five-star resorts at home and abroad while the common people are suffering with their poverty and poor living-conditions.

The citizens and most foreign investors in socialist countries know very well the fact that briberies and corruptions are everywhere. Briberies and corruptions occur from the judiciary systems to the police departments, from the public services to the land administration, from tax administration to custom administration, from public procurement to the natural resources, from legislation to civil society...

The scales of briberies and corruption are not really revealed yet because the judiciary system in the socialist countries can only bring disciplines to the grass root officials in the lower ranks but the judiciary system can hardly and cannot touch high-ranking officials in the state-owned enterprises, government departments, provincial offices, national ministries, and entities of the central government.

These are the elected and corrupted officials of the political party and there are still millions of those elected and more corrupted leaders who are still sucking bloods of people and corrupting public wealth or social wealth for their wealth. These high-ranking leaders are so powerful to be touched by laws because they are still above the laws. In most cases, their subordinates would be sentenced on their behalf.

The corruptions for wealth, promotions or positions of socialist leaders took place in all levels of the party organizations, and public operations. Yet people could only see the tip of a corruption iceberg. How big, how wide and how deep is the corruption? People could only guess from the luxurious lifestyles of the wealthy socialist leaders, their children, relatives and the sufferings of the victims.

The briberies and corruptions are the results of various factors such as the human greed, the loopholes, the culture or the system. They are also largely the results of social ownership. The socialists greatly employ the concept of social ownership to convince people to eliminate the exploitations of the rich over the poor and to carry out their idealistic plan of wealth distribution to people from the social wealth.

The socialists believe that the monopolies of private corporations and industries are at the disadvantages of the employees because the elites could treat the employees unfairly and the elites could exploit the labors and the talents of the workers for their gain and wealth while the workers are often left their in poverty, unstable lives, and unstable jobs with low or underpaid wages.

The socialists believe that the elites are so powerful and the government would comply with the will and the demands of the elites. The government would protect the benefits and the wealth of the elites above the benefits and well-beings of the employees. This is also the cause of the social classes, social strife and social unrest when the gap between the rich and the poor becomes wider.

The socialists believe that the workers or employees are just the slaves and the instruments of the elites and are following the orders of the elites. The employees have no voices in the decision making process and no equal shares in the wealth that they created. They receive little when the employers get too much and this is unfair, unequal, and unjust and unacceptable.

The socialists believe that the elites are corrupted because they could manipulate the top leaders through their many offers for the financial and political opportunities. In turn, the elites are to be set free from many legal, social and political restrictions. This favor would corrupt the justice system and making the elites above the laws and the injustices would happen to the workers.

The socialists believe that "capital and factor markets would cease to exist under the assumption that market exchanges within the production process would be made redundant if capital goods were owned by a single entity or network of entities representing society, but the articulation of models of market socialism where factor markets are utilized for allocating capital goods between socially owned enterprises broadened the definition to include autonomous entities within a market economy" according to Wikipedia on Social Ownership.

So the socialists could provide the perfect answers to the dilemmas that the capitalists could not solve to give better benefits and justices to the employees. The socialist solution is through social ownership and this means that all the wealth are to be shared by the people equally according to their needs or merits. As the result the wealth gap will be eliminated and there are no social classes and strife.

The workers would no longer be mistreated and exploited because they have their equal economic shares in the social ownership. The workers would no longer be exploited or mistreated because they have their voices in the decision-making of the social-owned corporations. Everyone is equal so there is no need to corrupt the government or to seek the government favor for better benefits, wealth or positions.

For social ownership to be realized the private ownership of productions, means and modes of production, or the private enterprises and private lands, assets, properties, resources and equities must be abolished so that everything must be socially owned and shared by people. The government on the behalf of the people would facilitate the modes and means of productions, resources and properties.

The histories of more than 40 former socialist nations revealed that when social ownership was carried out at the reign of socialism and the socialists in these former socialist nations, it was true that the capitalists and the bourgeoisies were eliminated. The capitalists and the bourgeoisies were punished, tortured, imprisoned, or killed and their properties and businesses were socially owned.

But the social classes and social strife never disappeared and there is an emergence of new semi-feudal ruling classes or the socialists, the socialist elites, the socialist princes and princes, the socialist leaders and the socialist subordinates, and ruled class or the working class. The ruling classes are basically corrupted and greedy for powers, positions and wealth, and the ruled class were obviously suffered the most.

It was true that the lands were distributed to people before but the distribution of social wealth and profit surplus were never realized. Unfortunately, the lands were given to the people so that people labored on the lands for the socialist government and the produces from the land were to be submitted to the government. The lands did not and do not belong to the people but the country owns the lands.

It was true that the socialist governments did promise the people for equal shares of the surplus of wealth but unfortunately, the people were not able to share the wealth, the prosperity or the happiness. The people did share equally the poverty, the famines, the exploitations, and the injustices. The people did share equally the many losses, the oppressions, the loss of human rights and freedoms.

What the socialists believe to be bad about capitalism and capitalists, they are now doing those things to the people and they are even a hundred times worse than the capitalists. The socialist leaders exploit people to the bones and take people's freedom away. They oppress people and do so many injustices to people. They make the economic gap between the socialist elites and the people wider.

Yet, the American socialists are eager to see social ownership to be realized through the New Green Deal and socialist agenda. The Democratic Socialists of America made clear that, "The Pittsburgh Local of the Democratic Socialists of America seeks to facilitate the transition to a truly democratic and socialist society, one in which the means/ resources of production are democratically and socially controlled."

When social ownership was to happen in America, the millionaires and the billionaires like Jeff Boss, Bill Gate, Warren Buffet, Mark Zuckerberg, Larry Page and million people would be the among the first people to be executed by the socialists. Their properties, wealth and corporations would be taken over by the socialists and the workers would loose millions of jobs as the transition was to be taken place.

How truthful and successful is the implementation of social ownership? How wealthy and happy the people are when the people have their shared power and shared wealth? What will happen to social-owned properties such as land, resources, businesses, and corporations? Do the people really have their voices and powers to make decisions on the things that they share and own?

"The goal of social ownership is to eliminate the distinction between the class of private owners who are the recipients of passive property income and workers who are the recipients of labor income (wages, salaries, and commissions), so that the surplus product (or economic profits in the case of market socialism) belong either to society as a whole or to the members of a given enterprise" stated Wikipedia.

Wikipedia stated the five major benefits of social ownership or society-wide ownership of productive property according to economist David McMullen, "first, workers would be more productive and have greater motivation since they would directly benefit from increased productivity, secondly this ownership stake would enable greater accountability on the part of individuals and organizations."

The third major benefits of social ownership is that it "would eliminate unemployment, fourth it would enable the better flow of information within the economy, and finally it would eliminate wasteful activities associated with "wheeling and dealing" and wasteful government activities intended to curb such behavior and deal with unemployment" according to Wikipedia.

Unfortunately social ownership only happens in the socialist golden theory and it was and is still very far from reality. Indeed, the five socialist benefits presented by David McMullen are better true in the capitalist economic system. In fact, social ownership is the bait to attract and to gain the support of the people because it sounds great and the people would support for it as it brings benefits to the people.

Sadly, social ownership leads to corruption because the socialist leaders had free accesses to social ownership.

Sadly, social ownership leads to corruption because the socialist leaders had absolute power to control social wealth and resources

Sadly, social ownership leads to corruption because the socialist leaders are not accountable and transparency system is not available.

Sadly, social ownership leads to corruption because the socialist leaders build up the justice system in a way that the leaders are not to be touched.

Sadly, social ownership leads to corruption because the socialist leaders structure their hierarchy in such a way that corruption is inevitable.

The full-scale of corruption could only be known and be dealt with when the free press, free speech, civil right freedom and political freedom in the socialist country are available and powerful enough to address the wrongdoings and corruption of the corrupted leaders; and when the law enforcement agencies are powerful enough to hold the high-ranking government officials accountable before the law.

The reporter recognized, "There were, however, several limitations to the process, including the sluggish conclusion of inspections and ineffective anti-corruption methods, the leader continued. There were also issues in coordination between different agencies, which led to problems including the escape of suspects." The leader wanted to say that it is difficult to deal with so many high-ranking officials.

Social ownership does not make the workers to be more productive and motivated
Social ownership does not enable greater accountability
Social ownership does not eliminate unemployment
Social ownership does not facilitate better flow of information within the economy
Social ownership does not eliminate wasteful government activities

The victims are still the common people. They are being exploited of their economic opportunities while the socialist leaders and their party members are getting richer and powerful. Whenever the common people voiced out the corruption or wrongdoings of the socialist leaders, and the poverty, the people were arrested and imprisoned because they went against the will of the socialist party and leaders.

Social ownership becomes a perfect way for the socialist leaders to exploit people and their economic opportunities because the socialist leaders, their family members and their subordinates would have first accesses and first hands on everything before goods, products, relief packages, services, benefits could reach to people. So they could take all the opportunities for their businesses and wealth.

The socialist leaders also could decide on how to distribute or to carry out the benefits, relief packages, economic opportunities, and policies... and thus corruptions take place again as people must look for the leaders for the favors. The people are still the victims and they are being exploited from equal opportunities for businesses, for the development of their potentials or social welfares.

In fact, the move from private ownership to social ownership is the move from anti-corruption to corruption or from a law-abiding state to a corrupted state. It is the move from the stable jobs, increasing incomes and good lives to underpayment jobs, exploited incomes and struggling lives. It is also the move for elected socialist leaders to control people, to corrupt and to collect wealth for themselves.

My argument and upbringing in socialist countries see socialism is just an offshoot of feudalism or a semi-feudal form of government. Though the socialists try to polish their theory to be better than capitalism, socialism is still far from capitalism. I believe, Richard Wolff should revise his proposition as, "Socialism not Capitalism is unstable, unequal, and fundamentally undemocratic."

The socialists often advocate for the role of the big government so that the socialists could help people to realize the equalities and freedom. Yet big government turns out to be a disaster to the general public because the people are so weak now to voice out their concerns, or to have enough power to exercise their precious human rights and freedoms at the cruel suppressions of big government.

2nd Freedom: Freedom from Oppressions
Big Government and Suppressions

Americans and nations have been taught that because the government has limited control over the economy, mode of production, and distribution so the wealth is in the hands of the rich and they are so greedy that they are not willing to distribute wealth to people. The power then is better in the hand of the government so that the government can equally distribute wealth and the opportunities to everyone.

As the government is able to control the economy and wealth, people would enjoy equality, justice, freedom, prosperity and happiness when the wealth is being distributed equally to everyone through the collective efforts of the government. This sounds great, but it is too good to be true as this had never ever happened in any socialist countries since the birth of socialism until now and forever.

In reality, there is no socialist country in the top list of the countries with freedoms in the world and their promises never come true when their promises are checked. When a government has power over the economy and the mode of production as they do, the economy could hardly thrive with socialist economic principles and it produces more corruptions, the abuse of power, inequality and injustices.

BE FREE OR NOT BE FREE

A simple Google or Yahoo search with the following questions would reveal that the socialist countries are always among the top countries of the world to go against their sounding promises. What are the top countries in the world with poverty, inequality, massacres, injustices, oppression, and persecutions? What are the top countries in world with the violations of human rights and freedom?

Why do the leftwing democrats and especially the socialists always want to propose more government control or big government? They argue that when the government has more control over the economy, and wealth, the government would distribute wealth equally to every American. There will be no more wealth gap, job gap, and race gap when the government has more power to do so.

So the socialists painted a perfect picture of socialism and socialist Utopia through Green New Deal where every citizen would be provided with a stable job and high wage. They believe that the Green New Deal would break all inequalities and the controlling power of the bourgeoisies. The Green New Deal would solve all the social issues of inequality, exploitations, unstable jobs and economic pressures.

The socialist dream is always beautiful and it is nice to think of but the reality is always different from the unrealistic dream. There are great dreams and they are worth for our pursuits but there are also dreams that lead to bankruptcy, evils and destructions. The dream for big government would lead to limited freedom, huge abuse of power, injustices and tyrannies. This is for sure and certain.

The Framers of the U.S Constitution already predicted the greed of people for power. They knew that when the State is so powerful to control the mode of production, means of distribution, economy, military, media, land, and power then the head of the State becomes "king or boss" and the people just become "subjects or maids" as they have nothing left in their hands and suffer with many injustices.

First and foremost, socialist countries are known with the violations and suppressions of human rights, free speech, religion, and free press.

As you notice that so far we do not specify certain names of some socialist countries, leaders and the real names in many stories because these people are still there in the socialist countries, their lives will be at stake if we do that even now, the 21st century.

How many peaceful gatherings for human rights have been well received by the socialist authorities? How many peaceful demonstrations to fight for injustices have been answered by the government? How many thousands of people were and are incarcerated when they talk about the truth of corruptions and the oppressions of the socialist leaders? People ask for justices and they are suppressed by injustices.

At the close of 2019, a senior pastor was sentenced to 9 years in incarceration in a socialist country. His church had been in operation for many years and suddenly the government came and ordered the pastors and leaders to close down their churches and they were no longer allowed to gather for Sunday services, Bible study, small groups or prayer meetings at their church or even at their homes.

When the pastors, the leaders and church members refused to comply with their ridiculous requests quoting the religious freedom and human rights, hundreds of church members including leaders and the pastors were arrested and detained. Do many Americans really know that it is so common that pastors and Christians are being persecuted, tortured, humiliated and even killed in socialist countries?

They are put behind the bars for years not because they violate the laws but just because they exercise their rights, belief and religion. They are under surveillances not because they are doing something wrong but because they preach the Gospel. They are being fined and their things are confiscated not because they rob someone but just because they share God's love to and pray for others to be healed and better.

Their human rights are harshly violated, their dreams are dashed by the injustices and their future is darkened by incarceration. Can any socialists help explain how socialist countries, socialist believers and members can promote freedoms, human rights, equality and prosperity to the thousands of people who are receiving the cruel treatment, the humiliation, the injustices like this pastor is going through?

Do we find much coverage on the recent ruthless persecutions of the people of faith and the horrible violations of human rights in socialist countries on mainstream media? The many leftists and the liberals in America are now the socialists so they do not want to expose the flaws of their allies; the weak and wicked sides of their ideologies, so they better cover it up. That is one of the characteristics of socialism.

Secondly, the control of power leads to so much corruption as the government leaders begin to exploit the economy and use their power to get wealth at the losses of the people. The higher the positions the leaders are, the richer they become. The corruption in socialist countries is so rampant and so huge yet the people could not do anything because the leaders are so powerful and the power is in their hands.

The leaders are busier to accumulate their wealth and power that they have no time to care for the economy, business establishment and the well being of the people. The leaders know they will be in this position only for a while so they just take opportunity to accumulate their wealth and power so they may attain to a higher level of power, position and prosperity as they rise higher in political power.

In socialist countries, when the top leaders give a command, everyone must take actions immediately. No further discussions or public opinion needed at the centralized power of government. Members of parties dare not say anything. In America, any members of political parties can say what they think about that command, and they can analyze the strengths and weaknesses of that command.

After President Trump delivered the speech at the State of the Union Address 2020, the media was flooded with the improper behavior of Sen. Nancy Pelosi who tore the copy of President Trump's speech in half at the end of the address. In socialist countries, if she did this or even just showed disrespect to the top leaders she would be soon removed from her office or something bad would happen to her.

The leftwing leaders in the U.S. have been trying to apply that power of big government to remove President Trump from the office because he displeases them and he blocks their ways. They have been trying all the possible ways and more ways to come to attack, to discredit, to go against and hopefully to stop him from his presidency because he wants to protect the Constitution with small government.

President Trump is a thorn in their eyes as he discloses the lies, lawlessness, abuses of power, failures, crookedness, and corruptions of those leaders so they dislike him and hate him. If the leftwing leaders were to succeed, there would be no one in the future that these leftwing leaders could not remove. That would be the beginning of a new regime and the people would loose their freedoms and rights.

If Sen. Bernie Sanders or any socialist said Americans must change because the government is so corrupted, American people need to weight that statement again to see which countries have more corruption: America or Socialist Countries? Yes, we can find corrupted leaders in any country of the world but where do we find more corrupted leaders? In the socialist countries, it's for sure.

The socialist leaders could hide well their corruptions from one generation to another generation and they can play around the laws so they may go unpunished. If you apply well "It is not what you know, but it is who you know," you could be well protected. What happens to countless socialist leaders who found guilty with corruptions of millions and billions of U.S. dollars from all levels of government?

Most of the time, the subordinates of the leaders, not the leaders were prosecuted. The subordinates took their places because the leaders cannot corrupt, if they do how it is possible for them to convince people about justices and equality. Others are given warning or transferred to a lower position and waiting for the time to go to higher position than the position where they were charged with corruptions.

In America, there are corruptions and corrupted leaders who are good at hiding the evidences. But generally, the corruptions will be exposed and most of them will be prosecuted according to the laws in a matter of time. They would be removed from the service or they often volunteer to step down from the positions and admitting their wrong or corruption. You could hardly find this in socialist countries.

Thirdly when the big government takes control of the economy and the mode of production, it leads to the loss of passion, motivation and creativity, which are the important factors to thrive the businesses or the economy. Gradually it leads to the collapses of the businesses, the industries and then the economy. This is because many political leaders are not up to the positions they are assigned to be in charge.

They are assigned to be the head of that business establishment, industry, department or ministry or whatever the powerful positions because they are the seniors in the political party, or they are the children of the high-ranking officers, or they are the nieces, nephews, grandchildren, or relatives of this or that senior party leaders. Others climb up to powerful positions through corruption and bribery.

In most cases, these leaders do not have the related training, skills and experiences of the areas they are assigned to lead. They are in that position as a transition period to a higher position. Great ideas and innovations have been wasted, as they could not get through the bureaucracies and the political guidelines. If they could, the top leaders may not understand or do not have time to apply those innovations.

Even if many leaders want to care for the state businesses but many of them do not know how to do that. Others would think the businesses belong to the government any way and if the businesses are not doing well, the government will make subsidy. Some are capable and take good care of the businesses, but another new leader would come soon to take the position so they may go to better and higher positions.

The case of Hunter Biden who hold the senior position of Ukraine Burisma without any related trainings or experiences could be a good illustration. He could receive a large sum of money when people who were much more qualified than he was in terms of education, knowledge, skills and experiences could not. He was appointed because at that time his father was the former Vice President of the United States.

If his father was not the Vice President of the United States, then it was impossible for him to get that position. If there were no political power to back up Hunter Biden, and giving economic advantages to the operation of this foreign company, the company would not be willing to spend millions of U.S dollars for nothing especially to Hunter Biden who had no experiences and expertise in this field.

Fourthly, when the big government is so powerful to control the economy, the private sectors could hardly rise to place of prominence because private sectors are being monitored by the state. If the private sectors gain national influences and dominances they must agree to operate under the influences and the directions of the state if they want to continue to be in the businesses and thrive.

Many may say the socialist economic system is now working well in a few socialist countries and one of these socialist countries is among the top powers in the world. Why American socialists do not use that country as a great example of socialist countries? They would not do that of course because these countries were known with many oppressions and violations of human rights.

These countries tried hard with many economic reforms based on precious principles of the socialist economy, yet their socialist economic reforms and revolutions could not help them out of the poverty, famines, death and collapse of the regimes. The socialist leaders in these countries quickly adapted the open-door policy and allowed the operation of free enterprises and market-oriented economy.

Yes, it was not the socialist economic system that saved these countries from the collapse as it happened to the former Soviet Union. It was and is the free markets or capitalistic economist system that saves these countries. The key elements and principles of capitalistic economy saved the devastated socialist economies and countries from fallen apart but they still do not recognize that.

Young generations in these socialist countries still do not know about the truth of the socialist economic failures because those failures were not written and are not allowed to be mentioned in the textbooks, publications or media. There were a few times that some leaders may admit the failures but they would renounce their words at the pressures of the political leaders. History is rewritten in their dictation.

The socialists are so powerful in their propaganda and brainwashing to indoctrinate the people that their today successes are the results of the socialist ideology and only socialism may bring about prosperity, freedom and equality when the truth is socialism had brought so many pains to the people and the socialists use the principles of capitalism to save its ideology and regime without any recognition.

Do not be deceived by socialists who propagandize that it is the principles of socialist economies that socialist countries are thriving today. It is the principles of capitalistic economy that socialist countries have been able to overcome their tough times. Many socialists are still applying capitalistic economic system as socialist economic system could hardly help them to survive well like Venezuela or Cuba.

They grow by stealing ideas and inventions of people. They learn secrets by inviting industries to come to invest in their places. They become stronger by stealing technologies of companies and corporations. They compete by making intellectual properties of nations as their own. They prosper because they know how to partner with great partners and then take over their business establishments soon.

Fifthly, when the big government controls the power, economy, land, mode of productions and means of distribution, equality and justices could never happen in socialist countries. As the leaders have power, they corrupt and accumulate wealth; they become the richest and the most powerful group of people in socialist countries, they create bigger gap between the rich and poor.

The wealthy people in America or free worlds become rich and wealthy due to their talents and hard works. The wealthy socialist leaders become rich thanks to social ownership so they could easily use their power and positions to get wealth for themselves. Thus they are very insecure because of their illegal activities, bribes and corruptions, so they would destroy anyone who challenged or threatened them.

This would lead to inequality. The Americans are told that the socialist governments would provide free health care, free education, social securities and free stuffs. Those are just theories and promises. It would be enough for us to say that there are more free things and benefits offered in America than any socialist countries. Americans, you better awake from and realize the unrealistic promises of socialism.

Yes, the gap between the rich and the poor is wider in the socialist countries than it is in America. Yes, the inequality rate in the socialist countries is greater than the inequality rate in America. Yes, the gap between the powerful and the powerless is a lot greater in socialist countries than it is in America. The wealth gap between the common people and the socialist leaders is huge as East and West.

Just take a look at people who came from socialist countries to America, Canada and other developed countries to purchase corporations, companies, properties and many more, who are they? For sure, many of them are the children and relatives of the top leaders from socialist countries. The responsibilities of the top leaders are to keep good image as model leaders but they in fact corrupted money for their wealth.

It sounds contradictory, how is it possible for them to keep good image in the public and at the same time to corrupt money? It is all because the power is given into their hands and they can move the table around as they want. Many Americans are planning to give more power to the government at the great offers of the socialists. But those offers would rob your power and economic opportunities in the long run.

Last but not the least, when big government is in place, democracy is lost. Democracy is only possible when people have their voices and power. Democracy is only possible when human rights are promoted and protected. Democracy is only possible when people are free to exercise their free speech, free press, and free trials by jury… Democracy is only possible when no one is above the laws.

Good governments always say, "No One Is Above The Law." This saying works better in the U.S. where people see and hear more often leaders and people talk more about the laws and implement the laws. In socialist countries, people often share their heads saying, "People can do nothing about the leaders, they made the laws and they are the laws." So injustices are the results of leaders who abuse power.

Thomas Jefferson said, "When the people fear the government there is tyranny. When the government fear the people there is liberty." In the socialist countries, the government is the hungry and angry tiger. Of course the king of the forest would not allow other to freely move in its kingdom. The roar of the tiger king is already enough to scare the subjects of the kingdom to death.

It is not uncommon to witness rampant suppressions in socialist countries. People would be suppressed when they want to exercise their freedom of press but this freedom is not possible because the press is controlled strictly by the socialist government. People would be suppressed when they exercise their freedom of speech where citizens are told and taught what should and should not be spoken.

People would be suppressed when they demonstrate peacefully for justices and freedom and injustices and incarcerations are often the answers to justice and freedom seekers. People would be suppressed when they want to share different ideologies because only socialist ideology is allowed to be practiced and promoted. People would be suppressed when they want to share the truth.

In 2013, 13 activists and one blogger were sentenced to prison from 3 to 13 years though many human rights organizations demanded the government for the immediate release of these activists. In 2019, three activists were put into prison from 8 to 12 years. They are incarcerated because they are asking the socialist government for human rights, freedom and for fighting against corruption.

To sum it up, everything that is done not according to the will of the socialist leaders, the socialist government, the socialist party and the socialist ideology will be definitely suppressed. Everything that is said against the will of the socialist leaders, party, government and ideology will be for sure suppressed. Everything that is believed to make the authorities unhappy will be certainly suppressed.

When the subjects are not free from exploitation and oppression, then they cannot expect to be free from many economic deprivations. This explains why there are so many injustices happened to the common people at the abuses of power by the socialist leaders. Common people in the socialist countries are not only deprived of their freedom but also their properties and economic opportunities.

Is it possible for the common people to possess wealth and to share wealth in the socialist countries? Wealth is always possible in every society, but if wealth is to be feasible to certain groups of people in the socialist countries, then those people must be related to the leadership or they must know how to please the authorities to get advantages and to exploit common people for their wealth.

3rd Freedom: Freedom From Deprivations
Wealth and Distribution of Wealth

It was no doubt that hundred millions of people in many former socialist countries were fascinated at the great explanations and passions of the socialist leaders in the many plans of getting the wealth of the rich people to share those wealth to the poor and making people equally rich and powerful. The socialists ensured the people that socialism would bring about equal economic opportunities to everyone.

According to the Communist Manifesto, "In communist society, accumulated labor is but a means to widen, to enrich, to promote the existence of the laborer... Communism deprives no man of the power to appropriate the products of society; all that it does is to deprive him of the power to subjugate the labor of others by means of such appropriations."

The socialist ideas of land distribution to the poor, wealth distribution to the common people, enrichment of the laborers, and promotion of the existences of the working class were caught by people like fire. Then millions of people in the early days turned to socialism and wholeheartedly supported the socialist leaders. They did not know that they turned away from the green pastures to the parched lands.

In that momentum, millions of Americans today are also turning to socialism with the hopes for better lives, better opportunities, better treatments, better living conditions, better benefits and better future. It seemed that Americans could find those great things in socialism and in the promises of the socialists alone. Millions of Americans do not really know and learn painful lessons from the socialist histories.

Michael E. Telzrow stated correctly that, "the working classes had much to lose under socialism, and for later generations the shackles of communism would weigh heavy; for in practice, a central person or group had to control the redistribution of the wealth, and under communism power was concentrated for the benefit of the few at the controls-at the expenses of the masses, no matter the harm and the suffering visited upon the masses."

Just like the hundred millions of people turned away from the many economic opportunities of free market enterprises to the economic deprivations of the socialist system, millions of Americans are also heading to that direction with their innocence and ignorance. Millions of Americans are not quick to listen to the stories and experiences of the socialist victims for their losses of lands, jobs and even lives.

Firstly, the socialist leaders deprive people of their innocence. They know the grave needs of the poor people for stable incomes and stable life so they employ many benefits and freebies to attract common people for their political gains, agendas and purposes. They use the media to manipulate common people by creating the hatred and the division between the rich and the poor.

The socialist leaders manipulate the trust of the people for them and the socialist ideology so that they could carry out the socialist agendas to get powers at the sufferings and misfortunes of millions of people. They hide the true face of socialism and its so many failures. They cover well the facts that socialism is the cause of more than 200 million deaths and the ruthless socialist regime.

Many American millennials are deprived of the true information and news about socialism and socialist nations. American socialists even misled people that the Nordic countries are the great models of the socialist countries but they are not. They also told the people that they do not need big government and abolishment of private businesses but their plans require big government and social ownership.

Millions of Americans are deceived by the leftwing leaders that capitalism has failed to create wealth, equality, social justice, and freedom when it is socialism that failed miserably. Millions of Americans are indoctrinated by the leftwing media, their lies and their great promises of wealth distributions and equality. Yet, the result is that thousands of Americans are rioting and destroying their own communities.

Secondly, the socialist leaders deprive people of their powers. They make use people's powers and full supports to make a successful political revolution and they know well how to unleash the powers of the people to win their battles at the great costs of human lives, sacrifices and sufferings. The socialist leaders successfully overthrow the democratic governments and destroy the powers of their rivals.

Is there any socialist country in the world without the operations of police task force? The socialist countries even have more policemen and policewomen. Yet, so many Americans are so naïve to believe the BLM leaders, the Antifa leader and the leftwing leaders that they need to defund and disband police department. Many Americans do not know that is how they would become powerless soon.

When the socialists are in power and in control of the socialist nations, the people loose their powers and the powers are no longer to be shared as the socialists often said but the powers are exclusive and precious properties of the socialist leaders alone. Then the people are left without power, without freedom and without opportunity to choose the leaders and the government they want for better lives.

Thirdly, the socialist leaders deprive people of their labors. They criticized the capitalists for the exploitations, sufferings, instabilities and poverty of the workers but those are the results of the socialists' corruptions, greed and abuses of power. Common people could become wealthy with the capitalists but that is not so with the socialists unless the people must corrupt and compromise with the socialists.

The people also loose their power to pursue high positions in the government offices, organizations or businesses. Many people are talented and capable yet they could hardly climb up the bureaucracies for better positions or better economic opportunities just because they are not the socialist members or they do not belong to any political organizations or they have no socialist leaders to back them up.

Whenever, there are many good jobs and business opportunities or business projects available, common people could never have chances to grasp those business opportunities or projects because they are not the members of the political party and they are not in the special socialist group. So when the announcement about business projects announced, everything is too late for them.

Thousands of talented people were wasted and their ideas and innovations were not appreciated. They had no opportunities to make their innovations and research a reality in socialist countries, so they went to the U.S and free nations where they could find better opportunities for them to develop themselves and to apply their innovations and researches, and where they are respected and treasured.

Due to unemployment and low salaries in the communist country, hundred thousands of workers went abroad to work in factories. They got better salaries so they could send finances home to help their family members but they were discriminated, poorly treated and attacked by gang groups. Millions of people run away from the socialist countries in search of economic opportunities and freedoms.

Mike was in a big management team of stock market in a socialist country and he was very successful. We were impressed and also surprised at the same time because we hardly heard that his team lost their investment but his team kept on winning every time. We wanted to learn about the secrets for the many and great successes of his team so we asked him from time to time about their secrets.

He did share many principles of success from hard works to team works, from right timing to right judgments, from keen observations to accurate evaluations, from good analysis to the great system and many more. Even so his team was so good on those things but many big companies that observed well those principles also failed from time to time. But that was what I learned from him.

Then we noticed that Mike did a lot of travels to meet business partners but he rarely talked about those meetings. Out of curiosity we also asked him from time to time about those people and we was surprised with the many top leaders that he frequently met. Then we realized a very important and the most critical principle of success that he shared but he did not explain much and we did not pay much attention to.

Mike said before that they had to be updated with information all the time and the leaders knew what would happen. This important principle is still very true because the top leaders could even influence the up and down of the stock market for their gains if they want to do so and the business partners must depend on them for the most update information before they could make the right decisions.

Then the common people are mostly still the losers in the games of leaders in power. People's investments in stocks, jobs, houses, businesses, and projects could be affected and even lost at the manipulations of the corrupted leaders. The common people toiled and sweated for years to save up some incomes for their investments but their toils could be gone at any time at the decisions of the top leaders.

Fourthly, the socialist leaders deprive people of their lands. Since the lands are socially owned so the lands do not belong to the people but the government. The people were told that the lands were socially owned by the people but that promise was just to make the people comforted. The people use the land but they have no right to own the lands even people purchased the lands with their blood and toil.

When the government wants to take back the lands for new developments or any purpose, the people must be ready to move to new locations. Their produces and their toils for years to develop the farms and properties could be ended at very poor compensations. Their businesses or economic incomes were greatly affected when they had to move everything to new places.

In most cases, the farmers could hardly find new jobs. They were the farmers and gardeners or livestock raisers for most of their lives and now they were moved to new locations where those jobs were no longer available. They had to look for new jobs and they were not good and not happy at the new jobs. Many people were unemployed and their family suffered poverty.

With the urbanization, the value of the land also increased but they were compensated unjustly. The lives of the people could be much better if they were duly compensated according to the real value of their lands. Then they could have more capital and resources to invest their money or to start their businesses. Yet they were brutally exploited and the future was uncertain.

Fifthly, the socialist leaders deprive people of their opportunities. When there are great opportunities for jobs, housings, positions, promotions and educations offered by the central government or the donors to the common people. These opportunities could bring about many economic benefits to the people but the socialists would get those opportunities first for themselves or their people.

The socialist leaders are even heartless to deprive people of their social welfares and aids. The welfares are to assist the suffering people to resettle their lives and losses after the floods, earthquakes or tragedies. Health cares packages or relief packages were provided to suffering people, yet the socialist leaders get half of the aids or more for themselves while the people were struggling with their needs.

The corruptions of relief and social aids are very rampant and the local authorities try every way so that they could get economic benefits

Those huge amounts of money were also wasted in relationship buildings, parties, drugs, briberies, vices, lobbies, gambles, mistresses and more. The wasteful resources could have been used to give poor children education scholarship and health cares so that they could head to a better future. The corrupted money could have been maximized to provide job opportunities so their lives could be stable.

Three decades ago, my parents purchased a small piece of land in a suburban area called Salt Farm district. The land was very cheap then because it was a farmland though the place was not very far from the city center. My parents' plan was that they would move out from the city life and they would build a small house there to enjoy their old age in the countryside later. My parents were happy about that plan.

But their dream could never be realized at the exploitations of the corrupted local leaders. The government soon announced that the Salt Farm district would be developed by the government as part of the urbanization for tourism and residency. This meant that many families in that district would soon be moved to a new area if they happened to live in the major areas according to the city planning.

Then massive developments for the roads took place first and the local people expected their new developed areas would soon come into reality with new roads, new building and new city look. The local people were also looking forward to new business opportunities generated from tourism and hospitality industry. But suddenly, the development just came to a sudden stop.

The local authorities did not explain why did the constructions stopped or projects were put on hold. The people were just informed to wait for further instructions. Since the area was planned according to the central government so the lands in the area could not be sold legally and the values of the land was depreciated and people could only secretly transfer the usage of land through written documents.

The local people and the investors waited and waited. They wanted to build up restaurants and shops while waiting for further instruction from the government but they were not allowed to do anything but wait. The farmers wanted to plant their crops but they could not do so. More years were to come and nothing happened so the lands were just left emptied and unproductive.

There were people who planted the crops or started their livestock farms at their own risks and it meant that if the construction suddenly began again, then the local government would not be responsible for the loss of damaging their crops and their farms. Others could not wait and they just transferred their lands at cheap price because the local government would not authorize the ownership of the land.

For almost 30 nightmare years since the government announced that plan, the people were not allowed to build their new houses and they could not develop the land by themselves. They could only maintained and repaired their own houses. They could not do business and their many economic opportunities were deprived in three decades yet there were no compensations from the local government.

For that long period of almost 30 years, the people were on strikes to seek the permission to sell their lands and houses legally but their strike was still aimless and there were no definite answer. They fought for almost 30 years so they could have the rights to invest and develop their lands but their efforts were in vain. They demonstrated for the rights to build new houses but they got no permits.

For almost 30 long-lost years, the value of the lands in the neighboring districts already increased three to five times but the lands in Salt Farm was depreciated. The economy and the environments in the neighboring areas are getting better and modernized but the Salt Farm area is still underdeveloped and the people lost so many economic opportunities to gain wealth in those long lost years.

For almost 30 suffering years, their business opportunities were taken away at the tricks of the corrupted socialist leaders who are only interested in fighting for their benefits but not the benefits of the people. For more years to come the people will continuously be exploited, their lands and properties will be exploited, their investments, their rights, their dreams and their lives will be exploited too.

For almost 30 traumatic years, their times, their youth, their recourses, their opportunities and their primes were wasted. If they had their rights to develop and cultivate their lands, properties and recourses, their lives and their children for sure could have had higher economic status. If their lives and lands were not being exploited by the socialists, they could have become millionaires like others.

In those 30 years, the socialist leaders and their members kept being promoted from one position to higher positions. They accumulated wealth and power wherever they went. They had to spend for and corrupted their higher leaders but that was ok for them because that was the process for their political gains and they could get more wealth from the people as they climbed up higher political ladder.

After a few decades, the socialist bourgeoisies, elites and leaders had too much wealth that they secretly transferred their wealth and businesses and they also migrated their children to free and developed nations. They knew very well that the socialist regime would not last long and they also know well that their power and wealth in the socialist country could be gone at any moment.

The socialist leaders sent their children to the prosperous Western worlds like the U.S. These are the countries that they once told the innocent poor people that these countries had so much poverties, inequalities and exploitations. These countries are the enemies of socialism and the socialists had the responsibilities to deliver the people of these countries from the control of the capitalists and capitalism.

The socialist announced loud and clear that the socialist government would free people from oppressions and capitalism, and now the socialists and the socialist leaders worry that their families would be persecuted in their socialist countries. They declared that socialism would rule the world and now they have to make safe plan for their families and themselves before the coming doom and fall of socialism.

If the socialist countries could really free the people from exploitations, oppressions, deprivations, poverty and inequalities, why do the socialist leaders send their children and transfer their wealth and businesses to the free nations that they once mocked at? Do you know that the children of the top leaders of the socialist nations are all in the U.S now and so many children of the socialist leaders are U.S citizens?

There are also wealthy people in the socialist countries and most of them obtain new citizenship in the western world and they also try their best to transfer their wealth abroad secretly. Why do they do so? Because they know that their wealth could be over in the socialist countries anytime when they do not cooperate with the socialists or when the socialist leaders want to destroy them for any reason.

This was what the socialists did to millions of the landlords, wealthy and business owners in their lands before. They were the ones who took away the wealth and the lives of these million capitalists. So they know very well that soon or later, the socialist government would carry out the plan of social ownership in the name of equality, then people's wealth would be taken away from them and the people.

Our grandparents from my wife side were also wealthy landlords. Just like hundred thousands of the wealthy families who were the victims of the socialists' social ownership, our grandparents were also persecuted and their wealth and properties were taken away from the patriotic socialists. The authorities rushed into their house and searched everything that they could find.

When they could not find any more things that they could see by their eyes, they broke the walls of the house into pieces to find gold and jewelries hidden. Then they dig the floor of their house to find more gold and jewelries there. They did so well that they totally destroyed the house and they dig two-meters deep of the floor and they sent the families to the countryside for hard labor works.

The socialist leaders know that this history of wealth acquisition by the government would be repeated. That is why the socialist leaders must find ways to send their children and their wealth to the capitalist countries, the "enemy countries" that they usually oppose to in their countries but these capitalist countries could always protect their wealth and their lives except the socialist countries.

Will this happen soon to wealthy Americans? Some cases already happened through the riots and violent protests mobilized by the socialists, leftwing democrats, trained Marxists, communists and terrorists. People's shops were looted, people's houses were robbed and many people were shot and killed. If the socialists were to take over the U.S., massive massacres would take place.

Kshama Sawant, Seattle City Council woman said, "I have a message for Jeff Bezos and his class. If you attempt again to overturn the Amazon Tax, working people will go all out in the thousands to beat you… And we will not stop there. We are preparing the ground for a different kind of society, and if you, Jeff Bezos, want to drive that process forward by lashing out against us in our modest demands, then so be it.

"Because we are coming for you and your rotten system. We are coming to dismantle this deeply oppressive, racist, sexist, violent, utterly bankrupt system of capitalism. This police state. We cannot and will not stop until we overthrow it, and replaced it with a world based, instead on solidarity, genuine democracy, and equality: a socialist world. Thank you" reported Ian Schwartz.

So why are million Americans yearning for the U.S to become a socialist nation when the socialist leaders of million socialist victims try to run away from insecurities, injustices and tyrannies of the socialist regime? If the common people in the socialist country are being exploited, oppressed and deprived of their economic opportunities and benefits, is it possible that people would enjoy great equalities?

4th Freedom: Freedom From Inequalities
Egalitarianism and Inequality

My grandfather from my mother side was quite a wealthy businessman. He owned vast farm lands and many fishing boats and of course many workers. During his time, he was considered as a big landlord with vast lands where the storks could freely stretch their wings to fly across his lands. His family and he were loved by the people in his town for their successes, kindness, hospitality and generosity.

At the rise of socialism in the land, the socialists started to kill the landlords and the wealthy people or to put them in the labor camps to carry out a classless society and the elimination of rich and poor gap. They would take away the lands, properties, and wealth and their family members were sent to labor camps, prisons, or new economic zones as farmers to suffer the poor living conditions, malaria and deaths.

One evening the socialists came to the house of my grandparents. At the unyielding and non-stop barks of the dogs and at the sounds of the gate breaking, my grandfather felt that something was wrong and the whole family asked him to hide immediately. The socialists broke the main gate and then the doors of the house and rushed into the house as they asked my grandmother, "Where is your husband?"

My grandmother and the whole family members were nervous and scared but they tried to keep calm as my grandmother replied the angry and bloodthirsty socialists, "My husband is not home yet." The socialists of course did not believe her and her words because they knew that he was surely at home. They searched every corner of the house and the garden but they could not find him and they were very upset.

The socialist soldiers went to the huge fishing nets to search for my grandfather but they could not find him either. They used the long drakes to spear through the nets and they even shot at the nets to see if my grandfather was hiding inside. It was only by God's protection that the rakes did not hurt him and the bullet did not touch him though he was hiding inside those nets or else that could be his last day.

My grandfather hid himself in the nets until early in the morning and then the whole family left their homes, lands, fishing boats, properties, businesses, assets, great life and everything behind to run for life. They came to a new area in another province where they started a new life as gardeners. My grandfather was able to survive and the whole family did not go through the horrible tortures and humiliations.

Yet million rich people and their families were not spared from the discriminations, sufferings, poverty, humiliations, robbing, raping, prisons or murders by the cruel socialist members and leaders. These wealthy people really went through hades on earth. They had to fight against the poor living conditions, the new environments, the hard labors, many sicknesses, and the strict controls of the socialists.

Unfortunately, the socialists did not show their gratitude to the landlords, the wealthy people and their family members like my grandparents who were the major supports for the existence and expansion of socialism and the socialists from their early beginning. The socialists received almost anything they needed from these rich people yet they returned nightmares, grieves, evils and murders to these people.

At least, the socialists could have appreciated these rich people or they could have treated these people equally like other people in accordance to their ideology. The socialists could just take away their wealth and properties and use their talents to contribute to the good and the development of the country. Yet, equality was never a reality to these oppressed people whose rights and lives were taken away.

Equality was never a reality to the ruled people. Equality may happen when there are mutual respect, mutual understanding, and mutual care between the government servants and the people. When the socialists and their family members consider the people as their slaves for wealth and power and the people as their objects to be abused and exploited, then equality was an unrealistic wish or dream.

Equality was never a reality to the masses too. The socialists live with their grand party life and luxurious celebrations but the majority of the people struggle for their daily living and many expenses of their children. The socialists possess so many lands, houses, villas and properties but the majority of the people could hardly pay their monthly rent so how could they afford for a house of their own?

Equality was never a reality to even the socialists. The socialists are fighting each other for powers and positions. They also form their groups and allies to consolidate their powers and positions. They also have their enemies in the same political party that they use all means to destroy their enemies and their threats. The socialist leaders do not want their socialist enemies to become equal in their powers.

Equality was never a reality to people in the socialist nations. From Europe to Africa and to Asia or Latin America, socialism always left the painful marks of tyrannies and unbridgeable gaps between the poor and the socialist elites. Socialism leads to the imbalance powers between the socialist rulers and the ruled people. Socialism never brings about the fair social justices to the people.

Are there equal wealth between the socialists and common people?
Are there equal treatments between the socialists and common people?

Are there equal social benefits between the socialists and common people?
Are there equal job opportunities between the socialists and common people?
Are there equal education opportunities between the socialists and common people? For sure, you know well the answer to these questions.

Who are the richest people in the socialist countries? It is no doubt that the richest people in the socialist countries are the socialist leaders, their children and relatives

Who are spending the most in the luxurious resorts? It is no doubt that the richest people in the socialist countries are the socialist leaders, their children and relatives

Who is the majority of the foreign students from socialist countries in the U.S. and the Western world? It is no doubt that the majority of the foreign students are the children and relatives of the socialist leaders.

Who are the people purchasing corporations, businesses, and large properties in the U.S and the Western world in the recent years? It is no doubt that most of these people are the children and relatives of the socialist leaders

Who are spending millions of U.S dollars in casinos around the world? For sure, you already know the answer now.

People are unequal in their wealth in the socialist countries
People are unequal in their benefits in the socialist countries
People are unequal in their positions in the socialist countries
People are unequal in their treatments in the socialist countries
People are unequal in their opportunities in the socialist countries

The great promises of the socialists could not be seen from the positive sides of the promises as they said but the negative ones because the socialists are known to promise heaven to people but they deliver hell. They assure people with many freedoms and people receive oppressions.

They present to people with many rights and they can exercise many rights that the people cannot.

The egalitarian principles of socialism are well applied in producing the equal disastrous consequences across the former and current socialist nations. The people in these nations went through similar cases such as equal failures, equal humiliations, equal tortures, equal pains, equal sufferings, equal hunger, equal desperations, and equal suppressions.

It is sure that the ruled people are equal in their poverty
It is sure that the ruled people are equal in limited freedoms
It is sure that the ruled people are equal in underpaid compensations
It is sure that the ruled people are equal in their losses of human rights
It is sure that the ruled people are equal in many injustices and sufferings

There is a great parable of old telling us a great and powerful lesson. One day a bear caught a rabbit. The pitiful rabbit was frightened at the thought of death and trembled in the paws of the bear. The bear looked at the rabbit and decided not to eat the rabbit. This was not because the bear felt pitiful for the rabbit at her look but because the rabbit was so skinny and she could not be a great meal for him.

The bear thought, "I would feed her and when she was fat up I could eat her at anytime." So the bear talked to the rabbit, "I will not kill you, we are good friends and I will take care of your needs. Do not be afraid." The rabbit was so happy and she was more than happy to become his good friend. They indeed had a good time together as they could run and play together and communicate to each other.

The rabbit soon became happier, more beautiful, and fatter. One day, the bear called the rabbit to come close to him and as he looked at the rabbit something just came to his mind and he asked the rabbit to wait for him. The rabbit felt so touch at his melancholy look and was eager to see what the bear was going to give her or to do as she waited. Mr. bear came back with a red veil and he put over her head.

The rabbit was so thrilled and so happy. She thought, "Wow, at last he wants to marry me." At that moment of her happiness, the bear ripped her head off and enjoyed his long awaiting meal. This is a sad and cruel ending but that is the truth about socialism. You may wonder what is the meaning of the red veil or why did the bear covered the head of the rabbit with the red veil?

In many Asian cultures, the parents covered the red veil over the head of the bride on the wedding day and the bride is sent to the house of the bridegroom. On that night of their wedding, the bride would sit at the wedding bed with the veil covering her head and wait for the bridegroom to come in. As the bridegroom entered the room, he would take off the red veil from her head and the honeymoon began.

The socialists offer people with the red veil of happiness to make people happy for a while, yet their real purpose is to take advantage of the innocence of people, their wishful thinking of a great future painted by the socialists. Then the people would become the preys of the socialists when their right time comes. They would make people to feel touched, cared and loved before the nightmares to come.

Do Americans really know that America has always been the fertile and dreamed land that the socialists have been dreaming for?

Just as the bear would not spare the rabbit because they are not the same species and size, the socialists would not spare anyone who is different from their ideology and they are willing use people as their ladders for their searches, satisfactions and successes. If the socialists could cruelly executive the innocent ones, what else would they not do to people who are disagreeing with them or against them?

Are you still dreaming for America to become a socialist country to see that your properties and wealth to be robbed, exploited, to become public properties so that the socialist leaders could transfer those wealth to their pockets? Are you interested in discovering how justices are carried out in the socialist country? How do the people apply freely their freedom of trials by jury?

5th Freedom: Freedom From Injustices
Judiciary Fairness and Social Injustices

My hometown is known for the many beautiful beaches and islands. Due to the urban and tourist developments, many local communities and people were forced to move from their homes and lands to new areas so that the government could give the lands to the developers for the building of the economic zones, the constructions of resorts, or the development of tourist zones and sceneries.

In most cases, the local leaders would move more people out from their communities that were located near to the new developed areas even though those people and their communities were not supposed to be moved out to new locations according to the projects approved by the central government. But the local leaders would do that because the lands in those areas would soon become more valuable.

Then the local leaders would give those lands to other investors or developers and of course they could earn a lot of money from those lands and lots. Yet the local people often did not know that they were tricked by the corrupted leaders. Supposedly, local people could become a lot richer if they were to sell their lands to the developers but they were often exploited by the corrupted and greedy leaders.

The socialist leaders got more money from the investors or developers for every tree, resources and property on the land. They could ask high prices and compensations and of course great commissions from the developers because the leaders had the power to bargain for great deals as the developers mostly needed the great lands in strategic locations and the leaders could make that decision.

People in the slum areas were often happy to move to new areas because they did not have many things to loose but people who owned bigger lots of land and properties were often the victims of the poor and underpaid compensations by the local leaders. Whether people own big or small lots of land, the compensations were almost the same. Their duly compensations were deprived severely.

As people knew that injustices happened to them and they started to ask and kept asking for the due compensations but justices could hardly come to them. For 20 years, the local people were on strikes but there was no solution to their situations. They have been filling many lawsuits to get back their lands, properties or to ask for proper compensations but the judiciary system and justice are not on their sides.

In the socialist countries, since people have no right for the private ownership of land because the land is socially owned. The truth is the land belongs to the government and determined by the government and not by the people who are often told that the people are the owners of the land but the reality is opposite. When the government asked people to move to new places, people must obey.

If people really had the shared power and shared ownership of the land, then their voices should have power and should be respected. If people do not comply to the orders, the local government know well how to use different ways to deal with these pitiful people until these powerless people had to leave or they would be forced to leave when the government begins to develop the places.

This is totally different from the free worlds like America because Americans have absolute power and right to their lands and properties. It is not by forces and threats that Americans would leave their lands and their houses but it takes a mutual agreement, understanding and duly compensations. Americans even had the right to shoot down people who invade their homes, lands, and properties.

This is a great reminder to Americans and people of the nations who still want socialism and the socialists to rule and to rob your many rights. Once you agree for social ownership then you would loose your power and right for private businesses and private ownership of your land and guns. You would loose your power and rights for arms and armies. You would loose your powers and freedoms.

Though the socialists always say that socialism does not need to abolish free enterprises and private ownership and they do not need big government. But they have been using that trick for a century long and they are not going to change their trick. The socialists must say that way to make people feel more secure and people would be more comfortable to vote for them and support them.

Americans may say, "Why didn't these people apply freedom of trials by jury?" Common people in the socialist nations also want to do so but most of the people do not even know if they have that right or if that right is possible or not. In reality, people would wonder if the right is really needed here because the people know very well that the lawyers, judges or juries only listen to the higher leaders.

The socialist judiciary system is **firstly** to protect the socialist ideology. The socialist ideology not the people is the most and foremost important thing in the socialist country. Socialism is the heart and the focus of the country and it is the only way that people could find freedom and happiness. So socialism must have the first priority to be protected and defended in the judicial system.

The sad truth is that the socialist country can sacrifice people but the country cannot sacrifice the socialist ideology. People must sacrifice to glorify and to protect the ideology. People are willing to sacrifice themselves if the ideology is going to bring about the wellbeing of the humanity and they would not do so when the ideology is to against the humanity and to build regime.

Are people willing to embrace the socialist ideology in the socialist countries? They did embrace but the majority of the people suffered too much from socialist regime. People are now forced to accept the socialist ideology and those who oppose the ideology would be punished severely. The people are bound and controlled by the ideology and the political party. This is the cause of tyrannies and regime.

The socialist judiciary system is **secondly** to protect the political party. The political party is the guiding star and the sun. The socialist party is the only party that can lead people to discover the truth and the light of socialism, and to create a socialist utopia. The socialist political party must be long live so that it could lead people to freedom, equality and happiness.

If there is an only choice to choose either the socialist political party or the people, the country still has to choose the political party but that is only the choice of the corrupted socialist leaders who are thirsty for power over the sufferings of the people. People in the socialist countries today are demonstrating to remove the socialist political party but they could not do so because they have no power.

The socialist judiciary system is **thirdly** to protect the socialist leaders. The socialist leaders are the laws, the lawmakers and are above the laws. Thus the justice system could never touch them unless certain leaders are no longer in favor of the socialist political party and these leaders must be purged and punished as great example to warn people the consequences of disloyalty to the ideology and the party.

Unfortunately, the big criminals of the country are also the leaders of the country. The socialist leaders are the people behind the vices and the crimes. They are the unseen leaders of vicious operations such as sex trafficking, drug dealings, gang groups, and corruptions. They are the causes of the sufferings, murdering, humiliations, oppressions and injustices of the people.

The socialist judiciary system is **fourthly** to protect "birds of the same feathers." The judiciary system is obviously operated on the principle, "you are with us or against us." It would not accommodate people who are against the will and the guidance of the socialist ideology and leadership. It would not accommodate people of different ideologies and their political agendas.

The leaders must also protect one another or else they would be charged with many crimes because they are all corrupted. They must protect one another so that they could gain wealth and power illegally. They must protect one another so they could survive together. They apply well the principle "united we stand, divided we fall" to corrupt the wealth, exploit people, protect their benefits and control powers.

The socialist judiciary system is **fifthly** to protect the socialist powers. It must be in favor of the executive power, judiciary power and legislative power. These powers include political power, economic power, media power and the military power and any power that is protecting the existence and the goal of the socialist regime. Without powers, the socialist system is paralyzed.

Unfortunately, these powers are connected to uphold the socialist power and the socialist regime. The powers are employed to oppress innocent people and to control their rights. The powers are used to maintain the brutal regime and to cover the evils of the socialist leaders. The powers are manipulated for the gains of the corrupted socialists and for the sufferings of the people.

In any case, the people are the least to be protected in the socialist judiciary system. When the legal system and justices are not mainly to protect the people, then the people would be at loss for the justices and the people are the pitiful victims of the socialists' abuses of power. This is one of the main reasons why the socialist countries are always the top countries that violate human rights.

If social justice provides the equal access for common people to the rights, wealth, opportunities, and privileges within a society, then there would not be many injustices in the socialist countries. While socialism and the socialists always hail socialism for equality, justices and freedoms, yet the socialist countries always deliver limited freedoms, rampant injustices, and extreme inequalities.

Who are the wealthiest people in socialist countries? The socialist leaders, socialist members, their families, their relatives and their subordinates are no doubt the richest and most powerful people in the socialist countries. The socialists promise equal wealth distribution and social ownership of wealth but that promise is true for the socialists but not for the people. The people are equally poor and exploited.

Who have more opportunities in the socialist countries? The more opportunities are also given to the socialist members, the socialist leaders, their families, their relatives and their subordinates. They have more opportunities for better educations, faster promotions, top positions, powerful political power, greater wealth, and more luxurious lifestyles, people's opportunities are exploited then.

Who have more privileges in the socialist countries? For sure, you now know the answer. Supposedly, the poor and the underprivileged people should have more opportunities and privileges so their lives could be improved and their families could become better. Unfortunately, the opportunities and the privileges of the people are also robbed, exploited and manipulated by the greedy and evil socialists.

Then these countries are no longer the socialist countries and there should be no socialists. In its true sense, there is only one socialist country, but other countries prefer to call themselves socialist countries because the socialist ideology and the socialist party give the leaders absolute authority and power. They are already addicted to power and controlled by the power.

The socialists could not let go the powers because they know that their lives would be over when the powers are no longer belonged to them.

They are the victims of powers because they wrongly use powers to crimes, injustices, abuses of power, corruptions and murders. When the powers really belong to the people, then the socialists are the criminals and punished with many crimes against humanity.

Their hands have been stained with so many innocent bloods in their crimes for their political endeavors, brutal fights for their political positions, and vicious acts for their wealth accumulations. Their lives are now full with many rivals and enemies who are willing to take them down at anytime. Thus, they must protect themselves by becoming stronger so they could save themselves and their people.

During my university days, there were some scholarships for the students in the university to go abroad to study. The requirement was that the students must have good English skills to participate in an English examination given by the donor institution and the top ten students who passed the exam with the highest scores would be elected and would be sent to study abroad.

The students were very happy because this was a golden opportunity for them to go and study abroad and especially the scholarships were great because the scholarships were given by the foreign royal family so the scholarships covered everything and of course those who could graduate from the famous university would have greater opportunities for better jobs and future.

Just like many students, I also participated in the exam and I was glad that I was also among the top-ten students who passed the exam for the scholarship. I was happy and waited for the university to prepare the documents needed for student visa and I was looking for the day to go abroad. But no one from the university contacted me or updated me about the process or the procedures for visa application.

So I went to the school office and asked for the information and the staffs told me to wait and the school would instruct me about the procedures to apply for student visa when the time came. So I waited again for a few more months and then the semester was over but there was still no news from the university office. So I could only hope that the news would come soon after the summer break.

The new semester began after the summer break and the classes went on, and then the students suddenly talked about the students who went abroad. Of course I was also shocked when other students asked me why I did not go abroad with the scholarship and the same question was asked with another student on the top-ten list of the exam that I knew.

I went to the school office to ask for the truth but the faculty and the staff did not know what was happening. So I went to meet the president of the university and he simply said that the teachers made a wrong calculation of the exam and I was no longer among the top students. The same answer was given to the other student I knew and maybe the same answer was given to all the students on the top list.

Now you would understand why it was not necessary for me to sue the president or the school because I would not win the case anyway even I did sue them. My voice was too weak to be heard by the judiciary system then and the judiciary system was and is still not interested to defend the rights of the weak people. In so many cases when the victims sued the socialist leaders, more tragedies happened to the victims.

The students who robbed our scholarships and went abroad on our behalf were the children and the relatives of the socialist leaders. How could we win the lawsuit when the power was in their hand? How could we win the cases when they could easily change the documents? How could we defeat the socialists when the judiciary system is to protect the socialist leaders and their people?

The unfair judicial and justice system is also the direct result of the big government. As the saying goes "In the kingdom of the blind, the one-eye man is the king." In the socialist countries, the strong ones would win and the justices belong to the strong and powerful ones. The poor and weak people could only put their blames on fate for the many sufferings and injustices that come along their paths of life.

Though Americans still complaint about the racial issues due to clashes, fighting and murdering cases with the police task forces. Yet, Americans are still well protected by the judicial and justice system that put the rights, freedom, safety, security and benefits of every American equal and first priority while the judicial and justice system of the socialist nations put the socialist leaders above the law.

In the free world, when people feel that their rights and freedom are compromised, damaged, or threatened by others, people could file their complains to the court and to ask justices for their losses, hurts, wrong accusations, grievances. People could repeal or they could present their cases to the Petite jury and the Grand jury. People often receive fair judgment on their cases by attorneys or judges.

In socialist countries, when injustices happened the people and the justice often does not come to them because of the corruption of the leaders and their powers. People have no choice and from time to time they gather to demonstrate and to demand justices. The socialist leaders send gangsters and mafias to threaten people and even beat the victims of socialist injustices so that the victims just keep quiet.

That is justice in the socialist country.

Some may argue, "even though the people may face with exploitations, oppressions, economic deprivations, inequalities and injustices, but the people would have not many pressures because the people receive so many social benefits and that their lives would be enjoyable and comfortable." Our next session, Freedom From Many Burdens would give the readers more insights on the matter.

6ᵗʰ Freedom: Freedom Freedom From Multi-Burdens
Social Benefits and Distortions

My team and I visited elderly homes from time to time and blessed the elderly people with some foods. When we came to an elderly home and it was almost noon and we brought the gifts to the elderly people at their rooms. As I approached a room, I saw an old man who was sitting by the door. He did not notice that we were coming close to him, as he was busy doing something.

The old man was scattering the rice on a small tray and trying to pick out small rocks from the rice. I looked at the rice and I saw that rice was already partially dark and moist and it was supposedly to be thrown away or to give to animals. I was thinking that he may use that rice to cook for his dog or he may have nothing to do so he was just playing with it. I asked him, "Uncle, what are you doing?"

He said, "I am preparing rice to cook for my lunch." I immediately asked him, "Are you cooking for your lunch with this rice?" He said, "Yes." Automatically I said, "Uncle, the rice is not good, just throw it away or else you may get sick when you eat that rice." Upon hearing what I said, he just looked at me and his puzzling eyes made me realize that I should not speak those words.

His puzzling and shocking eyes expressed well what he wanted to tell me, "Are you kidding me? If I throw this rice away what am I going to eat? How am I going to survive today? That is all I have for today." I looked at his bag of rice and it was empty. The humidity of the room made the rice moist and partial dark, but that was his life and that was how he lived his day in darkness and loneliness.

To the well-to-do people, that rice was good for nothing but to throw away but for this old man and millions of people who were under poverty, the little foods and things that they had meant everything to them. It was their life, hope and the remaining temporary happiness that they had. When they finished what they had now then they would struggle to find foods for the coming days.

We may provide them some foods now through the supports of generous Christians, but how were their lives throughout the years and years to come? These elderly people were either abandoned by their children or they had no children. They were so poor that they had no place to live. The government built a place for them so they could at least have a place to survive their days.

The government also provided them some basic supports but the little support from the government to them was mostly robbed by the local authorities. Each elderly person had only a small room to live and they cooked and lived by themselves. They were on their own without health service, medical supports or sports and entertainment activities. Are these elderly people happy and satisfied?

Please do not compare these elderly homes with elderly homes in the U.S. That is a totally wrong comparison because Americans may tend to think the elderly homes that are well equipped with many facilities and services. You may compare the lives of these elderly people with homeless people in America but at least these homeless people are served with free meals and they could apply for social security disability.

My coworkers and I visited many elderly homes supported by the local government, we could only see the happy smiles of the local authorities and they were happy to welcome our teams but we could hardly see the smiles on the pitiful faces of the elderly people whom we visited. Even they tried to smile but you could tell how hard it was for them to smile as layers of sufferings were engraved on their faces.

That is just an example of the social welfare in a socialist country in responding to the many great promises of the socialists to make America a great socialist nations with many great social benefits that could lift almost the burdens from people's lives through basic incomes, stable jobs, free health care, free education, free daycare service, free debt and many freebies.

In America, millions of illegal immigrants are still able to receive the social welfares, free health cares, and food stamps and other free services. Their children would receive free educations, free after-school tutoring, and free foods at schools. Is there any socialist countries in the world could provide so many good offers as America does? People in the socialist countries now must pay for everything for services.

The leftists, the socialists and the democrats who support the socialist agendas for the many said freebies but they are also the ones who turn their states to be mostly populated with so many homeless people who are suffering with many economic hardships and sufferings. That is also the prospect of a socialist America in a near future as it is with some socialist countries in Latin America.

Just take a look at a socialist country in North Asia; the country is so poor that people could not eat even three meals a day and the people are suffering greatly. Foreigners are basically not allowed to go beyond certain cities. The extreme socialist government still tries to cover the truth about the poverty even though almost the whole world already know how poor the country is.

The capital city looks gorgeous with the high-rise buildings and modern facilities. But what is the reality of life beyond that beautiful capital city?

People from former socialist countries and third-world countries who went through famines and poverty could easily imagine and identify with the hard life and the many worries or burdens of the citizens in this socialist regime.

Foreigners who dare to go beyond the areas allowed would be arrested and may be even disappeared forever because they are considered as spies and because the real poverty situation of the country and the sufferings of the people are not allowed to be known to the public and nations. Thus, security guards and policemen are everywhere to watch over the movements and cameras of foreigners.

Tourist foreigners must be traveled in a group with tour guide and with transportations arranged by the tourist company. They are not allowed to use public transportations without tour guide. They are not even allowed to make long conversation to local people except some greetings. They are not allowed to say anything against the socialist rule or show disrespect to the socialist leaders.

With the strict control, foreigners could hardly get information about people's life and the majority of the citizens do not know about the prosperity and freedom that many nations have. The majority of the citizens were so deprived of the truth and the true information that they believed their economic situation is the best in the world and their mission is to set the nations free from poverty and inequalities.

The citizens of this socialist regime were promised decades ago about the prosperity, equality, happiness and so many social benefits and freedom as American socialists are now making generous offers to Americans. Do the citizens in this socialist country really enjoy so much the many economic blessings and are they really free from many burdens to enjoy their great and happy life?

Unfortunately, the capital city of this socialist nation and its modern facilities are to impress and deceive the world and local people with their fake glory and prosperity. The poor people are eager and consider it is a privilege to visit the capital city and to see by their own eyes the glory, the beauty and the enjoyment of the modern facility that they dream for and believe only their country could have those facilities.

The glory of the city is also a reason for the poor people to strive harder to be loyal to the socialist leaders and its ideology because that glorious and beautiful city is only for the socialist leaders, socialist elites, outstanding socialist members and talents of the nations. So if people want to leave their poor living conditions to the capital city, they must work harder to climb up the political ladder for that privilege.

How is it possible then for the people to be free from many burdens when poverty is still threatening their lives? How is it possible for the people to be free from many burdens when the monitoring systems or the securities keep watching over your moves and lives? How is it possible for the people to be free from many burdens when their economic opportunities and means of living are deprived and exploited?

In the socialist countries, who could realty enjoy the great services and benefits from the government social welfares and benefits? People whose status start with "socialist" such as socialist elites, socialist members, socialist leaders, socialist relatives... For the common people, "Money Must Comes First Before Any Service Offered" or "No Money, No Service."

Today, American millennials are passionate and curious about the idea of democratic socialism because they want to try new things as the nature of their age and they all want to have free college education, free health care, and free social benefits, free debt so democratic socialism sounds appealing to them. They do not think much if socialism could make those promises possible.

The millennials are fascinated at the 21st Century Economic Bill of Rights proposed by Sen. Bernie Sanders including: 1. The right to a job that pays a living wage; 2. The right to quality health care; 3. The right to a complete education; 4. The right to affordable housing; 5. The right to a clean environment; 6. The right to a secure retirement. Who would pay so that Americans could enjoy all of these rights?

New immigrants who do not really understand American politics, the skillful manipulation and the powerful control of mainstream media, are of course attracted to the many freebies offered by the democrats, leftists and socialists. They are willing to vote for those who are willing to give them more benefits as they heard from the news or from their national peoples.

Yet, it is really a pain for America when so many people are "educated" by words of mouth with the greedy thought and greedy habit of people from socialist and poor countries, "it is free, why not?" It is really a burden for America when many people are able but they don't want to work or they are so lazy to work and they just take advantages of social benefits and social welfares for their living.

It is also unethical for many people who apply for social welfare and yet they are not really poor because they know how to play around the policies. It is a real danger and corruption when lawyers, doctors lead people wrongly how to get funds and supports from the available sources so both sides could get benefits from the social funds. It is unfair to millions of people whose tax funds are being misused.

Who does not want to support the Democrats when the recipients are entitled to many benefits such as food stamps, social housing, free medical care and now free tuition for college education? Who does not want to live a life without any burdens or pressures? I happened to see an interesting word picture and I would like to paraphrase the content as follow:

This is why many people support free "Medicare for All" and free "College Education for All." Each month, a recipient may be entitled for $900 for child support, $600 for food stamps, $300 for cash assistance, $1200 for rent subsidy, $200 for utility assistance, $700 for daycare assistance. On top of those benefits, they received free medical, free public transit pass, free Obama cell, and free college tuition.

All they need is to work part-time of 20 hours per week and tax-free. Many of them work more hours and get cashes so they don't have to pay tax and still enjoy social benefits. The message in the picture stated, "Thanks to our tax she gets $3900 a month tax free, plus benefits. The average person drawing from social security gets $1200 a month... Does anyone wonder why thousands want to crash the border?"

Though the above example showed the negative example of peoples in the U.S. who take advantages and abuse social welfares but it also showed the abundance of social welfares in the U.S. What could people in the socialist countries get from social welfares when the socialists always promised many things? They have almost no social welfares so how could they take advantages of the welfares.

Millions of Americans still do not know the truth of many burdens behind the socialist offers yet due to the misinformation and the half-truth messages conveyed by the leftists, the liberals and their mainstream media. And they do not know those free lunches and free stuffs have been given for the political purposes and are well covered under the nice cover or mark of human rights and charitable acts.

As the saying goes, "There is no free lunch" and this is also true here. There is always a price for the free stuffs and the price is the sweats and toils of millions of American workers to provide free stuff for the comforts and enjoyment of millions of social-benefits recipients. It also makes more people to be lazy and to be dependent on social welfares. It also produces many social burdens, insecurities and crimes.

In reality, the majority of the people in the socialist nations could not enjoy so many rights and benefits and they are so burdened with the many exploitations, oppressions, injustices, poverty, fears and uncertainties. The people are so burdened with corrupted leaders, wrong accusations, limited freedom, human right issues, imprisonment and negative future.

The people are so burdened with government interferences. The control and monitor in the socialist nations are excellent but that is not for people's safety and security but it is to limit people from many things that people are not allowed in the regime. Their social media was checked, their videos about the truth of the government were removed, and their phone calls are monitored.

The people are so burdened with unsafe services from the government. Health services are filled with fake medicines, with long list of prescriptions and with unnecessary medicines or with expensive medicines. The food services are unsafe with many chemicals that are the real causes of many cancers and sickness. The environment is so polluted, the air is unclean, and the water is contaminated.

The people are so burdened with issues of human rights. How do they sleep well when their lands are taken away from them? How could they find security when their daily needs are not met? How could their voices be heard when the press is not in their favor? How could they find justices when they are mistreated and misjudged by the authorities? How could they be free when there is fair public hearing?

The people are so burdened with potential imprisonment. The judiciary system is not for the justices of the masses. People post facts and true news and people are being interrogated and threatened by the authorities. People go on strike and they are detained. People ask for political freedom and they are put behind bars. People demonstrate for duly compensation and they are imprisoned and tortured.

The people are so burdened with their looming future. The prices for living keep on increasing and yet their salaries stay the same. Jobs are so hard to find so life could not be stable. The inflation is so high that they could afford to buy many things. Able people tried to run away from the socialist regime leaving behind the hopeless people under the merciless hands of the socialist tyrants.

Unfortunately millions of Americans are still ignorant to the many costs and dangers at the wicked deception of the leftists and the liberals. When socialism is realized in the soil of America, it will not only bring many burdens to Americans but it also costs the precious rights of Americans. It will cost great dreams or previous live as it happened, has been happening in many nations, and is going to happen again.

Will Ashworth from Canada suggested that Americans should embrace socialism for the following 7 reasons: Happiness like the people in Nordic Countries and Canada; Less Crime, More vacation, Capitalism in its Purest Form Has Failed, Millennials Love It, Social Security and Unemployment Insurance, Greater Equality. These reasons sound great but unfortunately those are just the empty words.

Those were also the many reasons that socialism was welcome in nations before. The socialists asked the poor people to support them and fight together with them to get the lands from the landlords and wealthy people then they would distribute the lands to the people so that everyone would have his or her own land. The people would become the owners of their land and to freely cultivate lands, as they wanted.

People could determine their destiny because they were no longer dependent on the rich people and there were no longer under the control of the bourgeoisies. They were no longer slaves and they could determine their own future. Of course the common and the poor people could not find and support any better idea than these great promises, that was how socialism took over many nations before.

The corrupted socialists robbed people's bloods, toils or livelihoods. The greedy socialists take every opportunity to get something from the people. Someone wants to make a new identification, the socialists would ask for some money to speed up the process. People want to get married and they need to contribute something to the socialists in order to get a married certificate.

If you need to change your date of birth or name, that is possible too with some gifts. Policemen officers stopped you and checked your driving license, you better give some money and go even though you violate nothing. They stop and check you, in most cases, not because you are wrong but because they need cash. If you don't give, they would find reasons for you to pay fines or to waste some of your time.

Someone needs a job for certain positions in the government factories or offices, that is not difficult too, it is just depending on the amount of money that he or she is willing to "contribute" or the leaders that he or she knows. The bigger the job positions, opportunities, favors or projects, the bigger the "gifts" of the "offers" that the "seekers" should make to relevant people or agencies.

In the last one decade, thousands of the minority people lost their lives due to ethnic discrimination, social injustices, religious and political persecutions, and land issues. Thousands of people from these minorities run for lives to the neighboring countries. Some of them were able to make their way to America through asylum seeking or petition programs by churches and human rights organizations.

Yet thousands of them are now the illegal immigrants in the neighboring countries. They made many petitions to the United States and free nations in the West to help them and to give them the opportunities to make their new lives in the free world like the U.S. just as the U.S. and many nations of the world already received millions of socialist nations to their nations before.

Ironically, while socialist victims are hoping to have their new lives in America, the American socialists are trying to get people's supports so that they could run the socialist agenda and in turn they would take over America and Americans. Then they could take over people's lands for their securities, people properties for their wealth, people's guns and arms for their powers, and people's lives for their control.

This the reality of social benefits in most of the socialist countries and this would happen soon in the U.S. at the ignorance and naïve of millions of Americans when socialism was to take over the U.S. The exclusive people includes mostly the socialists and their family members, relatives, and their people.:

Free Housing Benefits: Only For Exclusive people
Free Health Care: Only For Exclusive people
Free Medication: Only For Exclusive People
Free College Education: Only For Exclusive people

Free Food Stamps:	Only For Exclusive people
Free Transportation:	Only For Exclusive people
Universal Income:	Only For Exclusive people
Childcare Benefits:	Only For Exclusive people
Child Supports:	Only For Exclusive people
Elder Supports:	Only For Exclusive people

In the next section, the readers would come to know that in socialist nations, the level of unhappiness and unsatisfactoriness is very high among majority of people. This is because the people have to face so many insecurities in their lives and because they are under so many pressures, oppressions, injustices, burdens, evils and unhappiness. This also leads to many immoralities and moral declination.

7th Freedom: Freedom From Unhappiness
Morality and Evil

In the second quarter of 2020, the chief judge of a province was caught with adultery with his staff and they had multiple sexes in the court office. The pictures and the videos of the intimate relationship were posted on the social media and of course those pictures and video clips went viral and it was a real shock to the people. The government had no choice but to investigate the incident.

When the case was brought to the attention of the public on social media, and when the authorities took actions to develop the case, another man sued the chief judge for having an affair with his wife, and the judge was also found guilty in the second adultery affair. The affair already happened a long time ago but the man's voice could not be heard earlier because the chief judge was so powerful to deal with.

There was also another similar case of another judge in another province who was also brought to the public and the government attention with his adultery acts through social media. The government leaders got involved and the leaders found out that the judge was having an affair with a college student. The leaders also discovered that the judge had multiple adulterous affairs with other women.

What would happen to the chief judge and the judge and the millions of the socialist members and leaders when they were caught in these kinds of scandals, abuses of power and corruption? Yes, the adulterous case is really considered a scandal but were these leaders charged with sexual allegations? Were they charged with their abuses of power and positions? Were they charged with sexual abuses or raping?

How did the public know their scandalous cases? Were the cases revealed by the government services or by the intelligent agents? Nope. Were the cases discovered by the rigorous investigations or by the diligent public servants? Nope. In most of the adulterous or corruption cases like these, the courts or the government agencies would solve the scandals internally and quietly or secretly.

The details of the cases would mostly not be known to the general public through the reports of the mainstream media. If there were reports of these cases on the news by the governments, it means that the leaders of those cases were abandoned by the top leaders or those leaders must be purged and punished for the political purposes of the party involved.

It is not an exaggeration but if the socialist government in Asia were seriously to investigate these kinds of scandals in the sexual affairs of their socialist leaders, the majority of the socialist leaders would not be clean from these sexual affairs. Thus, the government would not deal with these cases publicly because they are afraid that the image of the political party is to be destroyed by those scandalous cases.

The cases were revealed by people who were not happy with the socialist regime. The cases were exposed by people who were angry at the injustices, the abuses of power and the corruptions of the socialist leaders. These people wanted to reveal the truth. The irony was the people who took the pictures and posted on the social media were arrested and then they were put in prisons for discovering the truth.

If these people took these evidences and showed to the court, the evidences **first of all** would be destroyed by the authorities to protect the judges. It is not a joke to offend the judges because they have powerful back-up leaders in order for them to get to those positions as judges or chief judges. With this position, the judges could turn black into white and white into black.

Secondly, the people who showed the evidences may probably face the threats of their own lives and the lives of their loved ones. Instead of being appreciated for their courage to report the truth, these people may be attacked by the gangsters sent by the corrupted leaders. They would be the forever enemies of the powerful socialist leaders and their endings would not be that happy.

Thirdly, the victims would become the victims of injustices. If the victims do not keep quiet or comply with the demands of the leaders, the leaders had more than enough time to put the charges back to the victims. They were already the victims of their sex slaves, and they could become the next victims of imprisonments and "social justices" of the socialist countries.

Fourthly, if the cases were not brought to the public through the media with clear evidences of the pictures on the social media, the government leaders would not publicize the incidents in most cases. They could even dare to take away the evidences sent to them so that they could protect their leaders or comrades. That could also be another chance for them to earn some money.

If the country leaders are immoral and wicked and the laws also protect the leaders so that they could continue to live in immorality and to carry out their wicked plans, then great moral, justice and good consciences could not be evident in the country but evils and injustices. History proved clearly the fact that the socialist regimes brought so much evils and injustices to humanity.

Socialist regimes brought evils and injustices to political freedom fighters
Socialist regimes brought evils and injustices to peaceful demonstrators
Socialist regimes brought evils and injustices to human right activists
Socialist regimes brought evils and injustices to justice seekers
Socialist regimes brought evils and injustices to humanity

One of the famous socialist general talked to his parents in front of the public that "you are not my parents and I am not your child, we are the enemies of the social classes." Then he allowed his subordinates to torture his parents to death because they were the enemies. If he wanted to be in power, he must choose the socialist ideology and to destroy people who were against the ideology including the parents.

Another famous leader also said so to his mother, "you are not my mother and I am not your child." They were no longer related because he could only belong to the socialist party. His mother bit her tongue to commit suicide but she was stopped from doing that. Yet she was so devastated at the abandon of her son and the crazy ideology that she jumped off the bridge and died in her successful suicidal attempt.

What evil that the socialists would not do when they rejected and killed their own parents? What good morality that the socialists could educate the people and the generations when they are the examples of evil? What immoral acts that the socialists would not commit when they only care for their political party and their political power at the sufferings and deaths of million innocent people?

When the government and the leaders do not uphold justices but protect their powers and evils, then the people would have no great moral to live and to treat one another. People could not learn well how to become generous when they only see robbing is the way of life. They could not live in integrity when they only see corruption is the practice of social dealings. They learn more vices than good.

This was the heartbreaking story of Alexander, a powerful socialist leader. His father was a very powerful socialist leader. When the top leader of the country wanted to carry out another round of reform after the bitter failures of the previous ones. His father showed disagreement to the new plan to reform the country. Then his father was purged and the whole family also suffered.

His father was sent to the labor camp and his sister was beaten to death at the hatred shown to his family by the young radical guards. Alexander could have also been beaten to death a few times if he was not quick to escape the brutal attacks of these young guards. Just like the million children of counter-revolutionaries, rightists and dissidents, he was discriminated and mistreated.

Most of these children who were discriminated would just pretend to follow the guidance of the political party but in their hearts they really hated socialism and the socialists for the miseries they went through. But that was not so with Alexander. He showed strong supports and passion for socialism and he wanted to follow the socialist way for his political career.

One of the critical practices for people to pursue the political career in those days was to criticize, torture or even kill the dissidents of the socialist party and the counter-revolutionaries in the public. These criminals were mocked, humiliated, and beaten in front of the public as warnings to people. For Alexander he must renounce his father and his father's way to show his total loyalty to the party and leaders.

When his father was brought to the public for interrogation. The crowd shouted at and scolded at his father. They spit on him and the young Alexander must do something to his father to show his loyalty to the socialist leadership. He scolded his father as the betrayal of the country and renounced his relationship with his father. He said it was a shame for him to have such a relationship with his father.

But that was not enough to show his determination and passion for the socialist ideology, he kicked his father and his many kicks were so hard that he broke three ribs of his father while the crowd shouted at excitement and while his father rolled in pain. His father said, "Alex would become a great leader with his cruelty and determination." His father was right and Alex became a powerful socialist leader.

His father was right because without cruelty and evil determination in socialist countries, no one could be able to mount up to the top political ladder. It took a lot of evil planning and disastrous schemes to destroy the unfriendly friends, rivals, comrades, and enemies to reach the top political leadership. No one knew what was Alex thinking when he did those un-filial and violent acts to his father.

Did he really kick his father from his true heart and determination to follow socialism or did he really kick his father out of his self-defense, anger or desperation? One thing for sure it that the socialists teach their members well to use violence, punishments, coerces, and immoralities to object and destroy anyone or anything that go against the socialist power and controls.

As the result, the socialist country is rampant with vices. Drugs are rampant in this ungodly nation. The young generations are lost in the materialistic world, and power games. They may attain some positions and power but there is no satisfaction in their lives. So, they turn to drugs, alcohol and gambles to find the meaning of life. As the result, they are addicted to these vices and destroying their lives.

As the result, the socialist country leads to more crimes. Behind the drug cartels and drug dealings, and gang operation is the top socialist leaders. The cartels, mafias and gangsters are boldly doing horrible things in sex trades, human trafficking, shark loans, money launderings because they are well protected by the powerful leaders, and they are working with the leaders for mutual benefits.

As the result, the socialist country breeds ungodly morality. They want good people to be like them so that they would not feel guilty and their conscience will be at peace. They wanted and still wanted to legalize more abortions and the killing of million unborn babies. They want to fund more money to protect endangered species but to annihilate innocent unborn babies.

In America, the leftists and the socialists want to legalize late abortions and still want to legalize gay marriages. They want to legalize bigamy. They want to legalize incest. They want to legalize sex with animals. They want to legalize unnatural sexes. They want to legalize marijuana. They want to recognize pedophile as one of the sexual orientations. They want sex with different partners.

The removal of Christian education and biblical values in the public schools and societies in the U.S. have lead millions of Americans to the loss of their identity, morality and holiness. The removal of prayer and Bible studies has been filled the U.S. with hatred, un-forgiveness and violence. The removal of faith in God has led more Americans to injustices, lawlessness and immoralities.

Immoralities and evils find the fertilized soils in the socialist country because the leaders uphold atheistic view. This atheistic view is a denial and rejection of deities and God and the roles of religions. The opposing concepts of the fighting forces between good and bad, and the continuous conflicts between good and evil are the foundations of moral teachings of right and wrong, acceptable and unacceptable...

In Christianity, the moral teachings come from God's attributes of God that God is good, God is just, God is love, God is kind, God is peace, God is forgiving... and human being must act and live in accordance to those attributes for mutual respect and a harmonious society. When these moral teachings of goodness are removed from people's lives, the remaining is wickedness, evils, conflicts, division, and hurts...

Immoralities and evils find the perfect environment to growth in the socialist and atheist country because the leaders and people are driven by powers, materials and fames. The injustice system of the judiciary system allows people in power to oppress and suppress common people in the ways that they want and not in accordance to the laws that are protecting the well-beings of all people.

The continuous struggles for power lead to unrests, exploitations, riots and abuses. The socialist system does not bridge the many gaps between the people and the elites but it creates huge power gaps so that the socialists and the socialist party could stay in power to protect their powers. Consequently, the socialists and the socialist party are the causes of immorality, wickedness, depravity, and you name it.

Immoralities and evils find the great home in the socialist and atheist country because the leaders and people are forced to worship the extreme ideology. The idolization of the sole socialist ideology may require the rejection and elimination of many great moral and cultural heritages, literatures and legacies that have been considered the great pillars of civilization and social development.

The socialist ideology does not allow the socialist members and the people to accept the differences, thus they cannot appreciate the diversities. People in socialist country are only allowed to see things through the socialist lens. Consequently they perceive other ideas, ideologies, principles that help peoples of nations developed and prospered as evil or immoral but their destructive principles are great.

Immoralities and evils find the golden opportunity to be deep rooted in socialist country because the goal of life is materialistic oriented. If godly value guides human behaviors and relationships then evil could not take the prominent place but when everything is acceptable for the purposes of material gains then people don't find corruption is wrong as long as the participants are happy to receive something.

People are so busy and greedy to achieving material gains and wealth that they could no longer recognize that they have become the slaves of materialism. The outer appearances are now becoming more important than the inner beauty and people are willing to sell their virginity or bodies for a position, a property or a project. Marriages are broken at the rampant unfaithfulness.

Immoralities and evils of course find the greatest development in the socialist and atheist country because deception lies in all the socialist foundations because truth is not highly appreciated. The socialist party and the leaders could not accept the many truths that socialism fails its promises, socialism kills many innocent people, socialism breeds corruption, and socialism suppresses human rights…

When that deception is the foundation for every report, statistic and news, then positive changes are not possible. The deceptive report stated that the reforms delivered million people out of poverty and sufferings when the truth was millions of people were also died of hunger. The lies have been dominating for so long that the people could not even believe in the words and news of the socialists any longer.

The socialist leaders if not all are corrupted and wicked to the bones and vicious yet the news always praises them for their integrity and simplicity. They pretend to be so kind, considerate and virtuous yet they are the big bosses of drug dealings, mafia operations and unbelievable corruption cases. They always talk nice words and they lecture morals and ethics but poisons are all over their bodies.

The readers could imagine so far that the people in the socialist countries could hardly experience peace of mind due to exploitations and corruptions, oppressions and suppressions, economic deprivations and poverty, inequalities and injustices. These ill-treatments are also the result of the excessive abuses of power and the reasons for the repeated nightmares of the people.

Is this what Americans are looking for? Sadly, millions of Americans want to turn a great and moral America to a degraded and immoral America. How about you?

8ᵗʰ Freedom: Freedom From Nightmares
Shared Power and Abuses of Power

I had the first dental check-up in the U.S in 2019 and the dentist told me that I need a mouth guard for my teeth. I did not know what was the mouth guard for and why did I need it. So I asked the dentist, "Kindly explain why do I need the mouth guard?" The dentist explained that my teeth were damaged due to serious teeth grinding and the teeth grinding happened a long time as my teeth are wearing down to stumps.

She asked me, "Are you under many pressures from works or do you have sleeping disorder? I immediately responded, "No, I do not have any pressure at all and my sleep is ok." Yes, I did work a lot but I had no stresses and pressures from works. "How about family pressures?" she asked. I said, "Yes. I do sometimes but I don't think that family matters cause me a lot of pressures."

She said again, "Your teeth grinding is very serious and your teeth are damaged and you may be under many pressures but you may not realize that." I just thanked her and telling her that I would pay attention on my works and my sleep so that my teeth grinding would stop somehow. On the way home, I kept on thinking about the potential causes of pressures.

I suddenly realized that for almost 30 years, I did not just have pressures and stresses but I also had so many nightmares. Those pressures and nightmares did not really come from the workloads, ministries, mission trips or family matters or marriage issues, but they did come from the severe persecutions and threats from the socialist leaders that my family and I had been facing for decades.

It was stressful to keep thinking that when would the authorities call us or visit our home? We did not and still do not want to welcome this kind of visitation or call but we could not refuse just like millions of others. It was stressful to keep thinking that the authorities were following us and monitoring us whenever we go. It was stressful to be extremely careful about what to say even at our own home.

It was stressful for us to face with constant persecutions by the socialist leaders. It was very stressful for us to go through three to four hours of weekly interrogations with the authorities. It was really stressful for us to hear many threats from the government. It was extremely stressful for us when the authorities said that I would be deported and separated from my family.

Though God had given me strength to overcome the many fears and pressures from the serious persecutions but those stresses turned into pressures and they already entered my consciousness and my sleep and yet I was unaware of those things. My ears were so sensitive and alert to the sound of the police car when it happens to come by or the sounds of the door knocks as the results of their many visits.

How do you feel when you know that the government detectives follow you wherever you go?

How do you feel when you know that there is a spy sitting in the meeting where you are preaching?

How do you feel when you know that the policemen could enter your church or your meeting and take you away at any time?

How do you feel when you know that the authorities planted a chip in your home and your car to monitor your every action?

How do you feel when you must meet with four or five government officers every week for interrogations?

How do you feel when you know that every time you go for a mission trip or a leadership meeting and you may never come back home?

How do you feel when you the policemen come, surround you, arrest you, and handcuff you, and take you away?

How do you feel when you see that more than 120 policemen were running around in search of you?

How do you feel when you have to jump out of the window and the balcony to run away from the arrests of the authorities?

How do you feel when more than 40 policemen surround you and push you in their van and you are being taken to an unknown place?

The list could go on and I did go through all of those experiences and many more for years as a pastor, leader, and mission mobilizer. Life was not really easy at all when we must watch out if there were policemen following us secretly. Life was not easy when you knew that the policemen could come and take you away at any time. Those were the kinds of pressures that I had to deal with daily.

Since they were very young, our children had become our faithful coworkers to discover the presence of the authorities if they followed us when we drove the car to some places. When we got into the car, our children immediately tried to look on the right and left and behind to see any suspicious car that followed us and they would make a report about that. Those experiences could never be erased from memories.

That was also the story of my spiritual father, Rev. Dr. Paul and so many heroes of faith. When he was still in a socialist country, he always put a ready-to-go bag by his pillow before he went to sleep every night. That was not a bag of money, gold, jewelries, precious stones or important documents that he tried to protect but it was a bag of needed utensils for him to use in prison if the policemen took him away.

The inmates in America might not bother to prepare for them that kind of bag and daily utensils because the government provides the inmates almost things that they need for daily living. That was not so in prisons and detention centers in the socialist country. If you want to know what are exactly inside that ready-to-go bag, Rev. Dr. Paul could tell you personally if you want to him to share his many experiences.

At last, Rev. Dr. Paul could forget about that ready-to-go bag when he was finally deported out of the socialist country where he spent more than 10 years in prison and more than two decades of being monitored and controlled by the socialist regime. He could sleep soundly and he was no longer under the many pressures and nightmares of interrogations, persecutions, hardships, and imprisonments.

Just like Rev. Dr. Paul and million people of faith did go through the many trials, I was persecuted not because I did illegal things or did I violate any laws but because I wanted to exercise my freedom of faith and freedom of speech to share God's love to people. I was arrested not because I harmed someone or did I steal something but because I wanted to see the lost comes to life and the hopeless have hope in Jesus.

I was under many threats not because I engaged in counter revolutionary and revolting against the socialist government but because I wanted to see people's minds renewed and their pains healed by God's precious words. I was deported out of the country and separated from my family by force not because I went against the country or the leaders but because I wanted to see souls saved and loved by God.

Hundred thousands of leaders and believers were willing to pay the many costs of persecutions and imprisonment to preach the Gospels so that there would be an increase of 20% of the population in the villages, towns, cities, counties, provinces of the socialist nations and nations to come to know the Lord Jesus Christ as their Lord and Savior when the Body of Christ comes together in unity, missions and revival.

It was for the sake of the Gospels that millions people of faith have been going through severe persecutions, dangers, sacrifices and risks of lives. I was blessed and I am still glad and I am honored that I am among these people of faith who are blessed because they are willing to be persecuted for His name's sake and the expansion of God's kingdom. Will you be willing to be part of this blessing?

You may not need to face all the persecutions and risks. We need each of you to connect us to one church, or one company, or one organization or one donor, and this person could be you to support one church planter. If we have 2000, 5000 or 10,000 people like you to do so, we could support thousands of church planters to carry out Vision 20% in the socialist and Gospel restricted countries.

When we have thousands of people like you to stand together and to partner with us, we could save millions of lost souls who are suffering with so many injustices and pains in socialist and Gospel-restricted countries with God's love, God's power and God's transformations. Yes we need you to help us connect to at least 1 church or 1 donor, will you be willing to say Yes so that million lives would be blessed?

Keith Rothfus on Socialism Today stated, "The American people must be reminded that socialism is not a dream. It is a nightmare that is responsible for the deaths of tens of millions of people in the 20th century. Google it… Venezuela and North Korea, where people are literally starting, are the modern realities of socialism. Is that what we want America to look like?

Though it sounded horrible with the things that millions of people and I went through, yet I only paid just a small price because millions of people paid many high costs that I could hardly imagine if I could be still faithful to God and standing firm in faith until death if I were in their situations. The nightmares do not just come to people of faith but so many socialist victims suffered with series of nightmares.

Firstly, the socialist victims suffered the nightmares of suppressions. The brutal crushes and suppressions are still happening to this day. The people demand the transparency of information, freedom of speech, releasing of human rights activists, duly compensations of their lands and properties that were corrupted by the socialist leaders… through many peaceful demonstrations last for months.

But the socialist government did not usually back down at the reasonable requests of the people for justices. The socialist leaders must imprison or execute their socialist leaders at the justice demands of the people. Instead of responding to the pleadings of the people, the government used many tricks to stop the demonstrations through false promises, kidnapping of the leaders, threatening…

Many physical assaults took place and the people were beaten, arrested, injured, tortured, bleeding, imprisoned or committing suicides. On the protesting sites, the policemen fired tear gas, petrol bombs or shot rubber bullets at people to disperse the protests and demonstrations. The protests are still going through though the economies in areas where protests taking place are heavily affected

Secondly, the socialist victims faced the nightmares of persecutions. They were put in the detention centers where they were tortured physically and mentally. They were put in the labor camps to experience hard labors and poor living conditions until they faced exhaustion, sicknesses, loneliness, and frustrations. They were electrified and their fleshes were pierced in prison to agree things they did not do.

People are persecuted because they asked justices for their lands. People are persecuted because they sued the really corrupted leaders. People are persecuted because they pointed out the abuses of power of the leaders. People are persecuted because they wanted to speak with freedoms. People are persecuted because they presented evidences that their environments were destroyed and polluted.

People were persecuted because they asked the companies to stop releasing wastes to the rivers in their living areas. People were persecuted because they sued the children of the leaders who beat someone to death. It is sure that whatever justice they asked that is against the pleasures of the government, then the people would be persecuted. Do you still want socialism for America or your nations?

Thirdly, the socialist victims went through the nightmares of reeducation camps. It was not just about hard labors, ill treatments and humiliations in the camps, it was also the long and boring of daily lectures about socialism, the ideology that the prisoners hated and did not believe in. But the prisoners must learn them by heart and recite the greatness of socialism against their consciences and freedoms.

The victims were forced to be reeducated by the socialist leaders who did not even have proper education, higher education, or better talents, experiences, and knowledge than the victims who were forced to go through the reeducation. Unfortunately, the stronger people win so the victims just kept quiet and followed the education or else the victims would not have chances for freedoms.

Fourthly, the socialist victims were challenged with the nightmares of murdering. People lives are just hanging on a string of hair by the socialists. Human being is not different from an animal so people's life is not really appreciated but the socialist party and ideology. People were oppressed to death. People were hungry to death. People were tortured to death. People labored to death. People escaped to find death.

Tortures, imprisonments, persecutions, disappearing or murders are the common ways that the wicked and cruel socialists often employ to stop the voice of people whom the socialists are considered as their dissidents, human right activists, political opponents or counter-revolutionaries. How peaceful and happy life is when sudden death may come to people in the blood-thirsty regimes?

Last but not the least, the socialist victims survived the nightmares of strict surveillances. Will be you happy when your phone is monitored and the authorities could trace where you are and what you talk on that phone of yours? Yes your privacy is no longer private. Could you imagine that your offerings for churches and missions may be monitored and used as evidences against you as illegal?

This is because the freedom of religion is not really exercised and the authorities could come to your home meeting anytime and disrupt the meetings inside your house not because you cause social disorders or noise or security issues but because those religious meetings even in small groups are illegal. This is why the house church often moves from place to place to avoid government visits.

My team and I just entered a house church for an evangelistic meeting and we just minister to the people in less than 15 minutes, the senior pastor hurriedly came and told me that my team and I must leave the place immediately because the policemen were coming to arrest me if they found me there. Her friend, a local leader, called her to let her know the situation so my team and I were safe as we left early.

According to the plan my team and I went to another province the next day for a conference. When we just arrive at the place, the policemen invited me and my team for a "tea time" and we were told to leave that place and that city immediately. These few examples are to show that people's lives, phones, movements, social media, activities are under the radar of the insecure socialists and their leaders.

These nightmares are mainly the results the big government, social ownership, corruption in the judiciary system and the horrible abuses of power by the greedy socialist leaders. These nightmares are also the results of the great deceptive words and empty promises of the socialists that with socialism the people could have their shares in power, in decision-making, in pursuing their happiness and destiny…

These nightmares are also the results of what the socialists called as shared powers. The socialist leaders tempted the people that they should destroy the powers in the hands of a few capitalistic elites who controlled the national economy, the modes of productions, the jobs, and lives of the people. Then the people's voice could be heard in central planning or decision-makings with their shared powers.

The socialists have the shared power of the people thus they become stronger and more powerful and the people already share their power to the socialists thus the people loose their power. The loss of power leads to the loss of their voices, the loss of their rights, and the loss of their freedoms. The loss of power, then, leads to injustices, sufferings, hopelessness and nightmares of the common people.

Unfortunately that old same trick of the socialists worked well in so many countries, but the truth is that trick is the way to transfer powers from the kind hands of the capitalists to the destructive hands of the socialists. American socialists are still using that same old trick to call the people to make that transfer of power to be possible again and they have a large number of supporters to do so in a near future.

At the present, in the U.S and many free nations, the powers are not concentrated in the hands of a few elites or a group of politician leaders but are still largely in the hands of the citizens. The government powers are also distributed into the three branches of government so that the government leaders in the three branches of the government could co-check each other to make sure there are no abuses of powers.

Americans have the power to choose or remove their representatives depending on the performances of the representatives toward the will of the people. The powers that the senators and the congressmen have are then vested upon them and many public servants across the states by Americans. The people have real powers in voting for their representatives and the president of the U.S.

When a group of top leadership can manipulate or control the powers of the executive branch, the legislative branch, and the judicial branch without being checked or challenged by members of the three branches, then that is the sign of a big government. This is the aim of the socialists and the leftists, so they could easily make the policy, executive and implement the policies the way they want.

There are still many regimes around the world today where the authoritative leaders tried to change the Constitution so that they could control all of the powers in their hand. When they are able to control all the power, they would reign for a long time. Unfortunately, those who are thirsty for power would never allow freedom and democracy to be exercised but coercion and oppressions.

At that time, the people would loose their power because their representatives are now under the control of the big government and the top leaders. This is the reason why people in the socialist nations no longer have the powers and their voices could hardly be heard. As the result, the people must suffer with all the exploitations, oppressions, injustices, inequalities and nightmares.

Thus, do not be deceived by the socialists that the people would share their powers in planned economy and national management. Do not listen to their sweet words that the people would share power in the decision-making for judicial system and justices. Do not fall into the many traps of the socialists that the people would have their shares in social ownership and wealth distribution.

So far the readers could see clearly that the shared powers presented by the socialist leaders that the people could have are just the empty talks and the cunning tricks of the socialists to attract the attention, interests and supports of the people for socialism and their political revolution. Their deception is so disastrous to hundred millions of people around the world.

We are now coming to the last socialist freedom discussed in this book. The socialist promises are so great and powerful, yet unfortunately, none of the socialist freedoms that were promised has really became a positive reality to the innocent people. The people could only receive the empty freedoms promised and so many disappointments, frustrations and pains.

The socialist leaders deliver to the people the real stuffs of the socialist regime that are exploitations, oppressions, economic deprivations, inequalities, injustices, burdens, unhappiness, nightmares and lastly captivities. People in the socialist nations are really captivated in unrealistic dreams and they are also captivated in the many bondages and deceptions.

Americans are now facing critical situations with many riots and violence since the death of George Floyd. If the socialists' political revolution were to be successful in the U.S, many nightmares and limited freedom would be obvious to Americans in the days to come. The violence, lawlessness and murders by the socialists, trained Marxists, communists have become the nightmares of million people across the U.S.

Leftwing democrat leaders and mainstream media are betraying Americans by promoting and encouraging the riots and violence in the name of freedom, social justice, and eradication of racism. It is important that justices should be done and racism should be resolved. Those leaders just use those reasons as excuses but the real intention of the leftists and the socialists is to turn America to a socialist state.

Millions of Americans and people of the nations only know and heard that socialism and socialists would solve American and international issues of inequalities, economic gaps, exploitations, pressures and poverty... Yet millions of Americans never know that socialism and socialists have never been successful to carry out those promises in any country across the nations and continents.

Through out our discussion, people of the socialist nations could only experience exploitations and corruptions through social ownership, oppressions and suppressions through big government, deprivations and poverty through wealth distribution, inequalities through egalitarianism, injustices through judicial fairness, multi-burdens through social benefits, unhappiness through evil morality, nightmares through shared power, and now captivities through socialist party.

9th Freedom: Freedom From Captivities
The Socialist Party and Limited Freedom

In May 2020, another human rights lawyer, Lawrence, was suddenly disappeared after he sent a letter to the Congress through a social media. The lawyer addressed the internal issues of the national leadership and their responses toward coronavirus pandemic. The lawyer also pointed out the lack of the independent professional media to update the public with the real situation of the pandemic.

He also mentioned the tight control and suppression of the government over the people, media and the country. He called the people to exercise their freedom of speech, to voice out their ideas and thought and to make the freedom of speech a reality. His call for the people to exercise freedom and to talk against the suppressions and the control of the government is the counter-revolutionary crime.

His call was **firstly** revealed the ruthless suppressions and horrible raids by the socialists and the million deaths in the socialist countries for decades. That call for freedoms is not allowed and appreciated by the socialists and their leaders. That call is reserved and is exclusively for the top socialist leaders only and for their sole purposes to control and coerce people to follow the will of the socialist ideology.

His call revealed the reality of people's sufferings, interrogations, tortures, persecutions, imprisonments, detentions, and the executions of thousands of people in modern socialist countries. His call is not accepted because the leaders exercise their freedoms to accuse people wrongly, to change rights from wrongs or vice versa. They have freedom to implement laws and policies in their favors.

His call for freedoms is **secondly** a direct challenge to the sovereignty of the socialist regime. The socialist leaders know very well that they are still in control of the people as people have no freedoms and they still have the military power, weapon power and economic power at hand. If freedoms are to be exercised their powers are to be at stake because their lies, deceptions and evils are numerous.

The socialists never want to give up their powers and they know very well their loss of powers is equivalent with their unhappy endings. So they must do their best to deceive and indoctrinate people through media and education that socialism is the best form of government and socialism is the truth, the sun and the light to bring perfection, peace and prosperity to life at the many failures of capitalism.

His call for freedom is **thirdly** a great threat to the many fears of the socialists. They are in fear that their dirty deeds and corruptions to be discovered. They are in fear that their excessive misuses of power and injustices to be revealed. They are in fear that their cruelties and evils to be exposed. They are in fear that their positions and wealth are to be known as the results of their many corruptions and injustices.

They are in fear that their lives and their family members are to be executed one day due to their many crimes against humanity. The political party, positions and powers are their securities and they must cling on their party, positions, and powers even though they must sin against people or they must suppress and sacrificed the people at the people's sufferings, shocks and sadness.

His call for freedom is **fourthly** perceived as the intention to overthrown the socialist rule. That call shows the vulnerability and the tyranny of the socialist regime. The regime does not see the merits of people's ideas and their counsels. The regime is not willing to embrace the truth but to embrace their selfishness. As the result the socialists could only see the faults and wrongs of people.

His call is not perceived as the heart cries of the people to be free from oppressions and pains for so long. It is not seen as the desires of the masses for justices and happiness. It is not considered as a valuable reflection for the government to do better to improve themselves and to take the needs and the wishes of the people. As the result, the socialists rule the country with their fists instead of their hearts.

After decades of the socialist oppressions, the people in the socialist countries still do not have many freedoms. They could not freely exercise their human rights and their ideologies as long as they are still under the socialist rule and regime. That is the reality and that is the proven fact in more than 100 years of the socialist existence, reigns, rules, and controls of the socialist.

Ironically, Americans want the socialist freedoms when the exercises of the freedom of speech, free press and many precious rights are already so common at home that Americans may not even appreciate what they have. Millions of people from the socialist regimes run for their lives to the U.S so that they could enjoy the many great freedoms and rights that only the Western world like the U.S. could offer.

Ironically, Americans want to make America a socialist nation so that they would suffer the limited freedoms at their ignorance and stubbornness. Yet, in socialist countries, those freedoms are limited or even many freedoms are forbidden for people to exercise. Those freedoms are only real in theory, in imagination and in the propaganda of the socialists but those freedoms are far from reality.

There is only limited freedom in free press, freedom of speech, freedom to pursuit one's happiness and freedom to follow other ideologies in socialist countries. People who are asking and calling for the exercising of freedoms, human rights and political transformation are always punished and suppressed, and they also face the potential persecutions, imprisonments, disappearing, or murders.

Since 2017 these freedoms are again suppressed in some socialist countries and every year hundred thousands of people from the Soviet-type socialist countries found their ways to the U.S. and they do not want to go back to their countries due to oppressions, persecutions or loss of freedoms. Many activists and church leaders were also disappeared and no one knows how many people are imprisoned.

Freedom is always the signature promise of the socialists and socialism would set people free from the exploitations of the rich and the bourgeoisie and the capitalists. Yet in reality people in the capitalist countries enjoy more freedom and wealth than people in the socialist countries where the leaders are still praising and talking nicely about the freedoms that they offer to the people but freedoms are the jokes.

The socialist promises of freedoms are the just like the advertisements of a bald man who passionately promotes his medical treatment for hair growth or a barren doctor who tries to sell the medicines for pregnancy. At least people could easily identify the baldness of the seller and the bareness of the doctor but it is extremely to identify the tricks and the deceptions of the socialists at the beginning.

For a more detailed discussion on the freedoms offered in the socialist nations, please read our books, **The Twelve Commandments of Socialism** or **The Boat of Destiny**. These books would reveal to you how the many freedoms of speech, of press, of peaceful gathering, of travelling, of religions, of thought, of trials by jury and other freedoms are exercised in the socialist nations.

Michael E. Telzrow concluded precisely that, "all the socialist societies that came into being after the 1917 Bolshevik Revolution necessarily reflect some basic characteristics of the Soviet model-central control and coercion. In Russia the cruelties endured under the Tsar, which were to be replaced by equality and welfare, were merely replaced by a more brutal hierarchy and an economic system that crushed individual enterprise and guaranteed a dysfunctional economy."

The real answers to some of the following questions would provide the readers a better understanding about freedom in the socialist countries. These short answers would be enough for the readers to conclude that only limited freedoms are available to the people and to enjoy the limited freedoms and rights, the people must strictly observe the golden rules and follow the will of the socialist leaders.

Firstly, are the people in the socialist country free from the exploitations of the bourgeoisies? There are two groups of the bourgeoisies now and we may call them the socialist bourgeoisies and the capitalist bourgeoisies. The socialist bourgeoisies refer to the socialists who are now very powerful with their positions and wealth and they are even more powerful than the capitalist bourgeoisies.

The capitalist bourgeoisies are mostly the foreign investors and a small number of local business people. Whether they are the local or the foreign bourgeoisies, they must follow the rules set by the socialist bourgeoisies. Ironically that there are more social classes and hierarchies in the socialist countries than it is in the capitalist countries when the socialist aim is to destroy the social classes and gaps.

According to the socialist philosophy, people are exploited and suffered because of the existence of the bourgeoisies. Now there are greedier and more corrupted socialist bourgeoisies who are above the laws and the capitalist bourgeoisies who are under the law, so it is no doubt that the common people are being triply exploited and suffered more by socialist bourgeoisies.

Secondly, are the people in the socialist country free from poverty? Millions of people were not only free not from the poverty but also suffered and died from famines and the poverty due to the repeated failures of the socialist reforms and the poor socialist principles of economy. People were so hungry that they had to eat grass, tree barks, and even human fleshes to survive during the reforms.

Millions of people must leave everything they had then in the socialist country and run away from the socialist countries to other countries for economic opportunities or else they would also be the famine and poverty victims of the economic failures of the socialists. The socialist countries were almost collapsed at their idealistic, beautiful, and yet unrealistic dreams of equality and prosperity

Though some socialist countries now seem to be developed and prosperous but the majority of the people are still living under the poverty lines. Yet, it is the capitalist principle of free market economy that saved the socialist economy, the people and the socialist regime. The people are still not sure how long that socialist rule is going to last and the prosperity and happiness of the people are still in questions.

Thirdly, are the people in the socialist country free from religious persecutions? In the last few years, the socialist countries are on the top list of the countries that severely persecuted religious people. Due to coronavirus pandemic, gatherings are forbidden, and the believers worshipped online, yet they are not spared from being persecuted or at least they are blocked from joining online services.

In the last few years, the government crackdowns on churches and religious gatherings have become more intense. Churches were closed, pastors were imprisoned, believers were detained, their houses were searched, and religious items were confiscated. Thanks to the availability of social media, many uploaded videos and pictures become the solid evidences of religious persecutions.

Religious freedom is only allowed at a specific place and a specific time of a specific day approved by the government for the state-churches. Any other meetings are illegal. The house churched and underground churches often faced severe persecutions by the authorities. Religious workers, sermons and church activities are strictly monitored and many religious spies are inside religious meetings.

Fourthly, are the people in the socialist country free to gather for peaceful demonstration? This is among the least freedom that the people would employ when they have no other solutions. Their peaceful gathering always ended with violent responses from the government and the people are subjected to beatings, tortures, and impressments and even deaths.

Just like the call for freedoms and human rights as we discussed earlier, the peaceful gatherings are perceived by the socialists as the clear signs of threats and obvious intentions of challenging the sovereignty of the socialist regime. The peaceful gatherings also the sure indications that the people want to revolt and to bring about political change so the gatherings must be suppressed.

Through peaceful gatherings, people want to seek justices, yet injustices crushed on them at the merciless attacks of the socialist armies. People want to ask for reasonable human rights, yet their rights once again were deprived at the cunning tricks of the socialist leaders. People want to fight for peace, yet their hope for peace was shattered at the violent responses of the political party.

Fifthly, are the people in the socialist country free to pursue different ideologies? The socialist ideology is the one and only one. The pursuit of any ideology and thought is a rejection of the socialist ideology, a shame for the political party and a betrayal of the country. Socialism requires and demands people to devote their hearts and souls completely to the socialist leaders and the political party.

The socialists do not want the people to know more about other ideologies so that they could easily indoctrinate people and then control people's minds. Any ideology that does not support socialism is forbidden. Unfortunately, there are not so many ideologies that really support socialism but the socialist ideology is widely subjected to many negative critics due to its many flaws, repeated failures and havocs.

If Americans and people of the world want to freely discover, discuss and develop the great thoughts and contributions of various thoughts, ideologies, the socialists would not be happy with that but for the meantime the socialists are not strong enough to take over the country yet so they are just patient to wait for the time to come to rob people from their rights to follow other ideologies.

Sixthly, are the people in the socialist country free to fight for human rights? Socialism never promises people that the people would have their many rights for religion, free speech, free press, free trials by jury, free gatherings or others. The existence of the socialism is to destroy or control any rights that could potentially diminish its socialist influences, powers and political agendas.

Socialism only promises the rights for equality, socials welfares, and freedom from the exploitations of the capitalist bourgeoisies but not the exploitations of the socialist bourgeoisies, so please do not blame socialism and the socialist leaders and their strict controls of human rights they perceive could only do harms to the existences of their ideology, their political party and their leaders.

Americans and readers of the nations, millions of people suffered and died as the victims of socialism and the socialist leaders just because they did not read well and understand enough the tricky promises, the fabulous but cunning words, and the attractive but deadly agendas of the socialists. Hopefully, you are not going to fall into the same painful paths of the millions who went before us.

Lastly, are the people in the socialist country free to compose songs, writings or piece of arts that are freely reflecting their aspirations? Yes, they do but to praise the socialist leaders for their integrity when they are corrupted to the bones, for the great guidelines of the socialist party when it suppresses people, and for the greatness of socialism when it is the cause of million deaths and sufferings.

When someone writes or composes something negatively, he or she would be criticized by the socialists and that person is not grateful for the freedom that socialism brings to people when there is no freedom. That person would be punished for disrespect to the political party when the political party never respects people. Socialism can only get from people because it has nothing much to give.

So the golden rule for socialist freedoms is that people should only praise socialism, the socialist party, the leaders, their rules and their policies. Any negative comment would do more harm than good. For more discussions on the human rights in the socialist country, our book **The 12 Commandments of Socialism** would enlighten you with the realities of socialism and the many true stories of the socialist victims

So if people want socialism and if they want the socialists to get away their precious rights and your freedoms, socialism and the socialists would do that well. If people want socialism and the socialists get away their wealth and your power, socialism and the socialists are the experts. If people want socialism and the socialists get away your happiness and dreams, socialism and the socialists would welcome that.

The socialists are expert to turn your happiness to sufferings, and your talents to wastes. They are the professionals to transfer your wealth for your poverty, and your hope to hopelessness. They are the well-trained people to twist you from powerful people to powerless ones, and naïve people to the wicked ones. They are the powerful people to switch your dreams into nightmares, and joy to wailing.

The recent example of the impeachment and the recent resolution to limit the power of President Trump over Iran issues led by Nancy Pelosi, Adam Schiff and Democrat leaders in the U.S are the good examples of corruption of power and political positions. If the Democratic Party in America was the only one party as it is one socialist party in socialist countries, President Trump was already removed.

Americans may heard that there are different political parties in socialist countries and this is true but what Americans do not know is that those minor parties are just the shows, their party has no power and they are there in the countries and doing what the socialist party tells them to do. In the socialist countries, the power goes from the top down and thus corruptions and abuse of power are rampant.

As long as someone knows the top leaders, everything could happen if they want to. If they need to change bills, policies or laws, the leaders can do that easily. In America, the power is shared by the three branches of government and each branch of the government can voice their disagreements openly by their members, this does not happen in socialist countries because the power is from the top leaders.

The socialists always present the concept the shared power by the people but it is just like the concept of the shared wealth, shared power is another empty concept and that the socialists often used to persuade people to support for them. When they are in power, the powers are shared by the socialist leaders not the people. The people were tricked and then they become the slaves of the socialists.

In America, the branches of government often come in agreement for a bill to be signed or a law to be passed. This does not happen in Socialist countries, the government may take in the opinions of people, but when they make public a bill, a policy or a law, that is it. Those who voice their opinions against the decision of the top leaders, they would not be appreciated but will be apprehended.

Of course, things are changing now in America with the many lobbying policies of the leftists, liberals and the socialists for decades to prepare for the reign of socialism in America. The Democrats and the socialists wanted to remove the filibuster and increase the size of the Supreme Court so that they could easily move forward with their many socialist plans to make socialism a reality in America.

This is the main reason why President Trump was attacked so hard and he was falsely accused by the Democrats and the socialists that he abused power so that they could remove him as fast as they could. President Trump and his Administration fought hard to protect America and Americans from the corruption and the abuse of power by these corrupted leaders.

President Trump and his Administration have been fighting hard to protect and promote the precious freedom of America and Americans and to prevent America from the coming tyranny of socialism. He is fighting against the mainstream media, which have been promoting the progressive values and the socialist agenda. He also tries to stop the many democratic plans that are anti-Christian and anti-God.

Why are there many freedoms in the American? The founders and the framers of the U.S. recognized that those freedoms were bestowed on people by God and the freedoms are the precious gifts given by God and those freedoms must be well reserved and protected from generations to generations so the powers are shared by the three branches so that the people are well protected with their rights.

The ungodly leaders would not want people to have so much rights or else the evil and corrupted leaders could not get what they want. This is why they want centralized power so that they could be free from all the objections. As the result, the people could no longer be free and people are manipulated and abused for the purposes of the rulers and the political party.

What is freedom in the socialist country? As the saying goes "the survival of the fittest" so the stronger ones would win. The stronger would have more freedom and the weak would have less freedom and that is the reality in socialist countries where equality is promised and promoted. The socialists are the strong ones and the people are weak and the weak must serve the strong ones and oppressed by them.

The socialists often call the people to support the socialists so they could fight together to destroy capitalism and the capitalists who are considered the real cause of people's losses of freedom, wealth and happiness. In reality, people naively jump from precious rights, freedom, economic opportunities of the capitalistic societies to the captivities of the socialist culture at the seemingly great promises of socialism.

America and Americans, you are now in your heaven of freedom now, do not jump into the cruel traps and snares of socialist utopia.

It is great to conclude this session with the words of Michael E Telzrow as we continue to discover the perfect socialist countries, "Socialism saps incentive, destroy freedom, and leads to tyranny. Yet it continues to promise a Utopia to many despite the fact that every socialist experiment has ended badly from an economic and moral standpoint. It promises everything from the abolition of poverty to the destruction of bigotry and inequality. But it has never delivered."

CHAPTER 2

THE PERFECT "SOCIALIST COUNTRIES"

Years earlier, Senator Bernie Sander encouraged the U.S to follow Ecuador, Venezuela and Argentina for the socialist dreams as he said on his website, "These days, the American dream is more apt to be realized in South America, in places such as Ecuador, Venezuela and Argentina, where incomes are actually more equal today than they are in the land of Horatio Alger. Who's the banana republic now?"

Yet that socialist dream was dashed and turned into the nightmares for millions of these people and he never praised it again as these socialist regimes are struggling to survive with horrible situations of poverty, inequality, suffering, abuse of power, violence, and death. Now Sen. Bernie Sanders would not praise those countries but if these countries were successful with socialism, he would not deny them.

His team or supporters tried to explain that he was not the writer of the article. Even if he was not the writer, he endorsed it and he agreed with the message because it was clearly posted on his official page on August 5, 2011 and it was emphasized that this is a must read: https://www.sanders.senate.gov/newsroom/must-read/close-the-gaps-disparities-that-threaten-america

Jack Staples-Butler explained on Quillette, "However, a comprehensive search of Sanders' congressional records, speeches, newspaper articles, books, and the weight of opposition research against him, offers a rather different picture to that painted by his political opponents. The condemnation of his apparent praise of the Venezuelan regime, it turns out, is based on unfounded claims, unexamined sources, conclusion-jumping, intellectual laziness, and some pretty shoddy journalism."

Indeed, there is no need to do further research on this because that article on his official website alone was enough to understand that Sen. Bernie Sanders and the writer if Sen. Bernie Sanders was not the real writer, wanted to emphasize the fact that America had the jobs gap, the wealth gap, and the racial gap. These gaps brought inequalities so America dream was now realized in those countries.

The writer emphasized or Sen. Bernie Sanders agreed that the income equality in Ecuador, Venezuela and Argentina was better than the U.S. So the conclusion was America must learn from these countries to apply socialism in America as the solution to close the gaps, to bring about equality through socialist agenda, and to make American dream available at home.

Indeed, his message is still very consistent with his agenda and talks because Sen. Bernie Sanders always addresses the issue of the jobs gap, the wealth gap, and the racial gap in his speech. The difference was he did not believe that equality and the socialist dream could be realized in those countries anymore because they failed to do so, but the socialist dream could be realized in the Scandinavian countries.

During his presidential primaries, Sen. Bernie Sanders stated, "When I talk about democratic socialism. I'm not looking at Venezuela. I'm not looking at Cuba. I'm looking at countries like Denmark and Sweden." Since then, he had been using the Scandinavian countries as the great examples and role models for him and the socialists to promote his democratic socialism in America.

He said, "In those countries, health care is the right of all people. And in those countries, college education, graduate school is free. In those countries, retirement benefits, child care are stronger than in the United States of America, and in those countries, by and large, government works for ordinary people in the middle class, rather than, as is the case right now in our country, for the billionaire class."

Sen. Bernie Sanders said in an interview with Democracy Now in November 2006, "In terms of socialism, I think there is a lot to be learned from Scandinavia and from some of the work, very good work that people have done in Europe. In countries like Finland, Norway, Denmark, poverty has almost been eliminated. All people have heath care as a right of citizenship.

College education is available to all people, regardless of income, virtually free. I have been very aggressive in trying to move to sustainable energy. They have a lot of political participation, high voter turnouts. I think there is a lot to be learned from countries that have created more egalitarian societies than has the United States of America" reported Michael Kruse.

Thus, "One way to implement socialism in the United States would be to copy many of the economic institutions found in the Nordic countries of Denmark, Finland, Sweden and Norway. These countries, which consistently rank near the top of the world in happiness, human development and overall well-bing, have highly organized labor markets, universal welfare states and relatively high levels of public ownership of capital" said Matthew Bruenig and reported Charles Krupa.

The Scandinavian countries are in the Scandinavian Peninsula, the largest peninsula of northern Europe and they are known with spectacular views of many gorgeous mountain peaks, high plateaus, best places for skiing, dark winter, northern lights, Geirangerfjord and whale watching of Norway. Sweden, in addition, is known with the sandy beaches, Oresund underwater bridge, and the unique ice hotel.

Denmark is known with the beautiful ancient castles, royal gardens and of course the incredible Lego land, the home of the famous Lego and blocks. The Scandinavian peninsula are further beautified by the thousands of magnificent lakes and best places for hiking of Finland,

and volcanoes, the thermal groundwater, pools and the heated sidewalks by geothermal heat in the winter and the Blue Lagoon of Iceland.

They are among the best countries in the world with economic successes and welfare systems. Sweden is famous for innovation and inventions. "It is the country that first offered the perfected zipper, the marine propeller, the fridge, the heart pacemaker and even created your computer mouse. Not to forget the much-loved discount furniture retailer IKEA and fashion from H&M" according to Terri Mapes.

These Scandinavian countries are told as the great places to live even since 1930s and they are blessed with the best social welfare systems. The countries are nice and clean. "Norway topped the Legatum Institute's annual Prosperity Index for the seventh year in a row as the most prosperous country in the world. Denmark and Sweden came third and fifth" according to Vicky Spratt.

It is true that in comparison, by 2019, these Scandinavian countries are a lot better than the U.S in many categories according to the recent updated articles of Jason Knoll on The Nordics and The U.S. For a more detail comparison of the actual figures, kindly read his full article. For Jason, the Scandinavian are better than the US in UN Human Development Index, Life Expectancy at Birth, and Income Inequality.

They are also better than the U.S in Carbon Dioxide Emissions, Total Paid Leave Available to Mothers and Fathers, Child Relative Income Poverty Rate, Childcare Costs, Best Countries to Raise Kids, Environmental Performance Index, Gender Inequality Index, Gender Gap, Corruption Perceptions Index, Freedom in the World, Good Index Country, Overall Happiness, and Life Satisfaction.

For GDP per capita, USA ($55,681) was higher than Denmark ($47,673), Sweden ($47,194) and lower than Norway ($65,411). USA (3.9%) had the lowest total unemployment than Denmark (5%), Sweden (6.4%) and the same with Norway (3.9%). USA (3.2%) spent double Military Expenditure in comparing to Norway (1.6%), and almost triple in comparing to Denmark (1.2%), and Sweden (1%)

These countries spend more on Government Expenditure on Education, Public Spending on Family Benefits, Public Spending on Childcare and Early Education, Official Development Assistance than the U.S. does. In these countries, Individual Income Tax Rates is higher than that of the USA, which is at 37% while Denmark is at 55.89%, Sweden 57.19% and Norway 38.2%.

They also have long vacation with pay and the wage is beyond $15 per hour. Parents may take two-months leave or more with pay. Jobs are easy to find and education is free up to college and thus the literacy rate is relatively small. These are the dreams of Sen. Bernie Sanders for the U.S. But for those who do not like a lot of snow and the extremely cold winter, these countries may not the ideal places for them.

Benedicte said, "The welfare system in Denmark works really well and you can basically get money for doing nothing or be paid to study and you can live off that money. Healthcare is free too, maybe that's why everyone thinks it's so good here." These are the main reasons why Sen. Bernie Sanders uses Norway, Sweden, and Denmark as the perfect examples of socialist countries for America.

If the Scandinavians are socialist countries, as Bernie Sanders and the socialists said, then America may learn from the great examples of the socialist economy system from these countries and how to make those great things of economic prosperity, high wages and welfare system to become a reality in the beautiful land of America. What if the words of Sen. Bernie Sanders and the socialists are not true?

Are Scandinavian Countries The Socialist Countries?

Sen. Bernie Sanders said in an interview with the Guardian in November 2006, "Twenty years ago, when people here thought about socialism they were thinking about the Soviet Union, about Albania. Now they think about Scandinavia. In Vermont people understand I'm talking about democratic socialism" reported Michael Kruse on Politico. If socialism is great why it was rejected in Soviet Union?

It is no doubt that the Scandinavian countries offer the great social welfares. But are these countries the socialist countries? The socialists often mixed and played the two words social democracy and democratic socialism as if these two forms of government are the same or interchangeable but they are not, as explained later. Excuse me! Sen. Bernie Sanders, Scandinavians are not the socialist countries.

Norway, Denmark and Sweden, the beautiful countries are the successful examples of capitalistic countries. Norway, Denmark and Sweden all use constitutional monarchy with a parliamentary system. They are the strong capitalist countries with free enterprises and their countries are known with less of government's deregulations on the economy than the U.S government does.

Ralph Benko said, "The perennially happiest countries in the world, after all, such as Denmark, Norway, Switzerland, the Netherlands, and Sweden all were, last time this columnist looked, social democracies." These countries are not the socialist countries but social democratic countries and the socialists tried to twist the meanings as if social democracy was the same with democratic socialism.

Yes, these countries provide "free education, free healthcare, free childcare, free retirement, large unemployment benefits, lots of vacation time, and super-long maternity (and paternity) leave times. Add to that high wages, very low gun crime, low unemployment, and low incarceration rates. And how about low government corruption, very low national debt..." wrote John Larabell on New American.

But contrary to what Sen. Bernie Sanders, the socialists and the democrats said, Norway, Sweden and Denmark are not the socialist countries, once they were the socialist countries and struggled to survive, but their prosperity is the great successful example of capitalistic principles and operations. The welfare system was not developed thanking to the socialist ideology or socialist economic system.

If socialist economic system or socialist ideology were so good, why did these great countries stop applying those socialist principles? Was there anything wrong with socialist principles? Why did they change to capitalistic system for the growth of their economies? How do the economies of these countries were developed at the success of the capitalistic principles and are well maintained by those principles?

"It is incorrect, to refer Scandinavian countries as "socialist," given that no Scandinavian countries nationalize their means of production... are perceived as socialist because their citizens pay very high income taxes" stated Kelly McDonald on the Federalist. They were once very progressive countries and the heavily progressive tax slowed down their economic growth.

Though the Scandinavian Peninsula includes Finland and Iceland but the Scandinavia is commonly known as the three kingdoms including Norway, Denmark and Sweden, and "you will only find Danes, Norwegians, and Swedes referring to themselves as Scandinavian" reported Terri Mapes. What is the truth about the economic prosperity and social benefits of these Scandinavian countries?

Norway

Sen. Bernie Sanders said, he wanted the U.S to be more like Norway. "In Norway, parents get a paid year to care for infants." That is true but sorry Sen. Bernie Sanders, Norway is not a socialist country. "Norway is currently ruled by a coalition of the center-right Conservative Party, the libertarian Progress Party and the Liberal Party... It does not have a socialist government" according to Right Wing

The wealth of Norway is not achieved because of the application of socialism or socialist economic system. Norway is wealthy and the people are blessed because of their productivity which is the result of "a more educated work force; outsourcing low-wage, low-productivity labour; maximizing participation in the work force for skilled workers; and equal distribution" according to Esther Hsieh.

Denmark

In 2006, Sen. Bernie Sanders said on Democracy Now reported Michael Kruse, "In countries like Finland, Norway, Denmark, poverty has almost been eliminated. All people have heath care as a right of citizenship. College education is available to all people, regardless of income, virtually free... there is a lot to be learned from countries that have created more egalitarian societies than has the U.S."

That is true but Denmark is not a socialist country. "The largest party in Denmark is the left-wing Social Democrats, but the country's actually run by a coalition of the right-wing Venture, Liberal Alliance, Conservative and Christian Democrat parties, led by the very right-wing Danish People's Party. Non-socialist Norway, Sweden and Finland see Denmark as dangerously right-wing" according to Right Wing.

The Prime Minister of Denmark confirmed that Denmark is not a socialist country in his remark at Harvard's Kennedy School of Government, "I know that some people in the US associate the Nordic model with some sort of socialism. Therefore I would like to make one thing clear. Denmark is far from a socialist planned economy. Denmark is a market economy."

Sweden

Sen. Bernie Sanders said in an interview with The Washington Post in November 2006 reported Michael Kruse, "I wouldn't deny it. Not for one second. I'm a democratic socialist... In Norway, parents get a paid year to care for infants. Finland and Sweden have national health care, free college, affordable housing and a higher standard of living... Why shouldn't that appeal to our disappearing middle class?"

Yes he is a democratic socialist but that does not make Sweden a socialist country. "Sweden is a competitive and highly liberalized, open market economy. The vast majority of Swedish enterprises are privately owned and market-oriented... Sweden has achieved a high standard of living under a mixed system of high-tech capitalism and extensive welfare benefits" according to Wikipedia on "Economy of Sweden."

"Sweden's government is dominated by the Social Democratic Worker's Party, which is on the center-left – but it isn't socialist. Its policies are based on a capitalist economy generating wealth, which is then taxed to redistribute income. The SDWP has always rejected socialist policies like state ownership of the means of production. Sweden doesn't have a socialist government either" reported Right Wing

Finland

Oh yes, Finland used to be a socialist country in the past but socialism did not work well. And now Finland is not a socialist country either. Finnish parliament is a coalition of two conservative parties and the Greens. The country operates with free market and Finland does not have a socialist government so it is impossible that Finland is a socialist state as it is in other Scandinavian countries.

Sen. Bernie Sanders and the socialists may dream too much that that they perceive this beautiful country a socialist country in their fantasy. Yet, Finnish President, Sauli Niinisto, is an independent and is a social conservative and he is supported by the center-right Christian Democratic Party. Socialism once brought more harms to Finland before and it was abandoned and it is never welcome back to this country.

The "Socialist Economy System" in Scandinavian Countries

Sen. Bernie Sanders and the socialists tried to paint beautiful images of socialist Scandinavian countries. Unfortunately, as Americans or at least the readers now know for sure that these gorgeous Scandinavian countries are not the socialist countries. Sen. Bernie Sanders does not tell Americans that his idea of the socialist Scandinavian was of the 1960s. He would be correct if it were 30 to 60 years ago.

So to be fair with Sen. Bernie Sanders, it was true that these countries shifted to socialist agenda or socialist economy system in the 1960s but the socialist principles did not help these countries for economic prosperity but rather almost killed the countries. The great thing of Sen.

Bernie Sanders and the socialists is that they could talk things of 30-60 years ago as if it was just happening yesterday or today.

As Corey Lacono said, on the Foundation for Economic Education social democracy is not democratic socialism and "In the Scandinavian countries, like all other developed nations, the means of production are primarily owned by private individuals, not the community or the government, and resources are allocated to their respective uses by the market, not government or community planning."

Corey Lacono further explained, "an extensive welfare state is not the same thing as socialism. What Sanders and his supporters confuse as socialism is actually social democracy, a system in which the government aims to promote the public welfare through heavy taxation and spending, within the framework of a capitalist economy. This is what the Scandinavian practice."

Social democracy encourages limited government while democratic socialism or socialism in general fully supports big government. Socialism democracy stimulates the privatization of businesses and industries while socialism prefer the control of the government to the businesses and industries. The difference is just like East and West, yet it is a surprise that Sen. Bernie Sanders could not see the differences.

The governments of the Scandinavian countries did not impose minimum wages but "the wages are decided by collective-bargaining agreements between unions and employers... Union-imposed wages lock out the least skilled and do their own damage to an economy, but such a decentralized system is still arguably a much better way of doing things than having the central government set a one-size-fits-all wage policy that covers every occupation nationwide" reported Corey Lacono.

These countries once tried socialist principles, yet the socialist economic system almost brought these countries to collapse and economic crisis. So they had to turn to capitalistic principles to save the countries and to make the countries to become prosperous and wealthy as they are today.

They are democratic countries but the socialists made these countries socialist for their political purposes.

Jeffrey Dorfman said "it is worth noting that the Nordic countries were economic success before they built their welfare states. Those productive economies, generating good incomes for their workers, allowed the governments to raise the tax revenue needed to pay for the social benefits. It was not the government benefits that created wealth, but wealth that allowed the luxury of such generous government programs."

The governments of these countries encourage free markets and the operation of private business though low corporate tax. They do not interfere business affairs as socialist governments do to regulate the prices, wages, modes of production and distributions… They do not dictate or dominate the national industries. These countries do not even have minimum wage laws reported Jeffrey Dorfman.

If Sen. Bernie Sanders could praise Venezuela years earlier and avoid talking about it as if nothing was happened, how could he give the answer to million Americans about truth of the Scandinavian countries? In socialist countries, the leaders could lie everything and things just pass because people could do nothing about that when big government has so much power to control. Will that happen to America soon?

Another great thing about Sen. Bernie Sanders and the socialist is how they was able to twist the truth in such a way that only genius could do, to convince the people that these countries have both the equality and free things of socialism; and the prosperity and freedom of capitalism so that they could call these countries as the great examples of the socialist countries that America could learn from and follow.

Sen. Bernie Sanders saw the Scandinavia as the perfect example of the third-way economic model. He saw a perfect combination between socialism and capitalism; and the relationship between the rich, the government and the poor for the economic development and equality. Yet it is just like the polar differences between the Republicans and the Democrats and so it is with capitalism and socialism.

BE FREE OR NOT BE FREE

He wants the U.S to apply this third-way economic model to "reach the same socio-economic outcomes and prosperity by simply expanding the size of government. If one studies Nordic politics, economy and history in depth, however, it becomes evident that like with most urban legends, the reality of Sanders' utopia is wrong. Causality rather suns in the other direction" According to Daniel Schatz.

Yet Sen. Bernie Sanders and the socialists do not tell the truth that during the socialist eras, these countries were all suffered with economic crisis and they did not have many free things to offer to their people. Only when these countries shifted to the capitalist system, these countries were revived and they are now prosperous with many free things to their people today the nations are longing for.

Sen. Bernie Sanders is a genius to combine democracy, socialism, and capitalism to offer America and Americans a great democratic socialism. Yet he and the socialists still do not admit the disasters of economic crisis, corruption, abuse of power and inequality that socialism had brought to every country that applied socialism so far. And this will for sure happen to America when socialism is applied.

Did socialism really work? By 1960, Sweden turned to the high control of the government toward the economy, strong interferences of labor unions, and extensive social benefits. The tax was high and up to 50% of GDP. In the 1980s, the inflation became high, the real estate was hung, and the lending increased, and then the bubble busted. The GDP went down and the unemployment increased rapidly.

The investment became so low. The economy was at the hardest-hit crisis in the history of the country. "These socialist golden years, which saw a peak of big government, were not so golden for economic performance. While Sweden's growth was second in the world in 1970 (Japan was first), it had quickly dropped to the second-lowest within the OECD in 1990" according to Daniel Schatz.

"The 30 years to come were characterized by the growth of the generous cradle-to-grave welfare state which Sanders begrudges, based upon government intervention, an increase of tax rates and the re-regularization of previously free markets. The country's total tax burden reached a crescendo in 1990 at 52-3%, having a negative effect on business and job creation" according to Daniel Schatz.

"Sweden began to reserve its economic model during the 1990s by implementing reforms that would have made his Republican contenders proud: Stated-owned companies were sold and financial markets were once again deregulated while public monopolies were replaced with competition" said Daniel Schatz. Yes, capitalistic principle not socialism saved the country, the people and the economy.

"The welfare system that had been growing rapidly since the 1970s could not be used sustained with a falling GDP, lower enjoyment and larger welfare payments. In 1994 the government budget deficit exceeded 15% of GDP. The response of the government was to cut spending and institute a multitude of reforms to improve Sweden's competitiveness. When the international economic outlook improved combined with a rapid growth in the IT sector, which Sweden was well positioned to capitalize on, the country was able to emerge from the crisis."

Today, Denmark, Finland, Norway and Sweden are the great social democracy countries with capitalist economic systems. In the past Sen. Bernie Sanders used to praise socialist countries in Latin American and Southern America, and now he could not use the Scandinavian countries. Does he have any other socialist countries to serve as a good model for him to promote socialism in the coming days?

Geoffrey M. Hodgson on the Conversation also confirmed that, "The Nordic countries are all social-democratic countries with mixed economies... Nordic countries show that major egalitarian reforms and substantial welfare states are possible within prosperous capitalist countries that are highly engaged in global markets... They also suggest that humane and equal outcomes are possible within capitalism, while full-blooded socialism has always, in practice, led to disaster."

Maybe the next possible countries that Sen. Bernie Sanders may use to promote his socialism are some of the socialist countries in Asia. But so far Sen. Bernie Sanders still use these Scandinavian countries as the great example of socialist countries for his political propaganda because many Americans still do not recognize the truth yet. If Americans do, would they still trust him for the many social benefits?

Now that the Scandinavian countries are not the socialist countries, yet they are still among the best economic countries with the best social welfare states. Should Americans apply some principles of successes from these countries such as high tax? Probably, American socialists would skip using the Scandinavian countries again as the perfect socialist model as they did with socialist countries in South America.

Will The Socialists Follow The Scandinavian Examples?

Are Sen. Bernie Sanders and American Millennials serious to follow the successful principles of these Scandinavian countries especially Denmark or Sweden as he often said? That is what Sen. Bernie Sanders and the socialists have been talking all the time in their campaigns. If Americans know the true secrets of successes of the Scandinavian countries, will they gladly embrace and apply those principles?

Sen. Bernie Sanders said that people in these countries received everything for free and they don't even need to work. How do Sen. Bernie Sanders and the socialists convince Americans that these countries do not only apply almost 60% tax to the rich, but also the common people in order to provide free health care, free housing, free education or free childcare support?

In an interview with ABC, Sen. Bernie Sanders said, "In those countries, by and large, government works for ordinary people in the middle class, rather than, as is the case right now in our country, for the billionaire class… In Sweden, Norway, Finland, and Denmark, education is provided for free, social insurance is unimaginably generous, and times are good" reported Ryan Cooper.

Yes, it is true that the Scandinavian governments really work hard for the citizens. In addition, the citizens of these countries also work hard in order to make their countries great. The citizens of these countries do not just do nothing in order to receive social benefits and welfares, but they are also willing to pay high tax and work hard so the citizens and their next generations could enjoy the great welfares.

According to Chuck Collins on Institute For Policy Studies, "The Nordic countries-Norway, Sweden, Denmark, and Finland- typically have considerably less income and wealth inequality, thanks to both robust social safety nets and progressive taxation. They also top indexes of industrialized countries measuring quality of life indicators such as longevity, health, work-life balance, and vacations."

How less is the income and wealth inequality in the Scandinavian countries? In 2016, Elaine Schwartz on Econlife revealed that, "Sweden is less equal than most of us imagine… The numbers also demonstrate that Sweden has a relatively high number of millionaires and ultra high net worth individuals… and a happy middle class… For a small country, Sweden has a relatively high number of millionaires."

Elaine Schwartz also noted an important fact that, "In Sweden the middle class has more than one fifth of the country's wealth. Combined with upper class wealth, the total is almost 97 percent" of the country's wealth." According to the above information, the wealth and income inequality in Sweden is also big and Sweden also has many millionaires with high incomes and net worth.

So why do Sen. Bernie Sanders and American socialists only criticize America for the wealth gap? Why do they purposely falsely use the Scandinavian countries as model socialist countries? Why do they employ these countries as good examples of income equality for America to follow while the wealth gap in Sweden is even bigger than the wealth gap in the U.S? How about the truth of high tax in these countries?

What does the report of the OECD mean when it stated, "Copy the Nordic model if you like, but understand that it entails a lot of capitalism and pro-business policies, a lot of taxation on middle class spending and wages, minimal reliance on corporate taxation and plenty of co-pays and deductibles in its healthcare system" according to Charles Lane on Washington Post.

Then, America and Americans should learn from these Scandinavian countries with the rejection of socialism as these countries did. The experience of these Scandinavian countries with socialism failed miserably as many countries in the world did fail, so America should not follow the footprints of the socialist horrible failures. In fact, the U.S. is the great model of successes admired by nations.

American socialists have been praising the Scandinavian countries and using them as the model. Then, it is time for Sen. Bernie Sanders and the socialists to give up their ideology if they really mean to follow the Scandinavian countries, as these are not the socialist nations. Will they be responsible for what they said? For sure, they won't give up the ideology and still need it for their political purposes and gains.

Since socialism failed everywhere, there is no reason to believe that socialism would be successful in the U.S. If socialism always brought about oppressions everywhere, there is no reason that it would bring freedoms to Americans. Americans as well as people of world better walk out from that ideology and their deceptive talks and apply great lessons from the Scandinavian countries.

Should the U.S government apply high tax for all Americans as the Scandinavian countries do to their citizens? For sure American socialists would not want to talk about this or else how could they earn the votes from the people. Let us discover how is the relationship between high tax and the great social welfares offered in the Scandinavian countries?

The High Tax

Sen. Bernie Sanders and American socialists may forget to tell the Americans that Norway, Sweden, Finland and Denmark have highest tax rates in the world. In order for these countries to provide great social benefits, people must pay high tax for the great benefits and social welfare whether they are the tops rich, the middle class or anyone else. The people get what they have been paying for.

Social welfares of these countries do not just be dependent on the supports of the rich people alone. These countries have high total tax revenue and the total tax revenue is usually half of GDP. After tax, workers generally receive about 40% of their income. These countries know that wealth tax is great but if they only depend largely on wealth tax then the social programs would not be sustained in long run.

According to George Lakey, in his book Viking Economics and stated by Chuck Collins, "Residents in Nordic countries don't complain about their higher taxes because they clearly benefit from the expenditures. "For their high taxes the Norwegians have gotten overall affluence, stability, opportunity, a high level of services that make life easier and more secure."

Geoffrey M. Hodgson confirmed again the high tax and "the Nordic countries have achieved very high levels of welfare and well being, alongside levels of economic output that compare well with other highly developed countries. They result from relatively high levels of social solidarity and taxation, alongside a political and economic system that preserves enterprise, economic autonomy and aspiration."

"According to the OECD, Denmark (26.4 percent), Norway (19.7 percent), and Sweden (22.1 percent) all raise a high amount of tax revenue as a percent of GDP from individual income taxes and payroll taxes. This is compared to the 15 percent of GDP raised by the United States through its individual income taxes and payroll taxes for instance" according to Answers.com and Kyle Pomerleau.

"Denmark's top marginal effective income tax rate is 60.4 percent. Sweden's is 56.4 percent. Norway's top marginal tax rate is 39 percent… they tax most people at high rates, not just the high-income taxpayers" according to Answers. In other words, would Americans agree to be taxed at 60% if their income is $50,000 and above? If this were so, America would be filled with milks and honey of social benefits.

Kerry McDonald reported that, "According to the Organization for Economic Cooperation and Development, the average American spends 9.8 percent of his income on taxes; Sweden spend 12.3 percent, Danes 26.4 percent, Norwegians 10 percent, and Finns 12.9 percent. Perhaps because of these measures, government debt is less of a problem in Scandinavia that it is in the United States."

The high tax in the Scandinavian countries does not only offer great social welfares but it also relieves their nations from debts. The national debt of the U.S. is now over $20 trillions, so why American socialists do not propose high tax to all Americans so that the U.S would solve the national debt? American socialists also do not tell Americans that that high tax also leads Scandinavians to household debt.

Kerry MacDonald also revealed that, "Scandinavian rates of household debt are astronomically high. OECD figures also show the average Dance has a household debt equal to 310 percent of his disposable income; the number is 173 percent for Swedes. In America, the average is 114 percent... it is noteworthy that Scandinavia's progressive tax systems fail to protect their citizens from staggering personal debt."

These countries also collect sale taxes or VATs "levied on businesses throughout the production process. As a tax on consumption, VATs are economically efficient: they can raise significant revenue with relatively less harm to the economy. However, many (especially in the US) see VATs as a regressive tax because they more on those that spend a larger share of their income, mainly the poor" reported Kyle Pomerleau

"Denmark collects about 9.6 percent of GDP through the VAT, Norway collects about 7.8 percent, and Sweden collections about 9 percent of GDP. All three countries have VAT rates of 25 percent. The United States does not have a national sales tax or VAT. Instead, states levy sale taxes. The average rate across the country is about 7 percent. The much lower rate only collects about 2 percent of U.S. GDP in revenue" reported Kyle Pomerleau.

American democrats, liberals and socialists want to apply wealth tax on the top 1 percent but "Most Nordic countries, by contrast, have zero estate tax. They fund generous programs with the help of value-added taxes that heavily affect middle-class consumers. In Sweden, for example, consumption, social security and payroll taxes total 27 percent of gross domestic product, as compared with 10.6 percent in the United States" reported Charles Lane on Washington Post.

The truth or secret behind all of the good social benefits in the Scandinavian countries is that people pay high tax to enjoy their benefits. This is fair for the Scandinavians because they really pay for their benefits and they do not feel ashamed or guilty or being looked down to enjoy their great social benefits. They contribute to their rights as rights go hand in hand with responsibilities.

American socialists want to use the wealthy to give the rights to others but how long does this last? They only "inspire" people to get more money from the rich through wealth taxes for their political purposes. They do not tell the truth that when wealthy people cannot achieve the benefits that they want with the risks and investments, they would not invest or go to other countries to achieve the purpose.

This happened to America in the previous administrations when thousands of American companies moved their factories abroad. They closed down the factories and many operations at home and leaving America with high rate of unemployment and shaken economy. Million jobs were offered to nations yet millions of people in America struggled to look for jobs and to sustain their living.

Through low tax policy and reforms under President Trump and his Administration, thousands of companies are coming back to set up their factories in America. As the result, millions of jobs are coming back contributing and leading to the thriving economy and increasing wage to people without robbing the wealthy. Made-in-USA products are now available again when this was believed to be impossible.

Though the coronavirus pandemic heavily affects people and economies in America and nations of the world. Yet one must recognize that before the outbreak of coronavirus, president Trump did make America Great Again with his genius economic development plans through Opportunity Economic Zones and Pledge for America's Workers that brought America to the lowest record of unemployment.

Through tax-cut reform, more jobs were provided and more Americans have stable jobs to support their living and family. Importantly, the growing U.S. economy and the generated revenues before coronavirus pandemic showed that there was enough funding for social welfare to Americans. Thus the U.S. does not need to apply high tax to all American workers as Norway, Sweden and Denmark do.

Does high tax in Scandinavian countries affect the value of works among the Scandinavians? Do many able Scandinavians depend on social welfares or they really work and make contributions to others through their tax? High value of work is high commendable and is the value that people in the Scandinavian countries are upholding and it is also the secret of their prosperity and great benefits.

The High Value of Labor

Sen. Bernie Sanders and American socialists may not tell Americans that the Norwegians, Swedes, Finnish and Danish have high level of working ethics. According to Nima Sanandaji the Scandinavians have high levels of social trust, social cohesion, social responsibility and social ethics. All of these characteristics were already evident before the establishment of the modern welfare system.

Nima Sanandaji in his book, Debunking Utopia-Exposing The Myth Of Nordic Socialism, proved that "the reason for prosperity in the Scandinavian countries is not a social democracy, as the Left would have you believe, but a culture based on hard word, healthy diets, social cohesion and high levels of trust," and individual responsibility wrote Swarajya.

Daniel Schatz also confirmed that, "The relative success of Nordic countries like Sweden, in terms of being characterized by high living standards, long life expectancy and low crime rates combines with a considerable degree of social cohesion and even distributions of income, precedes the contemporary welfare state as well." That social cohesion is not only in term of race but also working ethics.

Scandinavians understand that for their countries to do well and for them to receive the great and excellent social benefits, each citizen must be social responsible and must contribute to the prosperity and stability of the countries. They have to work and they have to share social responsibilities. Their high ethical value of work and social responsibilities are the vital keys to their successes and prosperity

That working ethic is getting low here to millions of Americans, migrants and immigrants thanking to the powerful and bad influences of media propaganda by the Democrats, the liberals, leftists and socialists to encourage able people for free stuffs instead of hard works. They sent the wrong message that it is people's rights to have those benefits without much investment or sweats.

The U.S. has high level of unemployment and welfare recipients. U.S government spent about $1 trillion annually for poverty assistance programs and almost half of the fund is spent on Medicaid, about 30% is spent on family and children assistance. The rest of the fund is for housing assistance, unemployment, workers compensation and others reported to Lexington Law.

Lexington Law specified that 64,699,741 individuals were enrolled in Medicaid in October 2019, and an average of 35 percent of unemployed Americans received means-tested benefits, 43 percent of Americans signed up for welfare programs have been participating for over 3 years. The annual budget of $1 trillion supports "21 percent of Americans puts the large problem of poverty into perspective."

Unfortunately, many of the welfare recipients in the U.S. are people who are able to work but they are lazy or they just don't want to work. Many welfare recipients are not really poor and are also able to work but they prefer to receive social welfare and they secretly go to work part time and they just receive cash. By this way they could earn more, they could relax and they still enjoy many social benefits.

These able people add more social burdens to the government and taxpayers and they are also spending the big amount of financial resources that is supposedly used for the good of the majority people. They are not responsible to themselves and other people. If they work they could contribute more wealth to the nation as a whole, the wellbeing of Americans and needy people.

This is also the major reason why socialism and the socialist economic system did not work well in any former socialist countries before. People were not motivated to work because the lazy people received almost the same things as hard-working people so they did not need to sweat. The dependence of the majority on the government distribution led to economic crisis and the collapses of the countries.

The stimulus checks and unemployment benefits in the U.S. during the lockdown is great but it also points to the fact that socialism could never work in the U.S as well. If people just keep on living on unemployment benefits and social welfare, the U.S. would soon bankrupt and collapse if the country received no revenues and no contributions from the majority of taxpayers.

Social benefits and welfares are important and needed, yet benefits and welfares are not for able people who purposely take advantages of the welfare, and abuse and misuse public funds. Previous generations of Americans were well taught with the working ethics and social responsibilities through the biblical teaching and training. The current and the coming generations need to be cultivated with these teachings.

The Bible teaches and commands that, "If anyone is not work willing to work, let him not eat" (II Thessalonians 3:10) or "Let the thief no longer steal, but rather let him labor, doing honest work with his own hands, so that he may have something to share with anyone in need" (Ephesians 4:28). "The desire of the sluggard kills him, for his hands refuse to labor" (Proverbs 21:25).

These biblical teachings do not mean that God and Christians are not loving and caring for people and their needs. God is love and God's children are called to love and to help one another. That love of God could not just be seen and touched by empty words and literary explanations alone but through practical steps of giving, blessing, feeding, clothing, educating and sheltering people with those needs.

That love of God has been carried out through active actions of millions of Christian, charity and mission organizations that have been reaching out billion people around the world because "Religion that God our father accepts as pure and faultless is this: to look after orphans and widows in their distress and to keep oneself from being polluted by the world" (James 1:27).

These biblical teachings do remind people the importance, the value and the benefits of works so that every able people would not become a burden but he or she would become fruitful and helpful to others and societies. When people are not conscious of their working responsibilities and trying to avoid works for their gains, pleasures, and laziness, they are contributing many social issues to America and Americans.

Then, able people who just want to be dependent on social welfares would totally become dependent on the mercies of others. They would be dependent on the politicians. They would be dependent on government. They would be dependent on taxpayers. They would be dependent on everyone and everything and they are dependent on themselves for their own benefits and gains.

Able people who just want to be dependent on social welfares would learn to develop bad and negative habits. They are lazy, not motivated, passive, or at least they have the bad habit of depending government, social welfares and others and but not themselves. They might be prompted to make false statements and situations so that they could receive more social welfares.

Able people who just want to be dependent on social welfare also waste their talents. Their laziness or their unwillingness to work would stop them from developing their precious talents that could change their lives and the lives of others. They stop themselves from precious opportunities to be trained, equipped and to develop their potentials and talents toward better lives.

Able people who just want to be dependent on social welfare are not responsible to others. They are self-centered and they are not willing to become the channels of blessings to people who are in needs. Yet the opportunities for others may be affected when able people are taking the welfare portions that belong to other needy people who are really in needs of social supports, assistances and welfares.

Able people who just want to be dependent on social welfare give bad example to others. They do not just set bad moral and examples to their children but they also set bad examples to their circles of friends and families. They also influence people to take advantages of welfares. It is not easy to train people with virtue of works but it is very easy for people to learn how to take advantages of the social welfares.

Able people who are dependent on social welfares do not give fairness to millions of responsible Americans who have been working hard to pay taxes and to contribute to the prosperity of America. They are still risking their lives through economic crisis, pandemics to work so they could contribute wealth to America and supports to millions of welfare recipients while undeserved recipients just enjoy their lives.

Able people who are dependent of social welfare abuse the kindness of others. Millions of religious people and generous people are just being abused because they are kind and they are taught to show love and care to the neighbors and people in needs. They are willing to support government policies so that the country could provide better social welfares but they could be hurt upon knowing the truth.

Able people who just dependent on social welfare may affect the continuous supports to the needy people. These generous donors could be hurt and sad if they realized that so many able people are taking advantages of them and taxpayers. They may stop giving and donating and this would lead to many more issues when the needy people could not be helped and supported due to the lacks of funds.

Able people who are dependent on social welfare give burden to the society and taxpayers. Taxpayers must sweat and toil and sweat so that public funds are available to provide social benefits and welfares. The more welfare recipients, the more taxpayers' funds are to be used. The government also needs the contributions of the citizens so that more taxes received and more finances to develop the country.

Able people who are dependent on social welfare would not break themselves from poverty. Proverbs 14:23 say, "In all toil there is profit, but mere talk tends only to poverty" and "Whoever is slack in his work is a brother to him who destroys" (Proverbs 18:9). No country would help the able and lazy people to become rich so able people need to get on their feet and to change their economy and destiny.

This does not mean that God only wants people to work and work until death but God also teaches people, workers, and even animals to rest and refresh themselves as Exodus 23:12 stated, "Six days you shall do your work, but on the seventh day you shall rest; that your ox and our donkey may have rest, and the son of your servant woman, and the alien, may be refreshed.

These biblical teachings, trainings and practices made America prosperous and produced so many influential and great business people, researchers, politicians, lawyers, doctors and many famous and successful people. Those biblical teachings and principles of work ethics would revive America and make Americans prosperous again after the serious and deadly affects of coronavirus pandemics.

While American socialists are trying to impress Americans that socialism and the socialist do really care for the wellbeing of the people and socialism and the socialists may bring so many great things to people and to make their lives comfortable and enjoyable, yet people who grew up in the socialist countries never experience the economic and freedom promises of the socialists to be true ever.

In the past, millions of people were just dependent and waiting for the government to provide their needs. People just believed in socialism and thinking that they would not suffer poverty and hardships. It was true that they could receive some economic assistance in a short period of time. Then, the people faced economic crisis, poverty, famines, hungers and deaths in millions.

It's time for many Americans to restore social responsibility and high working ethics and not social dependences. It is time to pass these great values onto the next generations as John F. Kennedy once said, "My fellow Americans, ask not what your country can do for you, ask what you can do for your country." Americans can do this well because they did and were successful with that and they will succeed.

In addition to high tax for everyone in Scandinavian countries and high value of work, the wealth and the prosperity of these countries are also the results of free market operation not central planning by big government as it is in socialist countries. It is also the free market operation that saved these Scandinavian countries and many former socialist countries from economic devastations.

Free Market Economy

Sen. Bernie Sanders does not tell Americans that the Scandinavian countries of Norway, Sweden, and Denmark are not prosperous and successful thanking to socialist economic system and socialist ideology. Yet, these countries aspire innovations, economies and trades through free market not through the government controls of products and distributions which once killed their economies.

These countries had been deregulating the financial sector and promoting free enterprises, free competition and free trade since the mid-1800s by Swedish Minister of Finance Johan August Gripenstedt. "These reforms prompted Sweden's transition to capitalism which the Scandinavian country reaching one of the fastest global economic growth rates by 1890" according to Daniel Schatz.

Swedish government for example still wants to privatize partially or wholly some of the state-owned companies left. The reason for this is that the government does not want to leave the burden of debt for future generations and the government can also use the money to pay off the debt. The privatization of these state-owned companies include Telia Sonea for Telecom, and SAS Group for Airline.

The government ownership of companies post huge financial burdens on the taxpayers. The state-owned enterprises (SOEs) are huge in scales and yet they are often stagnant and the government basically must subsidize a lot of money to maintain state-own enterprises thanking to government projects, many resources, revenues and contributions from foreign investments and private enterprises.

Amir Guluzade noted that it is "the private sector's that contribute to Chinese economy: they contribute 60% of China's GDP, and are responsible for 70% of innovation, 80% of urban employment and provide 90% of new jobs. Private wealth is also responsible for 70% of investment and 90% of exports." Yet SOEs control most important industries of the country and the powers are in their hands.

It is important to note that, "Corporation tax levels in Scandinavia are low-much lower than in the USA. All of these countries are good places to run a business, and that's a deliberate policy to encourage private companies" reported Right Wing. If Sen. Bernie Sanders and American socialists want to learn from the Scandinavian countries they should drop their plans for social ownership and big government.

It is no need to discuss much about the concept of free market economy that is based on the principles of supply and demand here because America and the Western world have been applying the principles of free market economy successfully for decades. It would be sufficient to list down the advantages and disadvantages of the free market economy summed up by Louise Gaille on Vittana.

Free market economy gets rid of a significant amount of red tape. It provides more freedom to innovate. Customers always drive transactions in a free market economy, and customers always drive transactions in a free market economy. It naturally promotes equality and it regulates themselves naturally. It creates a rising tide that lifts all boats. Individual skills are what drives a free market economy forward, free expression is a natural component of this society.

Louise Gaille also listed the disadvantages of free market economy as profit is always the motive for success in a free market economy. Market failures can create severe recessions and ongoing economic consequences. A free market economy can provide limited product choices and it requires consumption to survive. Those who are unable to produce in a free market economy get cast aside.

Equality doesn't always equate to equal opportunities. The free market economy alters the priority of governing and it promotes the idea of monopolization. If large businesses fail in a free market economy, so does everyone else and the free market system restrains wages instead of encouraging them to grow. The socialist economists and leaders are always critical of these disadvantages.

Though the socialists criticize the disadvantages mentioned by Luise Gaille but they apply free market policy to save the countries from economic crisis. And it is the socialists that brings more exploitations of the workers due to corruption, the inequalities created by the socialists as big government control, the monopolization of industries and businesses, the orientation of profits, and economic consequences.

The remaining socialist countries now must operate on free market operation in order to survive from so many failures by the socialist economy and regime. This fact is enough to say that the socialist economic principle could not work well and it indeed never worked well in all former socialist nations and many current ones. It brought so much disasters and pains as discussed in the first chapter.

The socialist economy killed the creativity. Talents were not well appreciated and their contributions may be not accepted due to the restrictions of the socialist ideology. Talents were not in their positions to apply their findings and inventions because chances were mainly given to socialists. Talents thus were not motivated to think creatively and to develop their theories, models, inventions and researches.

The socialist economy killed the choice of the people. "The trademark of a free market economy is an absence of coerced transactions or conditions. Consumers have the right to choose what company provides them with the goods or services they require at any time" according to Luise Gaille. This was not possible when the government decides and provided the products they thought people needed.

The socialist economy killed the markets. The industries and modes of productions were controlled by the socialist government and private businesses could hardly survived the by the policies and corruptions. The socialist economic principle led to economic crises and the collapsed of many former socialist countries and leaving many current socialist nations in inflations and economic deprivations.

The socialist economy killed millions of lives. History is clear on this matter and it could not be wrong. Though current socialist countries still try to hide the fact that millions of people in their countries died due to poverty and famines alone, but they could not hide from the sharing of million victims who suffered the famines and who witnessed the million deaths of their loved ones, friends and neighbors.

Now that the socialist economic system has not been workable in more than one century and the Scandinavian countries were almost destroyed by the socialist economic system but these countries have been prospered by the free market operation as the U.S and many nations have been prospered, so why do Americans must take the socialist path of failures?

Indeed, the growth of the economic development that many nations and the growth of modern socialist countries are always the results of the free economic system with small government not the socialist economic system with large government. This flow of free market motivates healthy and fair competitions, job creation, creativities, passions, variety of products, and wealth.

Many people in socialist countries still remember the scarcity of products, goods and services during the time when socialist countries applied socialist economic system with large government. Common people had almost the same types of clothes, shoes, pens, bicycle, rice, and foods... There was almost no variety or quality improvement for each type of the products from year to years.

This was because all of the industries, goods and products were basically produced and controlled by the government. The government factories or industries had no competition and no pressure to make better products and service to attract buyers. The government controlled everything and products to be produced must be approved by the government but not the wishes and desires of the people.

You would see people wore the same kind of hats. They rode the same kind of bicycles. They wore clothes with the same colors and quality. It was like a bakery that produced only a few kinds of bread, and all the breads look the same. This is the same with socialism. It is then people are equal. Do you want that? Unfortunately, the leaders and the wealthy socialists received different treatments then.

At the present, there is not even one socialist country that is strictly applying this socialist economic system. You may do a Google search to understand how does life look like in a typical socialist country. You would find out the kinds of clothes and products that the people are allowed to have, the poverty life that people are facing and many more "weird" things that are unheard of in the free countries.

Americans and nations are blessed with the free market operation, freedom and many human rights. The free market allows the creativities, talents, intellectual properties, thoughts and opinions to be developed, protected and appreciated. As the result, it leads to the flourish of so many products, goods and services by individuals and businesses to meet the various needs of the people.

Of course every form of government has its strength and weaknesses, but one thing that hundred millions of people could say for sure is that the socialist economic system failed miserably wherever it is applied. Countries with free market operation or capitalistic economic system often produce more wealth, freedoms and equality to the citizens of a country than any socialist government did so far.

Not So Many Expenses

The American socialists may forget to inform Americans that America is the biggest spender in the world. In 2017, the expenditures of the U.S. was around $6.8 trillions while the expenditures of Sweden was around $275 billions following by Norway, $214 billions, Denmark, $173 billion, and Finland, around $137 billions according to Wikipedia on List of Countries By Government Budget.

The Scandinavian countries are not so burdened with huge and many expenses on immigration, illegal immigrants, international public relations, and militaries and defenses, but the U.S does cover large expenses for those areas. The amount of the U.S. expenditures shows that the U.S. has the capability to provide better social benefits when resources are to be well adjusted and managed.

The U.S. also spent more on health care per capital than the Scandinavian countries or any country in the world. In 2017, the U.S. spent $10,224 per person while Sweden spent $5,511, and other Scandinavian countries spent less than $4,000 per person as reported by Bradley Sawyer and Cynthia Cox on Peterson-KFF, Health System Tracker. The significant price cuts would make the U.S. healthcare better.

The U.S is also the largest defense spending in the world. In 2020, the U.S. spent $750 billions and the total costs may reach up to more than

$900 billion. The Scandinavian countries spent less than $22 billion annual: Norway, $7.179 billion, Sweden, $6.326 billion, Denmark, $4.760, and Finland, $3.570 billion according to Global Fire Power. Will the U.S. cut down some military spending for education?

According to Kimberly Amadeo on The Balance, "Almost two-thirds of federal spending goes toward paying the benefits required by Social Security, Medicare, and Medicaid. These are part of mandatory spending… that will cost $2.966 trillion in FY 2021. Social Security costs $1.151 trillion, Medicare costs $722 billion and Medicaid, $448 billion." The U.S. indeed spends a lot on social benefits.

Kimberly also reported that, "food stamps, Unemployment compensation, Child Nutrition, Child Tax Credits, Supplemental Security Income, and Student Loans… Retirement and disability programs for civil servants, the Coast Guard, and the military" cost a total of $645 billion. Illegal immigrants spent more than $250 billion annually from $448 billion of Medicaid and $645 billions of welfares.

Yet the number of spending could even higher because the number of illegal immigrants in American is almost the same the number of the population of three largest Scandinavian countries combined. The mainstream media and leaders reported about 10 million illegal immigrants when the number is between 15-20 millions and Sen. Bernie Sanders wants to add another 2 millions to the U.S.

The Scandinavian countries do not carry such a huge financial and social burdens for illegal immigrants but the U.S. does and illegal immigrants contribute little to the tax revenues. They also have small population. Norway has a total population of less than 5.4 million and Sweden has a population of about 10 million people. Denmark has a population of less than 5.8 million people reported Amanda Briney.

The small size of these countries in terms of population and geography would require fewer funds on the development of infrastructures, military spending, illegal immigration costs, and crimes. With the prosperous economy, high employment and high tax, Norway, Denmark and Sweden are in good standing to provide many free social benefits though they are under pressures now to provide those benefits.

Homogeneity is also a good reason and an advantage to apply social benefits in these countries because these countries may not face with many racial barriers as America has been facing. "Those facts are crucial in public policy – a cozy, tight-knit community will have a different opinion on centralized authority than a sprawling one filled with people from wildly varying backgrounds" stated Zeeshan Aleem.

Ryan Cooper is right to make this comment; "it is a proof-of-concept for policy, not a political blueprint. Each of these nations is quite small, with a vastly different social and historical context than that of the United States. Any implementation of Nordic policy here will be reached by a vastly different route-one rooted in American politics and institutions."

If each illegal immigrant costs American taxpayers a minimum of $2000 per month for social welfare and if we get the average number of illegal immigrants as 15 millions. Then, it would cost American taxpayers $30 billions each month. Every year, American tax payers lost this huge amount of money, which is supposed to be used to take care of their healthcare, education, housing, living conditions…:

$$\$30,000,000,000 \times 12 \text{ (Months)} = \$360,000,000,000$$

This minimal estimated amount is $360 billions for illegal immigrants in the U.S. and it is already larger than the expenditures of any Scandinavian countries or larger than the combined expenditures of the two small Scandinavian countries. The U.S. annual budget for military is even bigger than the combined expenditures of all the Scandinavian countries.

That amount of $360,000 billion is enough to provide free education to all American college students. If the democrats are willing to cut this huge cost from illegal immigrants, then America could solve major issues such as free college education, unnecessary building of the southern wall, releasing social burdens, decrease of unemployment rate, and other security issues.

President Trump addressed this issue of illegal immigrations at the State of the Union Address as he said, "Over 130 legislators in this chamber have endorsed legislation that would bankrupt our nation by providing free taxpayer-funded healthcare to millions of illegal aliens, forcing taxpayers to subsidize free care for anyone in the world who unlawfully crosses our borders."

If the Scandinavian countries take in 10 million illegal immigrants, would they be able to take care of these 10 million illegal immigrants with all the social benefits as America does? If they take in just 1 million illegal immigrants, would they be able to be the top countries with social welfare? Even if they took in half a million illegal immigrants, they could hardly take care the needs of such a big number of people.

Adding to the burdens of illegal immigrants, huge spending on military and defenses, and social benefit, the U.S. also has millions of Americans who were unemployed. The coronavirus pandemic made more than 40 million Americans filed for unemployment by the end of May 2020 and putting the U.S. economy into recession. Every year America also adds more than $1 trillion budget deficit.

This means that the U.S economy is so strong and capable to provide many needs and great welfares. If more able Americans were to go back to work instead of depending on social welfare under normal situation after the coronavirus pandemic, and the U.S government could reduce of the many big budgets, the U.S would be among the nations to provide the best social welfares in the world

Social Welfares

Sen. Bernie Sanders said, "What's wrong when you have more income and wealth equality? What's wrong when they have a stronger middle class in many ways than we do, higher minimum wage than we do and they are stronger on the environment than we are?" Yes, there is nothing wrong for Americans to receive more income and wealth. There are no problems to have a stronger middle class and better wage.

It would be wrong when taxpayers do not receive what they are being for. The Scandinavians are willing to pay high tax and they receive great benefits. A lot of money from taxpayers was channeled to Planned Parenthood for abortions instead of healthcare and services for taxpayers. Funds paid by taxpayers were fueled to the many costs for illegal immigrants instead of social benefits and infrastructures...

It would be wrong when able people are taking advantages of the social welfares, which are for the needy people. Many needy Americans are homeless and they are not able to receive proper health cares, medications and poor living condition, when illegal and able people are spending billions of U.S dollars that could be used to improve and to help needy Americans.

It would be wrong when the socialists try to apply a failed socialist economic system and deceive millions of Americans by saying that the socialist economic system is great and it would solve many issues of inequalities, poverties, and economic gaps when the socialist economic system is the cause of so many sufferings, inequalities, injustices and losses of many freedoms.

It would be wrong to use the freebies to attract people for political purposes. It is wrong to deceive people that it is socialism that could provide so many social benefits and to free people from so many debts and pressures, yet no socialist country in more than 40 former socialist countries around the world could do so in more than one century of the socialist history.

Since the focus of this book is to discuss about the reality of socialism not about the policies or the offers of social benefits or welfares, we would like to make a quick and short comments about the possibilities of Sen. Bernie Sanders' new bill of rights. **Firstly,** everyone needs to realize that though these rights sound good and needed but it always requires the finances to make these benefits available to Americans.

Secondly, in order to allocate the funds needed, the revenues that come from tax-payers to make those benefits available to everyone should be sufficient to ensure the continuity of the benefits. The funds may also come from the surplus revenues of the good economy and reasonable wealth tax. Do not just focus on taxing the top rich alone; this would kill jobs, economy and sources of funds for the benefits

Thirdly, a dying economy cannot provide free college education, healthcare or better benefits. A growing economy cannot be possible with the government alone, it also needs the contributions from businesses, corporations and individuals. If businesses stop the investment, no new jobs are to be created and if the workers are idle, then wealth could not be created. Then crises and chaos would take place.

Fourthly, it takes time to make those benefits totally free, the unrealistic application of these benefits would pose a strong burden on the nation's economy leading to inflation, crisis and even collapse of the economy as this happened in so many socialist nations. This benefit should go through a process by reducing the fee from 75% to 50% to 25% and then 0% as the resources and funds are available.

Concerning universal income, that is not a great idea for any country to apply as universal income would be a real burden for America. It sounds so good but it is going to destroy the U.S economy and put the U.S into more debts and the Americans into more sufferings. It would lead the majority of Americans to low-working ethics and dependences on taxpayers and the government for their living.

If each American is to be provided with $1000 monthly, then the rough cost that the government would be around $3.5-$4 trillion annually. Yet the annual revenues from taxpayers are less than $3 trillion. The government could only do so if the annual revenues from taxpayers could reach $8-$9 trillion because there are also many costs for social benefits and welfares.

Many people would have this tendency, "why do I have to work or to work more when I have money to spend, food stamps to live on and social housing to stay." Especially, millions of Americans are on drug now, and this universal income would lead them more into drug and vices rather than starting a new life and contributing their talents to societies because they still have regular finances for drugs.

As a minister, I encountered and prayed for some drug-addicted people. They said it would not take a long time for them to stop using drugs but it is tough to get rid of their desire for and their dependency on drugs. They wanted drugs to help them release their pains and uneasy feeling. They wanted drugs to create high feelings and happiness. That was the main reason why they kept coming back to drugs.

Another main reason that they continue to use drugs because of the available financial resources so they still afford for drugs. I asked them, "Where do you get money to purchase drugs?" The media and many politicians never wanted the taxpayers know that these drug addicted got money from social welfare. This is where social welfare may give more harms than good to these drug-addicted people.

Social welfares have been abused by many people who are well able to work and to contribute more to society but they are not willing to work to make their lives better and to be independent from the welfares. They might be hurt deeply by marriage failures, broken relationships, disappointments and the likes. They choose to live on food stamps and social benefit instead of getting on their feet again.

If the U.S. must make all other freebies as Sen. Bernie Sanders and the Democrats proposed, America does not need socialism to do so because no socialist country was able to do that. The U.S. economy could be strong enough to provide Americans better welfares in a near future when the U.S. government cuts many expenses on immigrations, abortions, military operations, and wars...

President Trump is also correct to point out that, "These proposals would raid the Medicare benefits of our seniors and that our seniors depend on, while acting as a powerful lure for illegal immigration. That is what is happening in California and other states. Their systems are totally out of control, costing taxpayers vase and unaffordable amounts of money."

On the overall, Americans may receive better social benefits when the expenses toward illegal immigration and illegal immigrants are controlled, the expenses of social welfares to able people is cut, and the expenses on militaries and defenses are reduced. Many high costs of education, healthcare, housing and prescription drugs also need to be adjusted so that more funds could be added to social programs.

In saying so, we don't mean to say that America would stop allowing immigration and welfares. America still needs immigrants for economic purposes and many foreigners also need America and Americans for humanitarian purposes as million people are still mistreated and suffered around the world. For the security and benefits of America and Americans, immigration needs to be done legally.

America and Americans should learn from Denmark, Finland, Norway and Sweden with characteristics of free market economy for the growth and thrive of their economies as well as of American economy. Then it leads to abundances of social benefits when the economy is prospering. America is now able to increase more social benefits to Americans by better management of tax revenues.

America needs to cut down the unnecessary costs on military spending. It is also important that America needs to control the many issues and expenses of illegal immigration then America could cut down a lot of costs, then more taxpayer money is allotted to increase the benefit investments in providing free healthcare, free education and even free housing to needy people.

America does not need to apply high tax to all people as it is in Scandinavian countries but reasonable wealth tax is possible but the revenues of wealth tax should be used properly for social welfares. Then the wealthy people are more than willing to do so because they have been doing that for humanity. America needs to cultivate the high moral of working ethics not the free-stuff ethics.

In saying so, we do not mean that social welfares will not be longer available to the underprivileged or needy people in the society. More benefits are to be given to the needy and every citizen of the country when able people are active in the work force. Their works and contribution would provide more revenues to be used to eliminate the wealth gap and inequality to people instead of just taxing a few.

College For All

Concerning College for All, in his speech at New Hampshire in 2016 presidential campaign, Sen. Bernie Sanders, "When we need the best-educated workforce in the world, yes, we are going to make public colleges and universities tuition-free." We have noted that the expenses for illegal immigrants are enough to provide free college education to almost 20 million students.

Sen. Bernie Sanders said, "Our job, if we are smart, is to make it easier for people to get the education they need, not harder." It was in 2016, Bernie Sanders proposed free four-year college education at public institutions for students whose household income was less than $125,000 per year, and free community college for students from all income levels reported by Mitchell Wellman. This is also great too.

Back in 2015, Sen. Bernie Sanders proposed College for All Act known as Senate Bill 1373 at the 114th Congress. This bill directs the Department of Education to award grants to states to eliminate tuition and required fees at public institutions of higher education. For more information on the proposed bill you may follow the following link: https://www.congress.gov/bill/114th-congress/senate-bill/1373

Just like his proposal of free healthcare, his promotion of free college education has been helping him to gain popularity and supports through the years and now at the 2020 presidential election among the millennials who love this appealing offer. A Harvard poll showed that Bernie Sanders got a 54% favorability rating among the 18-to 29-year-old and he is getting more momentum as the election approaching.

According to the 2019 statistics of National Center for Education Statistics, there were 50.8 million students in public schools and 5.8 million in private schools for PK-12 Education. In public schools, there were 23.7 million White students and 13.9 million for Hispanic students, 7.7 million for Black and 2.7 million for Asian students. The non-white continues to increase significantly in the coming years.

There were 19.9 million college students in the United States in 2019 and 12.1 million students attended full time. 14.7 million students were in the public institutions and more than 30% of students or 5.2 million students in private institutions. There were 16.9 million students in undergraduate programs and 3 million students in graduate programs in both public and private institutions.

The PK-12 Education is already free to American students and what will be the cost to make college education free? Statista projected that there will be 14.69 million college students in public institutions and 5.24 million college students in private institutions. The number of students in both public and private institutions will reach to 20 million college students by 2022.

Sen. Bernie Sanders tweeted on April 5, 2017, "We need millions of students to tell Mr. Trump and the Republican leadership, 'Sorry, we're not going to leave college $100,000 in debt.'" Yes, millions of students would do because no student wanted to have such a big debt and isn't that better if the education is free and they would be more than happy to vote for Bernie Sanders so they could have debt free?

Students are happy but million taxpayers may pay higher tax in order to provide that funds for free college education. The cost puts a huge financial burden to taxpayers and the government to make 100% free of college tuition for 20 million college students. If the education costs a student minimally $25,000 per year, then the government must be able to pay:

$$\$25,000 \times 20,000,000 = \$500,000,000,000$$

Sen. Bernie Sander also said, "Well, I'll tell you how we're going to pay for it. We are going to ask Wall Street to end their speculation. We're going to put a speculation tax on Wall Street." How is Wall Street going to pay for this? The speculation tax referred to the taxes on trade markets for each bond, stock or derivative they sell and is seen as "Robin Hood tax" according to Michelle Wellman.

When the military spending, proper control of costs on illegal immigrations, and more able people are going back to work, then the U.S could easily provide free college education to all student Americans or education with minimal payment from students. Free college education indeed frees so many millennials from debts and from the financial pressures so they could focus well on education.

Surprisingly, Sweden's public education system is ranked lower than that of the United States while Norway and Denmark are both ranked a little bit better than the United States. The educational institutions and schools in Sweden are not superior and better to those learning institutes in the United States even though more funding is given to Scandinavian educational system.

Surprisingly, education in the socialist countries are not cheap and education fee is still a great challenge to so many people. Even though, the PK-12 education in socialist countries is basically free, yet the schools and the teachers come up so many fees such as administrative fees, various contributions, uniforms, tutoring classes… that many families are still struggling with the financial burdens.

Million people in socialist countries also dream that one day their next generations could also receive free college education. Some former socialist nations also tried to provide free college education, yet their free education could not last long because the country economic ability was not able yet. Some socialist countries also applied free education but the quality of education was very poor.

When education is free, the quality of education may be at risks. While many students may be freed from the financial burdens, many students may not appreciate the free education that they have and they may not be motivated and diligent to make the best of their study. When free education is available, the country also needs to make sure the competitiveness in the work force.

Interestingly, the Organization for Economic Cooperation and Development (OECD) showed that the most-educated workforce in the world did not come from countries that offer free college education such as the Scandinavian and the Nordic countries but from Canada, Japan, Canada, then Norway, Sweden, United States, Finland, Slovenia, Germany, and Brazil reported Anya Kamenetz and Eric Westervelt.

Lastly, on health care, Sen. Bernie Sanders stated, "People who cannot afford health care don't deserve to die. We should not be spending far more, per capita, than any other nation for health care or be paying the highest prices in the world for prescription drugs. I believe now more than ever that the American people are ready to end the national disgrace of being the only major country on earth not to guarantee health care as a right for all of its people. Add your name if you agree."

Yes, we will be among the first of almost 330 millions of people to add our names to support for this bill if our votes are counted. Not only does this bill attract people who are unable to pay for medical expenses but also people who are financially able. Elizabeth Warrens, Bernie Sanders and democratic candidates gain many supports for "Medicare for All" even though their plans are yet feasible or realistic.

Survey Monkey Poll of November 2019 showed that 81% of Democrats supported Medicare for all, 64% of Independents and only 28% of Republicans also supported this plan. This added up to 55% of support, thus the majority of voters supported Medicare for all. The question remains how is it possible? What is the cost for free health care for almost 330 millions of Americans? Where do the funds come from?

Does Sen. Bernie Sanders really know that in socialist countries it is the people who have to pay almost everything from health care, childcare, education to housing? The irony is that the government officials and political members are the wealthy and powerful, yet these people, their children, their relatives and subordinates always receive the priority and every free thing they want to. That is equality and justice.

People in socialist countries must pay the fees for any social services first before they could get any treatment or service. If the patients, for example, do not have money, they can only wait for death without any treatment even they are lying in front of the hospital in their terrible conditions. Even when they have the insurance card but they have to pay the fee required first before receiving the health services.

Cuba may seem to provide free medical care to the citizens. The question is how is the quality of the health care in Cuba? Is it worth to receive the free health care with low quality but the people have to pay their lives under the suppressions of the government? Is it fair for the people to receive just a little from the government and they have to pay with lives and bloods?

Countless patients are helped and supported by Christians and Christian organizations that are willing to help these helpless people though they are still limited in terms of financial resources, facilities and manpower. Yet they have been doing fantastic jobs to either provide accommodations, foods, cares, counseling and financial supports to these patients during their treatments and tough times.

Most of the patients came from other provinces or the countryside and they were facing with various kinds of sicknesses and diseases from tuberculosis to various kinds of cancers, or chronic and incurable diseases. Most of them need urgent operations and they were short of the finances and the costs were not small. Thanks to the generous supports of believers, many made it to live and others to be gone.

Just like many Asians and immigrants from the nations to the U.S, we could not even believe at the beginning that the U.S government would pay monthly salary to either a father or a mother to take care of the ailing children, or to an adult child to take care of the ailing parents or family members. This is the real spirit of Christian nations. This has never happened in the socialist countries that I went through.

If this were to happen in socialist countries, then many Christians and Christian organizations may no longer need to provide many financial supports, housing or manpower to take care of these patients. If this were to happen then the countless patients and their families would not suffer daily with no jobs, no finances and no people to help them to overcome their tough situations.

My wife ministered to parents and their brain-damaged children or autistic children weekly and I myself was in the hospital for more than two months. Life would be different for these parents, and other patients that I met if they had monthly supports to take care of their ailing children or loved ones. It would take the socialist countries a long way to go to make that a reality.

Unfortunately, those basic social welfares are not really free yet even though the socialists often promised almost a century ago in socialist countries. America offers much better many social benefits and social welfares to the common people than any socialist countries could do so. I am sure that America could really provide many free services to Americans without the risky agenda and help of socialism.

The CDC on 2017 Health Expenditures reported that the total national health expenditures were $3.5 trillion and the per capita national health expenditures were $10,739. The total national health expenditures as a percent of Gross Domestic Product were 17.9%. 34% was spent on private health insurance; 20% for Medicare; 17% for Medicaid; and 10% for out-of-pocket according to CMS.

According to CMS, 33% of the expenditures were for hospital care; 20% for physician and clinical services; 10% for retail prescription drugs; 5% for other health, residential, and personal care services; 5% for nursing care facilities and continuing care retirement communities; 4% for dental services; 3% for home health care; 3% for other professional services; 2% for other non-durable medical products; and 2% for durable medical equipment

In 2018, the total national health expenditures were $3.65 trillion "according to a report from Axios. The amount is larger than the GDPs of such countries as Brazil, the U.K., Mexico, Spain, and Canada" reported Erik Sherman on Fortune. It was $3.5 trillion on 2017. Spending on prescription medicine would grow by 6% annually between 2020 and 2023 reported Todd Campbell

According to the CMS and reported Todd Campbell, "Healthcare spending per person is expected to surpass $10,000 in 2016 and then march steadily higher to $14,944 in 2023." By 2020, healthcare spending per American is more than $12,000 but "spending on health was about USD 4,000 per person (adjusted for purchasing powers), on average across OECD countries" according to OECD in Health At A Glance 2019.

The U.S. has the highest health care spending in the developed world according to the Organization for Economic Co-Operation and Development. The U.S spent almost 18% of its GDP while the Scandinavian countries spent less than 12% of their GDP, and the U.S spent almost double than these countries per capita when the U.S. spent more than $11,000 per capita.

According to the researchers at the Harvard Chan School and reported Yoni Blumberg, the health care prices were inflated across the board. "In the U.S., they point out, drugs are more expensive. Doctors get paid more. Hospital services and diagnostic tests cost more. And a lot more money goes to planning, regulating and managing medical services at the administrative level."

This was because the prices of health care services are very high in the U.S. General physicians in America made an average of $218,173 in 2016 while generalists received $86,607 in Sweden and $154,126 in Germany. The U.S. spent 8% of total expenditures but other countries only spent

1% to 3%. The U.S spent $1,442 per capital on pharmaceuticals, other countries spent $749 reported Yoni Blumberg.

Ricardo Alonso-Zaldivar reported on PBS that, "Medicare and Medicaid are expected to grow more rapidly than private insurance as the baby-boom generation ages... About 5 percent of the population-those most frail or ill- account for nearly half the spending in a given year... Meanwhile, half the population has little or no health care costs, accounting for 3 percent spending."

According to Kimberly Amadeo on The Balance, the two causes of the massive increase in health care expenses are the government policy and lifestyle changes. "The government created programs like Medicare and Medicaid to help those without insurance. These programs spurred demand for health care services. That gave providers the ability to raise prices."

"As of 2010, the health care costs of people with at least one chronic condition are responsible for more than 85% of health care spending. Almost half of all Americans have at least one of them. They are expensive and difficult to treat. As a result, the sickest 5% of the population consume 50% of total health care costs. The healthiest 50% only consume 3% of the nation's health care costs" reported Kimberly Amadeo.

According to 2019 OECD.Stat report on Health Expenditure and Financing, the total health expenditure of the U.S per GDP was the highest one in the world. It was 16.9% of 21200 US dollars in 2019 according to official data from the World Bank and projections from Trading Economics. The total health expenditure of Sweden per GDP was 11%, Denmark 10.5%, Norway 10.2%, and Finland 9.1%.

As the largest healthcare spending in the world, the U.S. could afford and provide affordable and better healthcare to all Americans. Greater healthcare services could be done when the pricing is well regulated and many cuts on the expenses such as drugs, individual services, rental costs of medical facilities, the investments in pharmaceuticals, high costs of researches and administration should be done.

In short, America does not need socialism to make health care available by spending more funds and to give more burdens to tax payers. America does not need socialism to turn private properties and businesses into social ownership in order to receive affordable health care but Americans would loose almost everything. America does not need socialism for big government to make health care available.

America is more than able to provide many universal social welfares that no socialist country could ever been able to do so. Americans already receive more and greater social benefits and welfares than any socialist country in the world could do. The government just needs to make adjustments to provide Americans greater services for free college, affordable housing and healthcare without socialism.

Do You Still Want Socialism?

At the rise of socialism in recent years, the conservatives, the republicans, and anti-socialism people responded to socialism through their many writings, blogs and media about the many failures, the sufferings and the tyrannies from the former socialist nations and nations that are still applying socialism or principles of socialism. But the young generations do not seem to take to hearts those messages.

President Trump also addressed the issues of socialism and determined to fight against the establishment of a socialist government in the U.S. Yet, many democrat leaders just disregarded his objection to socialism and they showed stronger support to the socialists and the leftwing agenda though they may not support the socialist ideology and that is an irony and even a contradiction to their convictions.

Socialism is still expanding its influences. More and more Americans are open to socialism nowadays and especially the millennials due to the great benefits offered. For Americans to really understand the reality and the failures of socialism, writings and education about the failures of socialism are significant important yet those writings might not be enough to convince Americans theoretically.

Americans need to see and hear the truth about socialism in such a way that they could feel the pains and horrors of socialism. Thus there is a great need for the writings and testimonies of socialist victims. Victims of socialist regimes need to share their stories and to be invited to media platforms to share their experiences, their thoughts, their feelings and their lives to live in the socialist regimes.

Movie and documents about socialist regime and victims would also play significant role in transforming Americans' perceptions about socialism. Unfortunately, the conservatives and the republicans are not very strong in doing so at the present. More efforts and funding should be invested in making real stories to come alive in the eyes, the minds and the hearts of the audiences.

Yet, the socialists still attract more people with democratic socialism though people may not know that when the socialist principles did not work in many nations, socialism was almost collapsed and the regime was about to end, the socialists immediately applied capitalistic principles of free enterprises and free markets. But they still maintain socialism because they could not admit the failures of socialism.

This new direction of democratic socialism is explained by Alexandria Ocasi-Cortez on Rachel Maddow Show, "socialists believe in collective versus individual ownerships, that collective can be the government, workers or citizens. Democratic socialists are different; they believe the government and private industries can work hand in hand to provide a better safety net for the citizens."

Thanking to the free market operations and free enterprises and foreign investments, some remaining socialist countries got over their tough times but they never acknowledge the credit and benefits of capitalism. They are using capitalist principles to produce more wealthy socialists and to control power. Yet, many Americans may not realize the role of capitalism in reviving socialist countries.

These socialist countries are not and never famous for democracy and freedom. They are always in the top list of the world for human oppressions, suppressions, and persecutions. They are known with injustices, sufferings and limited freedoms of press, speech, travel and others. But the millennials may not see those facts and the limited freedom in those socialist countries.

Unfortunately, the milliennials only heard the about the great promises, the economic growth and the great outlook of the socialist utopia. Unfortunately, Americans may not see the consequences and they do not realize that socialism is always the same in its nature of exploitations and suppressions. Whether it is socialism or democratic socialism, there is no difference in its nature.

This is just the play of word by adding the sound word, "democratic." Their purpose of controlling is still the same, but their ways are even more cunning and dangerous. In the current socialist countries, the socialist government allowed free enterprises so they government can learn from them. The government partnered with private industries to build up the experiences and strength.

The socialist government is willing to yield to the requests and requirements of private businesses so the government can learn, transfer and master their technologies and intellectual properties. When the socialist government is strong and able, then they begin to get rid of the private industries with the increase of high tax rates because the private enterprises and industries are no longer needed.

They use their policies and power to force private industries to follow their directions and to be under their leadership. If the private owners are not willing to do so they would be out of the businesses or bankrupted when private enterprises are no longer competitive in the same industries because they cannot compete the prices with the government agencies and businesses under the socialist direction.

The socialist government may take over the industries of private enterprises in many ways if the private entities are not willing to cooperate with the socialist government. If the government is kind enough the government may negotiate with business owners to become the majority shareholders of the private organizations or the government may purchase the private companies or the corporations.

In many cases, the government just finds ways to charge the owners with corruption and that would be the end of the private businesses because it is almost impossible for business people to do business without corruption in socialist countries. In other cases, the government just stops the private businesses from getting the projects from auctions, and then the private businesses would struggle to survive.

If the government wants they could also change the policy to make the private industries to go bankrupted. Then the government immediately takes over the industries, changing policies and reviving the industries. In many cases, the government just simply accused business owners with treasons, crimes of counter-revolutionaries or any crimes. That is the power of big government.

So many businesses and industries did not know the master plan of the cunning socialists so they have been the victims of the modern socialists. Of course businesses already realize this but it is already too late because their skills, technologies and secrets have been taken over by the socialists. In the past the socialist need them and now they need the socialists for survival and profits.

This also happened to all sectors including the educational sector. There were many private schools and institutions before because the government needed those educational institutes to meet the great needs of education across the land. Educational leaders, departments and ministry learned and adopted great educational systems from private educational system and international systems.

As the country became stronger with economic power, the government invested countless money to develop the country educational system and institutions. With the massive investments, educational institutes of the state became strong and these institutes did not struggle with financial burdens as the private institutes did. Then state schools purchased and took over many private educational institutes.

The private institutes that have been doing well and strong then must comply with the direction and new policies of the educational ministry if they want to exist. These private institutes have a strong tie and share with the government. Many institutes could be seen as private institutes but people do not know the real boss that is operating and controlling the education in those seemingly private institutes.

The deceptive nature of socialism would be the same whether it is the "Republic socialism or Democratic socialism." At the end it is still socialism and the socialists do always care for their political party, power, position and prosperity more than anything or anyone else. They are willing to carry out their unethical ways or approaches to achieve their purposes at the loss of pitiful and powerless victims.

In the U.S., leaders and members of Democratic Socialist of America train their members to get people's supports. When they talk to people, they would not say first they are socialist members, they just say first about their great offers to attract people first with their plans of free healthcare, free college education, New Green Deal. When people are convinced then it is time to tell people who they really are.

As you can see, even socialism has not been realized in the U.S., yet the socialists already learnt to apply the tricks and deceptions. If they learn well more tricks, America and Americans will be in great troubles. The bad news is they can learn the deceptive ways very fast because they are not driven by the heart to serve the countries, but they are driven by power and wealth. Americans, Please Wake Up!

The good news is that socialism is not possible with Karl Marx, Vladimir Lenin, Nicolas Maduro, Fidel Castro or Bernie Sanders. It is neither possible with any socialist leader of this world. Yet socialism could be possible with America when the government, the leaders and the people embrace God and the biblical socialism described in Acts 2 of the Bible and it is where equality really existed and practices.

As Dr. Jack Graham emphasized, "the Bible does not endorse any one political system. It does endorse freedom, and private ownership, and the value of work and a free market system that decentralizes economic power. By contrast, socialism suppresses the poor, steals from the rich, legislates theft, and encourages envy. It confiscates what people have sweated to earn and achieve and then distributes it to those who have not earned what they have been given. Socialism focuses on the government and the state. Capitalism elevates the status of mankind."

Yes, that biblical socialism is only possible when God is the center of the government, families, economy, businesses, politics, education, societies, and relationships. When people and not just an elite group are willing to show their love and care and sharing their possessions to others until there is no one having any needs to be met. This happened in the early church and it is till possible today.

^{42} They devoted themselves to the apostles' teaching and to fellowship, to the breaking of bread and to prayer. ^{43} Everyone was filled with awe at the many wonders and signs performed by the apostles. ^{44} All the believers were together and had everything in common. ^{45} They sold property and possessions to give to anyone who had need. ^{46} Every day they continued to meet together in the temple courts. They broke bread in their homes and ate together with glad and sincere hearts,[47] praising God and enjoying the favor of all the people. And the Lord added to their number daily those who were being saved.

Equality and egalitarian societies are only possible when people daily listen and actively apply God's word to love and to care for others as they do love and care for themselves. Equality and egalitarian societies are only possible when people are coming together for fellowship, meals and for edifying one another but not for self-seeking, self-exaltation or for taking advantages of others.

Equality and egalitarian societies are only possible when people are willing to take care the needs of one another by God's love and God's command and not by selfish motives or political agendas. Equality and egalitarian societies are only possible at the miracles and the grace of God not at the wisdom, ideology or philosophy of any famous politicians, statesmen or philosophers.

Do you really want to experience the reality of that socialist society? Acts Chapter 2 presents a great example of a real egalitarian society is. The early Christians were the early socialists, Karl Marx and Vladimir Lenin learned this concept from the Bible but it is sad that they materialized the concept in a wrong direction as they rejected God. Yes, real socialism is only possible with the love and power of God.

When money and materials are the priority of any government, socialism could not be realized. When position, power and authority are the priority of any leadership, socialism could not be realized. When greed and self-interest are the priority of any management, socialism could not be realized. Socialism is possible with the love of God who cares and love everyone equally. This seems illogical but it is the true.

Do not wait and then regret because of our ignorance. "The Scandinavian countries all have far-left parties. Almost nobody votes for them. At the last Norwegian election the Socialist Left party got 6% of the vote. Denmark's Socialist Party got 4.2%. The Finnish Communists received

0.25%, while Sweden's Communists only managed 0.1%. Scandinavians don't want to try Marx's ideas" reported Right Wing.

Many years ago, my parents, brothers, sisters, and relatives visited a python farm owned by a cousin. My cousin introduced to us his python farm, the pythons and how did he begin with it. He shared to us the failures and successes and then he shared to us some of his favorite huge and long pythons that he often let his friends and guests to touch and to put around their necks and to take pictures with.

He said that these pythons looked scary but they were well trained and they were harmless so we should not be afraid of them. So the daring members started to touch the python, others put the python around their necks. The excitement and the funs began because the pythons were really harmless and were well disciplined. Everyone enjoyed the pythons and was happy at those big but harmless pythons.

Another cousin put a python around the neck of my younger sister and her head and they laughed at the nervous look of my sister. My sister was terrified and trying to get the python off her head and her neck. For some reasons, the python suddenly gave a hard bite on her cheek and began to squeeze her as my sister screamed. Her cheek was bleeding and her face turned pale in horror.

All the laughs and excitements ended immediately in shocks and fears. My cousin, the owner quickly removed the python from her neck and put all the big pythons back into the cage. The fun turned into the frightening moment, the harmless python turned into the heartless python. As the saying goes the curiosity killed the cat and this is also very true with the curiosity of million millennials toward socialism now.

Sen. Bernie Sanders said he felt "very good with the fact that we have now received some 2 million individual contributions." Tom Kertscher may have some doubt about the accuracy of this number in his article on Politifact.com on July 15th, 2019. Yet the number shows that there is a large number of Americans who are believing and supporting the realization of democratic socialism in the U.S.

It is important that these 2 million contributors and millions of others who believe in democratic socialism need to read this book or at least this part of the book on socialism so that they would make wiser decision in their voting. Mainstream media with their leftists, liberals, socialists and democrats has been deceiving Americans for so long with their lies and half-truth. It is time to put a full stop here.

Now, the socialist ideology is now turning into a movement of protests and demonstrations with thousands of American millennials, leftwing democrats and socialists across the U.S. As it always happened before, these protests and demonstrations turn into violent riots, lootings and killings with the presence of many communist leaders and trained Marxists, anarchists and even terrorists.

Socialism looked harmless just a few years ago with many promises of freedom, social benefits, wealth distribution and equality yet white lives are in danger when Black Lives Matter. Socialism is now turning many places and people into nightmares with their lawlessness, violence and brutalities. These mobs and lawlessness members brutally beat old and young people and murdered them.

They have so much hatred that they use freedom to ravage places and people. They practice social justices well by defunding the police, free the prostitutes and dismantle prisons. They carry out wealth distribution by looting stores and business. They exercise equality by revenging the white people and people they thought that did them harms, and Americans who fought for their freedoms.

They demand social justices by asking the white people to vacant their homes and give those homes to the poor African Americans. They demand equality by asking the white people to move out of certain areas so that the place could only be for the African Americans. They allow freedom of speech by shooting people who dare to say White Lives Matter or All Lives Matter as explained in Chapter 1.

Do not wait until socialism kills the jobs and incomes. Do not wait until socialism kills business and future. Do not wait until socialism kills economy. Do not wait until socialism kills the prosperity and stability. Do not wait until socialism kills your happiness and joy. Just stop it now. Socialism seemed to be a great theory but just like many unrealistic theories that sound great, socialism is also unrealistic.

As Tyler O'Neil wrote on PJMedia on June 27, 2018, "The Success of Socialist Candidates Would Mean a Return to Poverty and Tyranny." Tyler explained that the socialist ideology that Sen. Bernie Sanders has been promoting for an American socialist democracy, is "truly regressive, and would resurrect the age-old strategy of a pre-free market command economy with fewer options and more poverty."

Right Wing also confirmed that, "Over the past 120 years or so, socialism has been tried in a wide range of countries, from advanced industrial nations like East Germany to emerging former colonies in Africa and Asia. It's failed every time, inevitably leading to poverty, repression and violence." During that 120 years, hundred millions of lives died and suffered by socialism and that is true.

Sen. Bernie Sanders recent said, "We're very opposed to the authoritarian nature of Cuba, but you know, it's unfair to simple say everything is bad. You know?" Sanders said. "When Fidel Castro came into office, you know what he did? He had a massive literacy program. Is that a bad thing? Even though Fidel Castro did it?" reported Caitlin and Christopher on Yahoo News.

His praise about Fidel Castro, Cuban President for his social programs was immediately backfired by more than 2.3 million Cuban Americans and millions of people fleeing for their lives from socialist nations because most of them knew better the terrible Cuban social programs that brought them tragedies and their deadly escapes from Cuban to America and other nations in the 1960s and now.

Sen. Bernie Sanders praised the Cuban tyranny leader, Fidel Castro who created the horrible consequences upon millions of Cuban. Michael Bloomberg tweeted and confirmed, "Fidel Castro left a dark legacy of forced labor camps, religious repression, widespread poverty, firing squads, and the murder of thousands of his own people. But sure, Bernie, let's talk about his literacy program."

Regardless of who is trying to praise and to believe in the great success of socialism and the realization of the socialist utopia, socialist victims would tell you that, "Please do not listen to the nice word and fall into the socialist trap. Socialism could not be trusted and Americans should not put your wrong trust in socialism, an ideology that has bad and serious records of failures, and havocs could not succeed.

First of all, socialism could not be trusted. Millions of people went through socialism could testify about this fact and history can easily prove this fact well that socialism was never successful in any countries that applied socialism. The many falls of the great socialist countries such as former Soviet Union, Eastern Europe and the current turmoil of Cuba, Venezuela and others concluded that fact well.

Secondly, the socialist promises are great but they are not going to work well in the long term and socialism would turn America to be countries like Cuba, Venezuela and other socialist countries soon. Even if socialism were to take over America somehow, the conclusion would be clear and loud that Americans could not enjoy so many freedoms and human rights as Americans are enjoying right now.

Thirdly, the words of the socialists are not consistent. They used to praise former Soviet Union, Venezuela and others but now they just keep quiet about and avoided to talk about those countries as great socialist models. They admired the Scandinavian countries as the socialist nirvanas or utopia for America to learn from but these countries are not socialist countries but social democracy countries.

Fourthly, the socialists could make up stories for their gains. Jonah Goldberg also noted that, "Mr. Sanders, who favors single-payer health care, routinely says we should follow the example of Scandinavian and other countries. He recently tweeted a list of 27 nations with universal health care. But National Review's Ramesh Ponnuru pointed out that not one of the countries listed has single-payer health care."

"The egalitarian Nordic nations have as many billionaires, relatively, as the U.S. and more concentrated wealth, at least as measured by the share of wealth controlled by the top 1- percent." The Nordic countries are also free-traders and have many of the pro-business policies that Mr. Sanders despises here at home" according to James Pethokoukis and reported by Jonah Goldberg on Baltimore Sun.

Most importantly, America is already a great example of the economic success and freedom. This is why America has been the world leading economic power. Nations look up to America economic successes and they have been learning from America and her stories of success. People of so nations even the socialist nations are also longing for the freedom and human rights that Americans have.

In a nutshell, socialism has no reason to make America better when it was a grave failure when it was applied everywhere. The socialists are contradicting to themself because if socialism is rejected because of their failures to produce equality and freedoms in all former and current socialist countries, then, socialism cannot produce the freedoms and equality when its fruits showed the opposite ones.

Now that these Scandinavian countries are not socialist countries, do you think that Sen. Bernie Sanders and socialists and Democrats would follow these Scandinavian countries to apply the high tax and low immigration as these Scandinavian do or they just use social benefits to attract voters? If they impose high tax and low immigration then they have nothing to win the heart of the general publics.

CHAPTER 3

RELIGIOUS FREEDOM AND THE GREAT AMERICA

The First Amendment clearly indicates the freedom of religion, freedom of speech, freedom of press, freedom of assemble, and freedom to make petition. The forefathers confirmed the faith in God when they signed the Constitution, "Done in convention by the unanimous consent of the States present the Seventeenth Day of September in the Year of our Lord one thousand seven hundred and eighty seven."

The Paris Peace Treaty of 1783 or Treaty of Paris is the set of treaties that ended the American Revolutionary War and that granted American Independency. This historical document was another undeniable document that shows the Christian faith of the forefathers and of Americans in God. It clearly addressed the Christian God in the Preamble, "in the name of the most holy and undivided Trinity."

Yet the leftist leaders, the liberals, the socialists and many millennials want to challenge that faith, the Constitution, the Declaration of Independency and even want to change those precious rights. They try to replace the precious American faith, values and cultures that once made this nation strong and powerful with progressive values and atheistic ideology that are now tearing this nation apart.

Dr. Jack Graham warned Americans "against the leftists corrupting American through the sinister ideology... What we are facing here is a culture war that is driven by those who hate Christianity and the Church of Jesus Christ. If the far left is successful in capturing the hearts and minds of Americans, the entire world will descend into a spiritual darkness unlike anything that has ever been seen" reported News Division.

The words and the promises of recent Democratic presidential candidates and Democratic leaders ring the alarms of how anti they are toward Christianity and people of faith. The socialist Bernie Sander wants to make this nation a democratic socialist country. What do you think a gay and gay activist like Pete Buttigieg would do to this country once he is elected as the 46th President of the United States?

Former Vice President Joe Biden at the Human Rights Campaign in Columbus, Ohio "declares his #1 priority will be the anti-Christian LGBTQ Equality Act… to silence Christians who believe biblical teachings on marriage and reject the view that boys can be girls and girls can be boys." according to Paula Bolyard on PJMedia on June 3rd, 2019. He also wanted to support Planned Parenthood and abortions.

As the top democratic candidate for 2020 presidential election, former Vice President Joe Biden will codify Roe v. Wade for unlimited abortion on demand, supporting the repeal of the Hyde Amendment to use taxpayer funding for abortion on demand, and restoring federal funding for Planned Parenthood through Medicaid and Tile X reported Karen Cross on Life News.

Megan Baily on Beliefnet commented, "While Christian persecution is widely recognized in other countries, most do not realize the persecution happening right at home… Traditional Christians are facing increasing intolerance in this country through fines, the lawsuits, the jobs lost, and the public disdain felt." These persecutions took place in politics, in businesses, in colleges and in public schools.

What exactly are these liberal leaders trying to do with this nation?

Denial of Christian Faith

Even many liberals and secularists tried to deny the Judeo-Christian faith and value, which laid the political, moral and spiritual foundations of the U.S. Yet they could never change the fact that the Puritan Separatists or the English Protestants first fled to Leyden, Holland from England in 1609 to exercise their religious freedom due to the religious persecution in England under Elizabeth and later James I.

Even the liberals and secularists tried to impose their view but they could never rewrite the history that the Separatists came to the New World to establish their new religious community and the Mayflower Compact signed by all the people on November 21, 1620 was the declaration of their Christian faith, "for the glorie of God and advancement of ye Christian faith" and their trust in God for their future.

The liberals and secularists could not disprove the fact that "the Compact was modeled after the church covenant that the Pilgrims had drafted and signed in 1607... For the next fifty years, the Mayflower compact served the Pilgrims well, and it became an important precedent for the idea of a written American Constitution at the Convention of 1787" according to Christanity.com.

The liberals and the secularists just consider Thanksgiving as a holiday or tradition, but they could not reject the gratitude of the surviving Pilgrims to God through their first Thanksgivings and the word of Pilgrim Edward Winslow, "And although it be not always so plentiful as it was at this time with us, yet by the goodness of God, we are so far from want that we often wish you partakers of our plenty."

The liberals and the secularists, regardless how hard they try to make Americans to be free from the religion particularly the influences of Christianity, could not remove the ultimate call of the founding forefathers to protect and exercise the precious religious freedom. Their abundant efforts to persecute the faith that formed and shaped America from the very beginning of its establishment will never prevail.

"There has been consistent push to remove all traces of God from government for many years. Our Pledge of Allegiance, for example, has been repeatedly been brought up saying that "Under God" needs to be taken from its text. Even American money has been brought into question, because it has "in God we trust" written on it" reported Megan Bailey on Beliefnet.

They want to remove the faith that is stated clear and loud "In God We Trust." It is this faith that united and made America to become the great nation of economic and political powers, land of freedom, religious liberty and high morals for decades. It is this faith that prompted the forefathers of the United States to risk their lives and to cross the Atlantic Ocean to make this great nation under God.

"In God We Trust" was the recognition that U.S. was not a heathen nation but it was a nation under the Almighty God. The Congressed passed the Act of April 22, 1864 to approved this motto to be printed on the U.S currency in from coins in 1864 to paper money 1957. It was the national motto and the reminding record for the coming generations that the United States was not a godless nation but under God.

This was confirmed by Salmon O. Chase, Secretary of the Treasury, "Dear Sir: No nation can be strong except in the strength of God, or safe except in His defense. The trust of our people in God should be declared on our national coins." This national motto of the U.S., "In God We Trust" was approved again through a Joint Resolution of the 84th Congress by President Dwight Eisenhower on July 30, 1956 according US. Department of The Treasury.

"In God We Trust" is the faith that empowered the Americans to overcome their tough and challenging battles for centuries. It is this faith that accompanied the Americans to go through their crises. It is this faith that Americans found wisdom, comforts and strength to face with their critical times. It is this faith that brought the peoples of America to come together as a strong and powerful nation.

"In God We Trust" is the faith that leads people to seek God and to live in His holiness and His image. It is this faith that brought people together in equality, humility, and love. It is this faith that inspires people to love, to protect, and to care for one another. It is this faith that formed the great ethical standards and high morality of America.

"In God We Trust" is the national motto of the United States. It is the national symbol for religious freedom. It is also the national affirmation of the United States of America to reject atheism. It is the national commitment that the United States of America is the land of freedom where peoples of faith freely exercise their religious liberty. It is the national declaration that the United States is the nation under God.

But now many Americans want to give up that faith. The rejection of that faith, "In God We Trust" leads to the great divisions and opioid crisis of the United States as it is today. The rejection of that faith leads to horrible immoralities of abortion and free sexes. The rejection of that faith leads to the low moral and ethical confusion of what is right and what is wrong.

The rejection of that faith leads to the down turn of America in terms of economics, moral values and identity crisis. The rejection of that faith also leads Americans to the high rate of divorces, crimes, and depressions. The rejection of that faith also leads people to violence, drug addiction, and suicides. The rejection of that faith also leads to the confusion of American identity and cultural disintegration.

The rejection of that faith leads to the thirst for power and control. The rejection of that faith leads to shameless acts and horrible morality. The rejection of that faith leads to incest and incurable diseases of HIV and AIDS. The rejection of that faith leads to generations of fatherless and irresponsibility. The rejection of that faith leads to so many wickedness, evils, tragedies and bondages.

Yet regardless of the increasing rejection of the faith, most towns and cities in the United States were pioneered and established by people of faiths. The names of those towns and cities had religious or biblical meanings such as Bethany, Bible, Goshen, Hebron, Jericho, Jordan, Lebanon, Los Angeles, San Antonia, and Texas. Names and places of the Bible could be found in every States of the United States.

It is unbelievable that many Americans are forsaking their own priceless beliefs and have been persecuting their own precious faith and values. On LifeSite USA of November 21, 2016, Jonathon Van Maren listed and described many cases where Christians were being persecuted for their faith though the mainstream media tried to cover up the truth by citing those cases as discriminations, bigotry, racism…

Jonathan shared the stories of Jack C. Phillips in Denver, Colorado who stopped to make wedding cake to be true to his faith instead of making wedding cake for a gay couple when he was ordered by the two courts to comply to the order of the gay couple for the wedding cake. Then, Elaine and Jonathan Huguenin in New Mexico were fined $6,600 for refusing to photograph a lesbian "commitment ceremony."

The University of Toledo fired Crystal Dixon because she rightly disagreed that gay rights movement could be compared to civil rights movement. She argued that she did not choose her minority status as a black woman, so why homosexuals do? LGBTQ make their own choices to be that way, and now they aggressively impose their choices on others and force others to follow their will.

The serious case was happened to Aaron and Melissa Klein who refused to bake a wedding cake for a lesbian wedding. The state of Oregon took their accounts and assets of $144,000 and their bakery was shut down. "Aaron Klein is currently on disability after injuring himself working as a trash collector to provide for the couple's five children. Their family was also the target of a vicious campaign by gay activists intent on destroying their business, regardless of the cost."

You may find more similar stories at www.lifesitenews.com. There are also many stories of policemen, coaches, fire workers, teachers and others who were fired because of their prayers and faith. Bushrod Washington reported on TheFederalistPapers.org the case of Joe Kennedy, the high school football coach at Bremerton School District who was fired because of his prayer with his players.

Coach Kennedy often went to mid-field and prayed with players after each game since 2008. He was ordered to stop the prayers in 2015 but he said that was the violation of his First Amendment rights. "Kennedy told CBN News the post-game prayers had been a good thing for the young football players because they helped to bring peace after the games" due to the high tensions at the loss or winning.

The Horn News emphasized the fact that "and in the face of criticism from the atheist organization the Freedom from Religion Foundation (FFRF), the school district demanded the coach stop... dozens of lawmakers in the Congressional Prayer Caucus sent a letter to the superintendent expressing support for the coach" but the school district kept their decision to fire coach Kennedy.

Coach Kennedy sued the district to get back his job, his rights of speech, religious freedom and prayer in the football fields. He said, "I want to be a coach. I want to be out there with my young men... I really believe (coaches) are one of the mentors for these young men to become somebody in society, to know how to be better young men" according to CBN News on June 13, 2017.

Almost half of decade, justice still remained silence to coach Kennedy. John Jessup reported on CBN News that the Supreme Court declined to take the case into consideration in January 2019. "Currently, the case is back in district court. Meanwhile, Kennedy has returned to the football stadium to support the team-but from a different perspective. Now he's watching from the stands."

Denial of Christian Contribution

Christian Good In Society posted that, "No single group in human has contributed more to education than Christian have. No group in human history has contributed more to healthcare than Christians have. Christians, more than anyone else, have contributed to the welfare and protection of children. No other group in human history has fought the slave trade more than Christians have. No other single group in human history could have contributed more to the cause of charity than Christians."

You may disagree or you may not believe those big claims but those are the truth and facts. You may not accept those claims as true because you may have prejudices about Christianity. You may be an atheist and you may not pay attention to the things Christians are doing around the world. It could be that you may only listen to negative things about Christians, yet those claims are not exaggerations.

Americans are **firstly** indebted to Christian contributions as most schools in the U.S began with Christian education and the U.S. founders "believed education that produced liberty must have its foundation in Christianity… Colleges and universities were started as seminaries to train a godly and literate clergy. In fact, 106 of the first 108 colleges were founded on the Christian faith" according to Stephen McDowell.

Those early schools in the beginning days of the U.S. had formed American culture, Christian education, godly government, biblical values, great wisdom, righteous thoughts and godly ways of life. Reverence for God, the Bible, church, prayer, worship and Christian counseling have been the vital elements of a compass to guide Americans to go through thick and thin since the establishment of the U.S.

With Christian faith and education as the foundation of the U.S., there are many Christian contributions to the U.S. and Americans in terms of moral standards, justice system, charity, philosophy, economy, politics, arts and more. Some of the major contributions are mentioned in the next paragraphs as the reminders to those who object Christianity and deny the roles of Christianity in the U.S.

In the campuses throughout the U.S. today, "outspoken Christians are regularly demeaned, debased and targeted for their beliefs. Many times these Christian college students will hear from others about how their religion only has hateful, bigoted, and privileged believers." Christian colleges were also asked to conform to secularist ideology or they would lose accreditation reported Megan Bailey

Secondly, great ethics and values are the greatest Christian contributions to Americans and people of the nations. Biblical ethics and values shaped the personal behaviors, social morals, justice system, appreciations of human rights, exercise of democracy and freedom according to a holy, just, forgiving and loving God. People are taught to love, care, and to forgive one another and live a holy life.

Communities and individuals that chose to walk away from the biblical ethics and values would easily open to immoralities of sexual pleasures, adulteries and abortions. The rejection of the biblical ethics and values lead to jealousy, violence, unforgiveness, self-seeking, rage, hatred, and greed. Consequently, that rejection leads people to crimes, vices and addictive practices for drug, alcohol, gambling...

Under the influences of biblical ethics and values, people are taught and called to love our neighbors as ourselves, to love our enemies as ourselves, to be holy because God is holy, to repent for the forgiveness of our sins, to work with all of our heart, to rob not our neighbor, to seek no revenge against anyone, to bear grudges to no one, to do to others as we would have them do to us.

There are so many great biblical ethics and values to guide people in their harmonious relationships, great marriages, integrity in businesses, constructive talks, fair judgments, godly living... In short, biblical ethics and values could be found and applied in all areas and walks of life and the could be summed up as "love does no harm to a neighbor. Therefore love is the fulfillment of the law."

Another great Christian contribution to Americans and the nations is the form of the U.S government that fights for the human rights and high standards of justice because God is just, God is holy and God is the Supreme Judge. This godly government would respect the liberty and many rights that God bestowed to human kind and that the human beings are created in the image of God and created equally.

This godly government would uphold justices, great morality and the compassion heart of God. This led to the abolishment of slavery, elevation of women and common man. Carson Holloway on The Daily Signal also confirmed that, "By teaching the equality of all men before God, Christianity laid the groundwork for the rise of a belief in equality of all before the law."

Alexis de Tocqueville in his book, Democracy in America, argued that America democracy "owes both its origins and its preservation to Christianity... he held that the spirit of Christianity helped American democracy to continue to flourish even after it had been established. For Tocqueville, political freedom requires an unshakable moral foundation that only religion can supply" reported Carson Holloway.

According to Faith Facts, the constitutional government had its roots from biblical doctrines. "There is no doubt that the concept of our Constitutional checks and balances system is a direct result of the biblical doctrine of the sinfulness of mankind... Many other aspects of our laws come directly from the Bible—for example the judicial, legislative and executive branches trace to Isaiah 33:22."

Benjamin Rush, one of the signers of the Declaration of Independence, said the government today wasted a lot of times, energies and money to punish crimes and the government forget that the principles of the Bible are the best ways to prevent those crimes. His words are still true and still relevant today. Should Americans and the leaders put his words into practice again?

"We profess to be republicans, and yet we neglect the only means of establishing and perpetuating our republican form of government, that is the universal education of our youth in the principles of Christianity by the means of the Bible. For this divine book (Bible), above all others, favors that equality among mankind, that respect for just laws, and those sober and frugal virtues, which constitute the soul of republicanism" wrote Benjamin Rush in 1806.

Benjamin Franklin also said, "A nation of well informed men who have been taught to know and prize the rights which God has given them cannot be enslaved. It is in the region of ignorance that tyranny begins." Yet the biblical truth shall set people free. Should Americans today stop trying hard to remove Bible, Christian education and Christian influences from schools and societies?

Lastly, Americans and nations often took for granted that clinics and hospitals were and still are among the greatest Christian contributions to humankinds. It was from the biblical teaching to take care of the abandoned, sick, needy, orphans, underprivileged widows that Christians started clinics and hospitals all over the world to show cares, love and kindness and to bring healing to these people.

In his book, "The Greatest Benefit to Mankind: A Medical History of Humanity (The Norton History of Science," Roy Porter, the author pointed out the significant contribution of Christianity in planting hospitals. That medical ethics coming from the biblical values to care and to love patients as the Lord Jesus loves them are still being carried out to the nations especially in North America.

BibleMesh.com discussed the Christian Origins of Hospitals provided and the role of the churches in developing hospitals from the early centuries to the present days. It stated, "the modern hospital owes its origins to Judeo-Christian compassion. Evidence of the vast expansion of faith-based hospitals is seen in the legacy of their names: St. Vincent's, St. Luke's, Mt. Sinai, Presbyterian, Mercy and Beth Israel."

In the Asian socialist countries, when a patient without insurance goes to a hospital for medical check-ups, a patient must pay first. Even patients with insurance, they still need to pay some fees first. Without money or payment, a patient just waited there even until the point of death. There is no free public clinic or hospital for the poor. In case of emergency, it is still money first or no services.

Sometimes, the media may report a special case where a patient was freely treated yet this case just happened once in a blue moon. The medical fee related in this case was basically not covered by the mercy or generosity of the public hospital but by the mercies and generosities of the general public and the media agency that made the donations to help the patient for the treatment through media channels.

Are patients well treated with respect and dignity at the clinics or hospitals? Yes, but the levels of treatment with respect and dignity would only come with the amount of money you pay for the services you want adding to the level of gift you offer to nurses and doctors or the relationships that you have with them. You still have a choice to make between the socialist healthcare values or the biblical ones.

Denial of Christian Practices

For decades, liberals and ungodly leaders tried to remove Christian great contributions from the public platforms in an effort to implement the policy to separate Church and States. The motive is to remove the influences of Christianity upon America and Americans due to political correctness as well as anti-Christian, anti-God and anti-church attitudes. Thus many Christian practices were banned.

Prayer has been part of the majority of American families. It was popular in most of the important events in the early days of America. It was not a surprised to hear prayers at governmental ceremonies or school events, and especially at the Inaugural Address where the new U.S President laid hand on the Bible as he sworn his oath of office, and then he would pray as George Washington did.

"It would be peculiarly improper to omit in this first official act my fervent supplications to that Almighty Being who rules over the universe, who presides in the councils of nations, and whose providential aids can supply every human defect, that His benediction may consecrate to the liberties and happiness of the people of the United States a Government instituted by themselves for these essential purposes."

According to Legal Information Institute "two branches of the Federal Government also have a long established practice of prayer at public events... Congressional sessions have opened with a chaplain's prayer ever since the First Congress... And this Court's own sessions have opened with the invocation "God save the United States and this Honorable Court" since the day of Chief Justice Marshall."

Prayer has been the powerful weapon of millions of Americans to fight over their relational, economic, emotional and political crises as well as the merciless attacks of the enemies and the power of darkness. Prayer has been the strength of millions of Americans to overcome their disappointments, depressions, fears and pains as well as the uncertainties of the present and of future.

Prayer has been the spiritual discipline of millions of Americans to help them live a loving, caring, uniting, forgiving, and godly life as well as a God-glorifying lifestyle. Prayer has been the sources of wisdom of millions of Americans to find the right solutions and directions to life, community, and national issues as well as to the challenges that they are encountering.

Prayer has been the channel of the supernatural power of millions of Americans for healing, deliverance, reconciliation, wisdom, strength, freedom and breakthroughs as well as great transformation of life. Prayer has been the daily expression of millions of Americans for the peace, well-being, prosperity, security as well as the pursuit of equality and human rights of America and Americans.

Prayer has been the effective way of millions of Americans to overcome sickness, hatred, divisions, poverty, sins, disasters, and oppressions as well as the many tragedies of life. Prayer has been the key of millions of Americans to victorious, happy, satisfactory and joyful life as well as a life of abundant blessings from God. Prayer works and the prayers of righteous people are effective.

Prayer is the channel of reflection and conviction of one's sins and wrongdoings to God and one another. Prayer has been the powerful way to lead people to confession of their sins, to forgive the enemies, and remind people to show care and to do good to others. Thus prayer modes and transforms people to be a better person, faithful spouse, exemplary parents, good child and great citizen of the country.

Today prayer is being attacked, criticized and removed from the public events, schools and even families. The students and millennials do not understand the power of prayer as they do not learn and apply the power of prayer in their lives since prayer is discouraged and not allowed in their educational and social settings and the failures of parents to teach their children to pray.

This is "What happened when a public school student sued over prayer." Kaylee Cole and her mother Christy filled a lawsuit against "Webster Parish schools in violation of the Establishment Clause in the First Amendment of the US Constitution" because the Lord's Prayer was observed at school according to Mallony Simon on CNN News on January 28, 2018.

At the absence of prayer, people are no longer to be reminded to be kind to and to protect one another. At the forbidden of prayer, people are no longer taught to forgive and to accept one another. At the disappearance of prayer, people are no longer become patient to one another. As the consequences, hatred increases, and vengeance becomes the norm, fighting takes place, and violence arises everywhere.

More than six decades earlier, the Johnson Amendment was signed by former President Dwight D. Eisenhower in 1954 and it prevented pastors, religious leaders and organizations with 501(c)(3) from political speeches if they wanted to keep their tax-exempted status. If leaders and organizations endorsed political candidates or participated in political campaigns, they may risk their tax-exempted status.

The Johnson Amendment was implemented and then the freedom of pastors and leaders for political speeches and issues was censored and apprehended. For 64 years, their voices on politics, political candidates, social issues and elections were unheard and depraved at the threat of the loss of tax-exempt status. When the moral voice was silenced, the immorality was on the rise to the extreme left.

The real threat was already given to the Landmark Church in Binghamton, New York when they ran advertisements against the then presidential candidate Bill Clinton before the 1992 presidential election. The other case was happened to All Saints Episcopal Church in Pasadena, California before the 2004 presidential election according to Los Angeles Times on November 7, 2005.

In the same article on November 21, 2016, Jonathan Van Maren said, "these things are happening to Christians. And whether you think these things are deserved consequences or irrelevant to whatever Oppression Scale you happen to use, they highlight why many Christians do feel as if their communities are being targeted. Disregard them if you like, but realize that just because you haven't experienced something, doesn't mean it isn't happening."

The Johnson Amendment kept churches, pastors and leaders from voicing out so many immoral and social issues. It also kept the churches and leaders from preaching publicly to support godly leaders or rejecting ungodly candidates. It also kept the churches and leaders from raising many national policies and issues. It also kept the churches and leaders from stopping many ungodly agendas and policies.

For more than six decades of silence, unrighteousness has taken over the U.S. For more than six decades, ungodliness has dominated American societies. For more than six decades, immorality has penetrated into American lives. For more than six decades, progressive value has occupied the minds of million Americans. For more than six decades, anti-God attitude has filled American education and culture.

Bible is often used when an elected president of the United States must lay hand on the Bible to sworn into office. The Bible was the main textbook of education when schools and universities in the U.S. began. The Bible was the moral textbook and moral guides for million people. Yet, public agencies in the U.S. today reject this precious and sacred book, the Bible.

The Bible is a book of faith but it can only now be taught as a classical literature in schools. The Bible is the book of wisdom but words of wisdom from the Bible is rejected by many educators and thus students. The Bible is the book that provides the highest moral characters or the highest morality, but it is now despised by the new generations and the ungodly leaders.

Pro Progressive Values

What are the progressive values? In fact, the progressives do not even know what are their values exactly except their redefinition and excessive use of freedom, identity and equality. The real discussions and excessive exercises of those progressive values only lead to what we know today as immoral values. They lead to abnormality rather than natural, and insecurities rather than securities.

If the progressives just put aside the Judeo-Christian values and values of various faiths, what values do the progressives have? They have almost no values but to borrow the pragmatist or socialist values or atheistic values. Unfortunately, the socialists and atheists do not have better values to offer except their borrows of previous values if these values support their atheistic views and political ideology.

If their values are considered as values, these values can only lead to corruption and immorality, remorse and gradually destruction. These values lead to totalitarian and brutal attacks and selfishness because these values are derived from self-center and self-gratification for power, authority, wealth and control under the name of freedom, equality, human rights and they are destructive in the long run.

What are these values proposing for? The progressive values that promote human rights for equality and freedom are leading the adherents to the limitless of sexes, abortion, adultery, and addictions. They are now leading the adherents to identity crisis and moral crisis. These values are breaking up relationships and families under the name of dignity and freedom to live and love in their definitions.

As the result of those progressive and atheist values, the United States of America are now filled with selfishness, addictions and opioid crisis. As the result, American societies are filled with lies, violence and crimes. As Americans are so free to exercise those values, America cities are now no longer different with the cities of Sodom and Gomorrah and American homes are filled with pains and brokenness.

In many schools, children and students are the victims of the progressive education. Students just failed their courses and they did not repeat the class. They failed and they did not need to be responsible for their failing. They fought with each other but teachers and schools do not have the right to teach them what are the right and wrong. Students are not responsible for their acts and the damages they made.

Liberal education is taking the students to far to liberate them from moral responsibilities and consequently leading them to moral confusions. Dr. James Dobson, the founder and president of Family Talk warned Americans and especially parents and children about the current American education that is strongly influenced by the leftists and socialist, he said,

"I am especially concerned about a generation of children who are being manipulated and warped day by day. These vulnerable boys and girls have no defense against activists and some liberal teachers who are propagandizing them. They see our kids as a way to guarantee their vision of a socialist future. Their goal is to recast America as a Marxist, atheistic, all-powerful form of government."

Children and students were destroyed by the progressive values as they just do what they think is fine for them and of course there are still many things they are still too young to distinguish what is right and wrong. They need to go to school to learn good manner, but they are the ones to teach teachers and others how to behave. Teachers and educators are exhausted at the situations and many just left.

In the classrooms, many situations are out of control when students are fighting in the class and in front of the teachers and teachers and the securities cannot do anything. When the policemen came, students would spit at the officials and shouted at them. These young children have no respect for the elders, the older and the authorities and they know no boundaries because of progressive values.

Teachers cannot discipline and protect students at what they called progressive values. Schools cannot protect students at what they called progressive values. Policemen cannot protect students at what they called progressive values. So students have to protect themselves. The stronger would win, so they have to form their gang and recruit their members to protect themselves and to destroy others.

What happens next? What we see right now is the violence in schools, fighting, mass shooting in schools. To become a gang member or to be protected by a strong group, the member must drink, smoke, fight and use drugs. That is the result of what they called progressive values. Progressive values put things in chaos and they only lead to more issues, destruction and violence. Consequently lawlessness is everywhere.

Yet, the Democrats and the liberals who caused the problems are always the people who put the blames on others. They never acknowledge the great harms that they have done to the young generations and the societies. They stopped prayers and Bible that taught and trained students with morality, humility, love and care for one another on behalf of freedom to moral decay and violence.

Americans, it is time to go back to the great traditional values of America and to get out of your moral confusion and chaos. It is time to break that socialist ideological deception and to consolidate the godly, biblical and conservative value and thought. It is time to say no to progressive values and to embrace the great biblical values. It is time to refute the atheist practices and to apply biblical principles.

It is not the progressive or socialist values but Christian values that form the moral heartbeat of American culture. It is not the progressive or socialist values but the Christian value of faithfulness that brings family together. It is the Christian value of the sanctity of life that life is well appreciated and protected. It is the Christian value of love that makes equality and care for the needy people a reality in this nation.

Promotion of Islam

While Christians are being robbed of their rights for religious freedom and jobs, Christine Douglass-Williams reported on JihadWatch.org, "US Supreme Court: Teacher who forced student to say Islamic conversion prayer did not violate Establishment Clause… the US Supreme Court declined to take the case of a public school teacher who required her students to recite the Islamic conversion prayer."

Caleigh Wood, the 11th grade student at La Plata High School in Maryland received a threat from his teacher that if Wood did not recite the shahada, "There is no god but Allah and Muhammad is the messenger of Allah," she would receive a failing grade." Wood was also forced to see "PowerPoint slides including one casting aspersions on Christians that said, "Most Muslims' faith is stronger than the average Christian."

Thomas More defended Wood and contended "the school violated the First Amendment's Establishment and Free Speech clauses when it ordered Wood to do an assignment that she could not complete without violating her Christian beliefs." Yet the 4th U.S. Circuit Court of Appeals ruled that the teacher did not violate the Establishment Clause.

On May 2019, Christine reported another case on JihadWatch.org, "Washington school district caught promoting Islam for Ramadan; lawyers send cease and desist letter." At the suggestions of CAIR to make "various changes in policy and practice that would benefit Muslim students," and "greet students in Arabic … as part of the Ramadan policy," the Washington school district issued the following policy

"The policy directs teachers to create "safe space" for Muslims, plan with Muslim students to let them "quietly slip away" from class for prayer, "privately offer information" about nutrition during their Ramadan fast, give "a lesson" on Ramadan and privately ask Muslim students what accommodations they want" according to the Northshore School District in Bothell.

The Freedom of Conscience Defense Fund wrote, "While students are allowed to practice their religion… "nothing in the Constitution prohibits public schools from accommodating students' religious exercise," public schools are not allowed to have policies or practices that "convey a message that a particular religion, or a particular religious belief," is favored.""

A few days earlier, the similar situation also happened at the Dieringer School District in Lake Tapps, Washington. Though the Freedom of Conscience Defense Fund came at the right moments and demanded these two school districts to revoke this favorable policy toward the promotion of Islam in public schools, yet the fight is still on as many attempts are taking to teach and promote Islam in public schools.

William Kilpatrick reminded Americans "While jihadists across the globe are busy slitting throats, American school children are taught that jihad is an "inner struggle" and Islam means "peace." The 9/11 event was just almost one decade ago and the recent battles between the U.S and ISIS and terrorists do not seem to remind many Americans about the many casualties brought by terrorists and their teachings.

William Kilpatrick continued to explain the misleading information, "While Muslim rape gangs destroy the lives of teenage girls in England, American teenagers learn that Muhammad was a champion of women's rights. And although American students are taught all the gruesome details of the Atlantic slave trade, they learn little if anything about the Arab slave trade which took many more lives."

The U.S Department of Education introduced "Access Islam" to public schools and the program has been used in so many states since 2005. The Bible is rejected and Christian prayers are banned and the recital of Ten Commandment or Bible verse in public schools is considered as proselytizing people. No course about Christianity or Judaism or Hinduism is allowed to be introduced this way in public schools.

But "Access Islam" is widely accepted and used. The content included religious traditions and holidays of Muslims. The lesson plans also included Muslim prayers, student learning in a Muslim college, tensions of Muslim immigrant and challenges faced by Muslims with terrorists. "The U.S. Department granted $166,000 in fiscal year 2005 and $8,000 in fiscal year 2005 for the program" reported Amy Sherman.

PolitiFact claimed that "The United States Department of Education has introduced an Islamic indoctrination program for the public schools, called 'Access Islam" is false. Yet, it cannot deny the fact that this course has been taught in so many public schools in many states. PolitiFact only quoted the words of experts but did not state many instances of students who were indoctrinated through this program.

Amy Sherman on PolitiFact said that it is not clear how many schools have been using "Access Islam." Meira Svirsky on Clarion Project listed many schools across many states that used this program and she stated that, "Parents charge that the course amounts to nothing less than proselytizing about Islam in public schools. In addition, they note that the Department of Education provides no comparative study or promotion of any other religion."

"A video from the course prominently features a Christian convert to Islam, who declares emotionally how he has found the true religion without any "intermediaries. In addition to videos, students are given worksheets to learn the Five Pillars of Islam and how to pray. Children are also expected to memorize verses from the Quran and know the meaning of those verses" reported Meira Svirsky.

John D. Guandolo pointed out the misleading teaching about Islam, "Maybe U.S. public schools have an understanding of Islam that is exactly opposite of the truth because the man who worked with the Department of Education to help them determine what information would go into public school text books about Islam was a financier for Al Qaeda who is currently in federal prison-Abdurahman Alamoudi.

In another article, John D. Guandolo also revealed that, "Through a massive effort by jihadi groups like the Council on Islamic Education (CIE) and their offshoots with support from many other Muslim Brotherhood organizations like Hamas doing business as the Council on American Islamic Relations (CAIR), the Islamic Counter-State controls the narrative about Islam on most college/university campuses, senior/junior high and elementary schools in America."

"Today, there are over 800 MSA (Muslim Students Association) chapters on nearly every major college/university campus in the United States, in a number of high schools, and now in an increasing number of junior high schools. Working in tandem with other Muslim Brotherhood organizations, like the Foreign Terrorist Organization Hamas/CAIR, these groups use intimidation, threats, and the U.S. court system to force their barbaric sharia into the U.S. while school boards, principles, state attorney generals and governors sit on their hands in fear of offending Muslims and being "divisive."

"Here is how it works. Saudi Arabia "generously" agrees to fund to expand or create a Middle East Studies program on a university/college campus, which college presidents fall over themselves to accept. Then, they "offer" to send over "guest lectures" to help get the programs jump started. Finally, they recommend a specific individual to chair the program, the university always agrees, and from then on, jihadis control the message every student on campus will ever get about Islam."

What if there are 30 million Muslims in the U.S. by 2040? This is not a hypothesis but it is a plan of the Islamic groups and the leaders made clear that Muslims do not need to use terrorism or weapons to take over the U.S. It is going to take over the U.S. by increasing their populations through birth and through migrations just as they are doing now in Europe aiming to make Europe as Islamic state by 2037.

Joseph R. John stated, "This Op Ed was written is to alert all American patriots of the immediate threat posed by Radical Islamic Terrorist organizations such as ISIL, Al Q'ieda, Iranian Republic Guard, Al Shabab, the NPA, the Muslim Brotherhood, Jamaat al-Fuqra, the Taliban, Hezbollah, Ansar Al Sharia, and so many others too numerous to list here." What do these groups do here in the U.S.?

"Those Radical Islamic Terrorist organizations are using online tactics to instruct the hundreds of Radical Islamic Terrorists "Sleeper Cells" already in the U.S, who, for the past 6 years, have been entering the US thru the wide open southern borders and setting up their terrorist networks, in order to strike the United States. That is the result of Obama's massive immigration of 6 million Muslim immigrates who didn't have their backgrounds properly investigated, as required by Federal Immigration Laws previously passed by Congress and signed into law by over 20 past Democrat and Republican US Presidents" stated Joseph R. John.

It is not clear if President Obama is part of the leadership of the Islamic groups but at least Americans must know that President Obama allowed the largest number of Muslims from almost all Muslim countries migrated to the U.S. It is important that Americans should at least read this article, "Obama's Massive Resettlement of 6 Million Muslims to the U.S." written by Joseph R. John on www.drrichswier.com

By the end of his presidency, almost 7 million Muslims were migrated to the U.S. and more than 1.1 million green cards were issued to Muslim migrants, yet millions of Christians who were persecuted and killed were not allowed to migrate to the U.S. President Obama helped the Islamic groups to accomplish almost 30 percent of their goal of 30 million Muslims with more than 8 million Muslims at the end of 2016.

Hope that Americans would not attack on President Trump anymore on his policies of Southern border, immigration issues, and restrictions of certain Islamic nationalities from entering into the U.S. This is because President Trump and his administration must deal with so many issues of national securities and terrorism to make America First and to Make America Great Again.

Preaching of Voids and The Vices

America is one of the major nations that God has mightily used in the past to bring hope and blessings to nations and to restore the morals of the people. Yet today America is seen as the hub of evils, immoralities and wickedness. America is used to be the land of freedom for many nations including the developed countries, yet today America is now turning to be the home of horrors, violence and nightmares.

When God is being rejected, hatred is filled in the heart of Americans.
When God is being rejected, violence is rampant in American dealings.
When God is being rejected, immorality penetrates into American lives.
When God is being rejected, deception covers American thoughts.
When God is being rejected, murder invades American societies.

When God is being rejected, humanism takes over American philosophy.
When God is being rejected, atheism attacks American faith.
When God is being rejected, materialism occupies American ethics.
When God is being rejected, cynicism holds back American future.
When God is being rejected, idolism is evident in American ways.

When God is being rejected, racism divides American minds
When God is being rejected, socialism replaces American rights.
When God is being rejected, Marxism controls American freedom
When God is bring rejected, anarchism destroys American government
When God is being rejected, terrorism oppresses Americans

Many Americans reject the Creator to worship the creatures.
Many Americans reject the highest moral to receive the low morale.
Many Americans reject the supreme values to the shameful values.

Many Americans reject the faithfulness of God to embrace furious things. Many Americans reject the living word of God to produce lies.

They reject His powerful deliverance to become the pitiful downcast and death.
They reject His glorious hope to become hopeless and heartless.
They reject His abundant protection to become the addicted and abnormal people.
They reject His power to become powerless and painful.
They reject His salvation to become sinful and sad.

They reject His mercy to embrace mourning, mocking and madness.
They reject His love to follow lusts, loneliness and losses.
They reject His grace to suffer with grievances, grinding and graves.
They reject His way to become the worst, wrong and weak.
They reject God to pursue girls, guys and ghosts.

In order to fill in that emptiness which, only God can do, human beings try to look for other solutions. They try drug and they become drug addicted, they seem to be free from God but they are not free from drugs. They try party life and drinking and they soon become drunkard and horrible victims of rapes and sexual assaults and they feel all the more emptiness. Why don't you let God to fill that emptiness?

In order to fill in that meaningless of life, which only God can do, human beings try to look for other ways. They try religions, philosophies, or political ideologies. They try new-age religions, atheism, and socialism. They seem to be smarter, more logical, and more persuasive, yet they still cannot find the meaning of their lives with their logical, rational, philosophical analysis. Why don't you let God reveal that for you?

In order to fill in that feeling of identity and gender loss, which only God can do, human beings try to look for other sensations. They try sex and they become sexless. They try unnatural and abnormal sex, and they soon become the victims of AIDS, HIV and other incurable diseases. Yet they are still more at loss and confusing their sex preferences. Why don't you invite God to replace that loss?

In order to fill in the satisfaction of love, which only God can do, human beings try to look for other temporary fillings. They try worldly love for powers, fames, and authority. They try the worldly love for positions, pleasures and wealth. They become hurts, disappointed, broken, depressed at the conditions required or set by that worldly love. Why don't you try God's unconditional love?

Kanye West, the recent new convert to Christianity who is against abortion and LGBTQ said rightly that "When you remove the fear and love of God, you create the love for everything else" so he is not worried that because of his faith his career will be affected, will be over or his appointments will be canceled. Yet the fear of God would give people the victory according to Will Maule on LightWorkers.com.

Before Justin Bieber became a Christian he was struggled, "with childhood fame, heavy drug abuse, and the pain the inflicted on the people closest to him." Now he encouraged his millions of fans to come to know God and "to consider the unfailing love of Jesus." Chris Pratt and Shia LaBeouf also came to Christ and also talked about their relationship with God like Miley Cyrus according to Trevin Wax.

There are many celebrities who came to God and shared their freedoms from drugs, fames, sins, pains, and hopelessness. They find their real meanings of life when they seek God. They find their relationships restored when they trust in God. They find peace in their hearts, minds and in their daily things when they begin to trust in the God who loves the world so much that He came to die for people and to save them.

As the result of the rejection of that faith, In God We Trust, the United States is making high records of divorces. Americans are now among the top in the world for immoralities. They are top in the world for crazy ideas. They are top in the world for abortions. They are top in the world for the fatherless generation. They are top in the world for opioid crisis. They are top in the world for abominations.

America is one of the top countries that have the highest crimes. BBC News Hub listed the United States of America is among the "Top 10

Countries With The Highest Crime Rates in 2019." The majorities of these top 10 countries are also the countries that are pursuing progressive values such as Belgium, Sweden, France, Columbia, Jamaica, Germany, United Kingdom, Brazil, India, and United States of America.

WhichCountry.Co also listed the United States is the top country in the "List of Top Ten Countries With Highest Crimes Rates" in developed nations. The number of 2014 crimes committed in the United States was 11,877,218 and this was almost double the number of crimes committed in the United Kingdom and Germany, and three times more than France, and 4 times more than Russia and Japan.

These crimes include felony, misdemeanor, and offenses against an individual and property, assault, murder or homicide, kidnapping, sexual assault, battery, criminal negligence, robbery, false imprisonment, and mayhem. They also cover corruption, money laundering, drug trafficking, human trafficking, rape, fraud; illegal arms dealing, illegal drugs…

World Health Organization ranked the United States Number 3 in the list of countries with the highest alcohol and drug use. The drug includes opiates, ecstasy, inhalants, pot, heroin and cocaine, prescription pill popping. "In the U.S. NPS use is 6.1% while 5% are dependent on alcohol consumption daily and 8% of the population buys drugs over the darknet" according to WhichCountry.Co.

The United States is ranked among the most depressed countries in the world according to the World Health Organizations. It "ranked third for unipolar depressive disorders, just after China, which ranked No.1 and India. India, China and the U.S. are also the countries most affected by anxiety, schizophrenia and bipolar disorder" reported by Deidre McPhillips on USNews.com.

How about raping? Congratulation! The United States is among the top 12 countries with highest rape crimes stated Bojana Petkovic on InsiderMonkey.com. "According to the American Medical Association, sexual violence and rape are the most under-reported violent crime…

the Centers for Disease Control counted nearly 1.3 million incidents" reported by Abayomi Jegede on Trendrr.net on September 13, 2019.

Yes, the United States is also known with the highest number of sexual assaults and the number is not decreasing each year. "Every 107 seconds, one person in the United States is sexually assaulted. Every year there are about 293,000 victims of sexual assault. 68% of sexual assaults are not reported to the police. 98% of rapists will never spend a day in jail" also according to Abayomi Jegede.

How about abortions? The United States is also the top country among the current socialist countries and former socialist countries of Russian Federation and Ukraine. In term of the number of abortion, China ranked first with 7,930,000, then Russian Federation with 2,287,300, Vietnam with 1,520,000, the United States with 1,365,700, then Ukraine with 635,600 according to CountryRanker.com.

How about human trafficking? Sex trafficking? Child sex trafficking? Congratulation, America is not far behind from other countries. "The U.S. is one of the highest, if not the highest, consumers of child sex" according to Timothy Ballard on Fox News on January 29, 2019. He said there were about 10,000 children being smuggled into the U.S every year to be sold as sex slaves thanks to socially progressive values.

The list can go on, yet that is also enough to conclude that the choice of progressive values and socialist values have turned the United States into one of the top lonely, painful, hurting, depression, unforgiving countries of the world. Are those values the good choices? We don't think so and we are sure you are now recognizing that those choices have been leading Americans and America to changes for evil not for good.

With all the powerful knowledge, great philosophies and incredible scientific development, yet one in five Americans today faces with mental issues. Samuel Adam, the father of the American Revolution believed that Christian education provided the principles and means to renovate the generations. Let Americans read his words written to John Adams who was the Vice President of the United States.

BE FREE OR NOT BE FREE

"Let divines and philosophers, statesmen and patriots, unite their endeavors to renovate the age, by impressing the minds of men with the importance of educating their little boys and girls, of inculcating in the minds of youth the fear and love of the Deity and universal philanthropy, and in subordination to these great principles, the love of their country; of instructing them in the art of self-government, without which they never can act a wise part in the government of societies, great or small; in short, of leading them in the study and practice of the exalted virtues of the Christian system."

Changes are necessary and needed sometimes but not all changes are needed. Changes are for the better not for worse. Changes are for good not for evil. Changes are for noble morale not for the shameful ones. Changes are for the greater values not for the less ones. Changes are for greater freedom not for the bondages. When the foundation is shaken, the whole building may collapse.

When kindness is no longer available, violence will take its place. At the lost of righteousness, unrighteousness will take over. With the absent of goodness, evil will dominate. When ethic is deteriorated, immorality will call its day. At the disappearances of great virtues, crimes become rampant. These are the consequences of choosing socialist and progressive values instead of biblical values.

These are happening in America now. Some people prefer the scary satanic worship than the worship of the loving and holy God. Other people tend to use violence and gangs to solve their issues than to deal their cases in love. Many people use deception, scams, false witnesses, lies to get what they want instead of using honesty and fair competitions. So many choose to stay away from others' injustices.

Then court cases required the removal of "In God We Trust" from the U.S currency and from government buildings. Then the fierce attacks turn on the Pledge of Allegiance. The Ten Commandment was asked to be removed from schools and public places. Prayer was forbidden. Bible classes were removed from school curriculum. If the Bible is to be used it must be seen from the literature viewpoint.

Then abortions and gay marriages are legalized in various states. The moral teaching of life and pro-life is being hated, yet the evil of abortion and murder of life are highly exalted. The life of certain species of animals are more valuable and important than the lives of millions of unborn babies because there are laws to protect them but the laws allow the killing of unborn babies.

Then unnatural sex is highly praised as the human rights. What were once and forever seen as immoral things are now being promoted as the rights so that those activists would feel better when they engage sexual activities with homosexuals or bisexuals or Barbie dolls, or even with animals. Will they go too far to fight for raping as the human rights after they approve pedophile as a natural orientation?

Then "the evolution" of sexes and sex preferences are now dominating media, public settings and schools. The moral and scientific teaching of only two genders is being attacked, yet the propaganda of multiple genders of GLBTQ is highly acclaimed. Sciences are being challenged to share the objectivity of sciences in favor of the propaganda of individual opinion.

Then there is the promotion of the scientific development of transgender operations. And now there is a widespread of Drag Queen Story Hour. DQSH said the goal is to inspire a love of reading, yet the main agenda is to educate children that there are more than two genders and children are helped to identify their sex preferences and transgender operation is offered to children if needed.

The moral teaching of faithful and life-long marriage is being mocked at, yet the divorce is praised as the way to set someone free from pain and unhappiness, and the decision for divorce is a courageous action instead of the decision to keep marriage. The moral teaching of privacy of boys and girls is being despised, yet the practice of all gender bathrooms is hailed as the sign of civilization and equality.

Today, many people with immoral behaviors are teaching about morality. Many racists are reasoning about human rights. Many faithless people are lecturing about faith. Many ungodliness leaders are educating people integrity. Many trans are promoting sexes. Trained Marxists are talking about freedom. Socialists are calling for human rights. As the result, the millennials can hardly tell right from wrong.

All of these progressive and socialist values have widely been promoted under the flag of freedom, equality, human rights and dignity. Mainstream media has been playing significant role in spreading far and near the progressive values and socialist ideology. Yet, if the progressive values are leading the peoples into shameless acts, immoral practices, and vices, we need to think twice about them.

We all love freedom and we all enjoy great human rights, but there is always a limit to every freedom and every right. Freedom is good but it cannot be devalued. Freedom is great but it cannot be manipulated. Freedom is powerful but it cannot be misused. Freedom is beneficial but it cannot be twisted. Freedom is useful but it cannot be violated. Freedom is a double-edged sword when it is used wrongly.

America and Americans are at least blessed to have many patriots and great leaders who are fighting hard to keep America and Americans from falling apart. The future of this land of freedom, the exercises of the Americans' precious rights and the prosperity of the nations needs more American patriots to be united and to protect the country from the many usurpations of the radicals, socialists and terrorists.

CHAPTER 4

THE REVERSING ORDER

As President Trump said, "our religious liberty is enshrined in the very First Amendment in the Bill of Rights. The American founders invoked "Our Creator" four times in the Declaration of Independent." And he said, "Don't worry we'll not let them change it." Yes, he did not just talk, he has been taking series of bold actions to ensure the religious freedom and the people of faith are protected by laws.

Right after President Trump was elected on November 2016, he openly said "Merry Christmas" and his favorite saying at the end of almost his speeches "God Bless America" to express his faith. During his presidential campaign, he said, "If I become president, we're going to be saying "Merry Christmas again" in responding to the political correctness related to "Merry Christmas" or Christmas War.

"**Merry Christmas**" was once the taboo that many leaders, business establishments, organizations did not want to speak it loud to others or to show the word "Christmas" in public settings because they worried that people of no faith or other faiths were to be offended by the word "Christmas" and its religious meaning. This also shows the anti-Christian atmosphere in the U.S, a Christian country.

So the word "Christmas" was "increasingly censored, avoided, or discouraged by a number of advertisers, retailers, government (prominent schools), and other public and secular organizations," and there were many debates and court cases to whether Christmas religious displays should be allowed in public schools and government buildings according "Christmas Controversies" on Wikipedia.

The anti-Christmas activists went further to object the participation at Christmas ceremonies, the decorations of Christmas ornaments, the government funding of public Christmas displays... President Trump just simply broke that taboo by saying "Merry Christmas" and the Christmas War seemed to be quiet for now. For more information, you may read the article "Christmas Controversies" on Wikipedia.

Though public restoration of "Merry Christmas" may be seem to be insignificant to some people. Yet, it brings back a piece of religious freedom that was intimidated and even prohibited for years. It also brings back the right for religious people to freely say from their heart, "Merry Christmas." It is also a declaration of faith that was suppressed for so long. It is also a beginning of the many great things.

Christians around the world have been praying for Israel and the peace of Jerusalem and Israel is at the heart of Christianity. Israel is also the important place that shows the fulfillments of many biblical prophecies, the end-time prophecies and the signs of the second coming of the Lord Jesus Christ. American Christians also expect U.S presidents to support Israel and President Trump is the strong supporter of Israel.

The long promise of many U.S. presidents to move the U.S. embassy to Jerusalem after decades of waiting was realized in 2018 by President Trump. President Trump "does not adhere to the belief that Israel is the source of the Middle East conflict." He also supported for "Israel at the United Nations and the firm stance against the Iranian threat" reported Haim Shine on Solve Israel's' Problems.

"In March 2019, Trump did what no other president had the courage to do: He recognized the Golan Heights as part of Israel and recognized Israel's, rather than Syria's, sovereignty over that area" and President Trump earlier declared and recognized Jerusalem as Israel's eternal capital on May 14, 2018 according to Mike Evans on The Jerusalem Post.

The Johnson's Amendment

On the National Day of Prayer at White House in May 2017, President Trump signed a new Executive Order to Protect Religious Liberty in America. This order is to "stop Johnson's Amendment from interferences with the First Amendment's Rights of free speech and religious freedom. This executive order directs the IRS not to unfairly target churches and religious organizations for political speeches." The Order stated,

"The Secretary of the Treasury shall ensure, to the extent permitted by law, that the Department of the Treasury does not take any adverse action against any individual, house of worship, or other religious organizations on the basis that such individual or organization speaks or has spoken about moral or political issues from a religious perspective, where speech of similar character has, consistent with law, not ordinarily been treated as participation or intervention in a political campaign on behalf of (or in opposition to) a candidate for public office by the Department of the Treasury."

President Trump said in a CBN Interview with CBN's founder Pat Robertson on July 12th, 2017 "I've gotten rid of the Johnson Amendment, now we are going to go try to get rid of it permanently in Congress, but

I signed an executive order so that now people like you that I want to hear from, ministers and preachers and rabbis and whoever it may be, they can speak."

"No Federal worker should be censoring sermons or targeting pastors. These are the people we want to hear from... As long as I am the President no one is going to stop you from practicing your faith or from preaching what is in your heart... We want our pastors speaking out. We want their voices in the public discourse. And we want our children to know the blessings of God" said President Trump.

In the past 63 years, pastors, ministers, preachers were not allowed to speak politically. President Trump confirmed, "You know, you couldn't speak politically before, now you can." Yes, that freedom is now restored and now speakers, pastors, preachers, rabbis and leaders of faith can do so freely and politically. They do not have to worry the tax-exempt status would be taken away from their organizations.

As the result, religious and non-profit organizations are no longer in silence and they begin to voice out their thoughts against social, national, and political issues, which are against their beliefs addressed by political leaders and especially recent presidential candidates. They express their views on the candidates and leaders. The freedom of speech on political matter and election is now being restored.

More and more top leaders and celebrities publicly share their faith in God recently than ever before. These people include Justin Bieber who shared his faith publicly and he even asked his 117 million followers to accept the Lord Jesus Christ; and Brad Pitt, the famous movie celebrity who used to called himself agnostic and even atheist and now publicly declares his faith according to FaithTrend.com

Recently Kanye West even "advised black Americans in an appearance in New York City not to vote Democrat" according to WND on November 8, 2019. Evangelist Franklin Graham, Pastor Paula White and many more leaders begin to speak the names of political leaders they want to oppose or support and calling believers to pray for these leaders. This was rarely happened in 63 long years.

Opponents oppose the removal of Johnson Amendment because the repealing "has serious potential consequences for our political process. It could open the door for mega-churches and religious organizations to funnel money directly into influencing elections, while their donors enjoy a tax deduction and can remain anonymous-another version of "dark money" according to Corporate Accountability.

In fact, the intention in opposing the repealing of Johnson Amendment is for the same purpose when the Johnson Amendment was enacted. Political leaders do not want people of faith to voice out unfavorable things against those leaders and to prevent them from the freedom to speak out what they want to say. So the best way is to rob the freedom and right of those leaders of faith to speak politically.

If leaders of companies, corporations, political agencies, civil organizations… can freely speak out what they think about the political leaders, elections and the candidates in their meetings, why leaders of faiths cannot do so? If those or your leaders can freely express their views in their offices, companies, cafeterias, why leaders of faith cannot do so in church offices, sanctuaries and cafeterias?

Tax code or anything else is just an excuse to rob the freedom of speech of leaders and people of faith politically. "Dark money" or anything else is just a cover to get away the religious freedom of leaders and people of faith politically. The threat to the separation of church and state or anything else is just the political scheme of corrupted politicians to remove this right from leaders and people of faiths.

If those or your leaders have their rights to support or oppose political leaders in writings, why leaders of faith cannot do so in writing? If those or your leaders have freedoms to make advertisement to agree or disagree with political leaders, why leaders of faiths cannot do so with ads? If those or your leaders are not restricted to share your views in media, why the leaders of faith cannot do so with media?

According to the White House, President Trump signed another Executive Order to protect religious freedom called the White House Faith and Opportunity Initiative during the 2018 National Day of Prayer at the White House. He said, "the faith-based and community organizations that form the bedrock of our society have strong advocates in the White House and throughout the federal government."

The aim of this Initiative includes the partnership between faith-based and community organizations to deal with poverty and to "apprise the Administration any failures of the executive branch to comply with religious liberty protections under law" and to make sure that the faith based organizations will have "equal access to government funding and equal right to exercise their deeply held beliefs."

During his speech at Faith and Freedom Coalition in June 2018, President Trump said, "we will always support our Evangelical communities and defend your rights and the rights of all Americans to follow and to live by the teachings of their faith. And as you know, we are under seized, you understand that but we will come out bigger, and better and stronger than ever you watch."

Anti-Abortion

The people of faiths are now coming out bigger, better and stronger as President Trump predicted. Now, there are more states that ban or criminalize the abortion or at least the late-term abortion of unborn babies such as Alabama, George, Mississippi, and Ohio... Earlier, abortion is legal in all the States of America and there is at least one abortion clinic in each State.

Heather Clark on ChristianNews.net listed "State-Level Bills to Outlaw Abortion, Criminalize as Murder Growing Nationwide." The bill "is increasing nationwide, with more lawmakers submitting legislation to ignore and defy Roe. Idaho, Texas, Oklahoma, South Carolina and Indiana are all currently considering legislation that would protect the unborn as persons and criminalize the act of abortion as murder."

Hundreds of abortion clinics were closed and Planned Parenthood is not allowed to use the funds from taxpayers for their abortion operations. Millions of unborn babies would be saved from now on and their right to live is acknowledged. Millions of mothers are also be set free from the guilt, shames and pains as the result of the abortions and they would enjoy the right of a mother to care for her lovely children.

Gaby Orr on Politico noted, "Three years into his presidency, the once-unapologetic womanizer has not only earned the trust of the anti-abortion community - he's irrevocably changed its standards for future Republican leaders… abortion opponents now unanimously regard him as their greatest converts and champion." President Trump is named the most pro-life U.S. President ever.

Gaby Orr also noted that, "Since his January 2017 inauguration, Trump has worked to regulate and restrict abortion access using a series of rule changes that restrict the way taxpayer funds flow to foreign and domestic organizations that perform or promote abortions." President Trump blocked the funding for the United Nations Population Fund (UNFPA) since 2017 after a few months of his presidency.

This blocked "US aid to any organization the US president determines is involved in coercive abortion or involuntary sterilization. Indeed, there could be no U.S. president in the last seven decades or so who could show strong stand on pro-life as President Trump does. Million Christians doubted that he could keep his promise on pro-life policy and now more Christians strongly support him and his agendas.

President Trump is the first U.S. president who was invited to speak at the 47th March For Live in Washington. He is famously said, "I notified Congress that I would veto any legislation that weakens pro-life policies or that encourages destruction of human life. At the United Nations, I made clear that global bureaucrats have no business attacking the sovereignty of nations that protect innocent life."

President Trump issued rule to guide the use of Title X taxpayer funding. The rule "will prohibit Title X recipients from providing abortion services entirely." This rule also informed family-planning clinics to stop referring patients to abortion clinics or abortion providers or else they would lose the federal funding. He also defunded Planned Parenthood that upset million leftwing democrats.

This rule gave a huge blow to Planned Parenthood and "independent abortion clinics that receive Title X funding will face the same choice… Hospitals that provide abortion services will also be in a bind, as they will have to choose between providing comprehensive care to a broad swatch of their community and receiving federal money that would enable these services" reported David S. Cohen.

He importantly repealed Roe v. Wade through the Supreme Court legal decision. This was thought impossible as abortion was already legalized in all states. He appointed 200 conservative judges and will be more if elected on the second term. These judges are also pro-life believers and the strong defenders of unborn babies including Supreme Court Justice Neil Gorsuch and Justice Brett Kavanaugh.

Religious Convictions and Businesses

Now, the fines against discriminations or the closing of religious businesses that refuse to bake wedding cakes, designing and printing cards or T-shirts, renting places for wedding and ceremonies or any orders that go against their religious convictions in businesses may be over now because "The Trump Administration has taken a stand on behalf of religious liberty in the courts."

Blaine Adamson and his printing company, Hands On Originals in Kentucky could have faced the same tragedy of being fined or closing their business just like business owners who refused their services to LGBTQ communities when he was sued by the Gay and Lesbian Services Organization for refuting to print T-Shirts for a gay pride event in Lexington according to FaithTrend.com on November 10, 2019.

Blaine Adamson was first found guilty of discrimination by the Lexington Fayette Urban Country Human Rights Commissions in 2014 but then Judge James D. Ishmael of Fayette Circuit Court overturned the ruling in April 2015. "The Kentucky Court of Appeals reinforced the decision in May 2018... The case was finally brought to a close in 2019" because the LGBT group does not have the statutory standing.

Bible and Prayer

Now, "Christian lawmakers in six Republican-controlled state legislatures across the country are pushing for legislation that would allow public schools to offer elective classes on the New and Old Testaments" according to Camilo Montoya-Galvez on CBS News. These states include Florida, Indiana, Missouri, North Dakota, Virginia and West Virginia, and others like Alabama, Iowa.

President Trump confirmed that "and we want our children to know the blessings of God. Schools should not be a place that drives out faith but it should welcome faith with wide open beautiful arms." It is time to let this generations and new generations about the faith of American forefathers and founders and how does that faith help the founders to build up a great America.

Kentucky already allows students in public schools to take Bible and Hebrew scripture classes when Governor Matt Bevin signed Bible Literacy Bill into law in 2017. President Trump tweeted on January 28, 2019, "Numerous states introducing Bible Literacy classes, giving students the option of studying the Bible. Starting to make a turn back? Great."

Yes, it is going to be great because there are higher moral and higher ethical living standards offered for living. It is great because recipients will have better and greater choices and values to make. The recipients would choose love instead of hatred, forgiveness instead of unforgiveness, giving instead of demanding. They would choose integrity over corruption, or kindness over violence.

It is great because clear moral distinctions are to be offered so the recipients may better identify what is right and wrong, what is noble and shameful, what is honesty and dishonesty. The recipients may have more choices between truth and lies, sins and holiness, freedom and bondages. They would be opened to clearer definitions of moral and immoral, normal and abnormal, ethical and unethical.

"Practical truths in religion, in morals, and in all civil and social concerns ought to be among the first and most prominent objects of instruction. Without a competent knowledge of legal and social rights and duties, persons are often liable to suffer in property or reputation, by neglect or mistakes. Without religious and moral principles deeply impressed on the mind, and controlling the whole conduct, science and literature will not make men what the laws of God require them to be; and without both kinds of knowledge, citizens cannot enjoy the blessings which they seek, and which a strict conformity to rules of duty will enable them to obtain."

Those are the precious words of Noah Webster written in 1839 to remind Americans of today. He spent his life to work on the reform of America. He concluded that education from a Christian perspective was the key to "provide a foundation of liberty, happiness, and prosperity for all citizens" as summarized by Stephen McDowell on Forerunner.com.

The words of Benjamin Rush in 1806 are also worth to be reminded "We profess to be republicans, and yet we neglect the only means of establishing and perpetuating our republican form of government, that is the universal education of our youth in the principles of Christianity by the means of the Bible. For this divine book (Bible), above all others, favors that equality among mankind, that respect for just laws, and those sober and frugal virtues, which constitute the soul of republicanism."

Now, the Trump's era will for sure usher a time of value and restoration, a period of social and spiritual reformation, a decrease of crimes and vices, and a long delay of the destructive democratic socialism. His era is promising a great time of prosperous economy, national security, and international influences. His era sees the fulfillment of his promise: Make America Great Again and Keep America Great.

Now, prayers are seen and heard in places that were previously banned or discouraged. Prayers are done in the White House, Office of the President, Cabinet Meeting, and Trump Rallies. Prayer signifies the coming powerful restorations of American homes, cities and societies. It is the channel to affirm and to consolidate the Truths stated in the Declaration of Independence.

The Declaration of Independence stated, "We hold these Truths to be self-evident, that all Men are created equal, that they are endowed by their Creator with certain unalienable Rights, that among these are Life, Liberty and the Pursuit of Happiness." The Declaration of Independence also holds that God is the Supreme Judge of the World and the U.S declares a firm reliance on the protection of Divine Providence.

On March 13, 2020, President Trump declared March 15 as the National Day of Prayer to ask God protection upon Americans against coronavirus. James P Moore Jr. wrote in his book, "One Nation Under God," "To dismiss prayer in the life of America is to embark on a fool's errand. Prayer has been and always will be an integral part of the national character."

"Such proclamations have frequently punctuated the pages of American history. If one thing has been proven to unity our nation in even the most uncertain times, such as we are experiencing now with the global COVID-19 pandemic. It has been a call to prayer by our leadership" from "long before America became a nation" to Presidents Harry S. Truman, Jimmy Carter, Bill Clinton… reported Robert J. Morgan.

Recently, President Trump also signed the Executive Order "that aims to prioritize religious freedom as a foreign policy initiative that includes requiring all civil service employees to undertake international religious freedom training." This Order aimed at deterring attacks on religious groups and enhancing security to places of worship reported Christopher Vondracek on Washington Times.

The Reaffirmation of "In God We Trust"

We make decisions to choose what to buy and why do we purchase certain items. We make decisions to choose what we do and why do we do that. We make decisions to choose our projects, services, transportations, staffs, workers, friends, and others; and we often make those decisions based on what we perceive as which one is better, safer or beneficial than the other.

Why don't we put the progressive values and the biblical values on the scale and make the decision again which one is better. Why don't we analyze if the socialist ideology is the greater choice or the biblical ideology is. Let us put aside all of our political views, misunderstanding, prejudices, negative experiences, uneasy feelings or even objections to religions… and make a fair choice.

Progressive values lead more people to abortions and guilt while biblical values protect lives and good consciences. Progressive values lead more people to drug addictions and emptiness while biblical values give freedom and meaning of life. Progressive values lead more people to broken families and hurts while biblical values restore families and heal the hurts.

Progressive values lead to free suspension, free of consequences and lawlessness. Progressive values lead to the free of responsibilities, free obligations and free guilt. They lead to chaos, disorders and violence. They lead to free sex, free gender, and free orientations. That is enough to call for a stop of those disastrous values and the call to go back to the biblical values that uphold high morality and responsibilities.

Progressive values lead more people to strife and selfishness while biblical values teach peace and generosity because it is better to give than to receive. Progressive values lead more people to fatherless home and struggles while biblical values bring children and parents together. Progressive values lead more people to suicidal attempts and sorrows while biblical values lead to life with joys and happiness.

Is there any organization in this world that has offered greater contributions and blessings than the people of faith? Is there any organization in this world that has offered greater care and love than the people of faith? Is there any organization in this world that has greater morale and morals than the people of faith? Is there any organization in this world that has greater forgiveness than the people of faiths?

Yes, there might be some uneasiness for you to choose and follow the biblical values and biblical faith at the beginning due to your prejudices and misunderstanding probably. Yet your decision today to follow the biblical values would produce greater goods, greater characters and greater benefits for you and people surrounding. Your decision would take you to higher perspective and destiny.

It seemed you maybe happy at first with the progressive and socialist values, but that happiness was short lasted and the negatives and pains as the result of those values became enormous and burdensome in your life. I am sure that many of you have already received and experienced those consequences with your progressive values and now you are struggling hard to overcome those negative experiences.

There are things in life that we do not want to do yet we have to follow to bring benefits to the whole. We may not like to go for weekly company meeting, yet that is how we are connected, informed and communicated. We may not like to stop at the traffic lights, yet that is how everyone is protected from accidents and even death. We may not like to pay taxes, yet that is how social benefits provided.

In the same way, biblical values may put a Big Red Stop Light to remind and to protect us whenever and wherever we are about to enter into unsafe, unhealthy, unbiblical, risky, dangerous or deadly zones. The following Scriptures may show a great description of the consequences or the fruits produced by progressive and socialist values at the rejection of God.

In Galatians 5:19-21, the Apostle Paul explained that, "The acts of the flesh are obvious: sexual immorality, impurity and debauchery, idolatry and witchcraft; hatred, discord, jealousy, fits of rage, selfish ambition, dissensions, factions and envy; drunkenness, orgies, and the like. I warn you, as I did before, that those who live like this will not inherit the kingdom of God."

The flesh symbolized the progressive and socialist values leads to death but the Spirit represented by the biblical values, gives life. When God is not in the center of our life, we are filled with all the fruits of the flesh as the result of the progressive values. Each act of the flesh is a red light and each red light reminds us that act of the flesh is not favorable, not good, not beneficial, not noble and not healthy.

We are being reminded to walk and led by the Spirit, so that we will not gratify the desires of the flesh. Yet the fruits of the Spirit are produced with love, joy, peace, forbearance, kindness, goodness, faithfulness, gentleness and self-control. These fruits shape the moral and philosophical foundation of America for decades in the past and will be in the future.

Dr. Jack Graham warned, "Socialism is fundamentally at odds with the Christian worldview because it seeks to suppress all people according to the dictates of the state. No one serious about their Christian faith can accept socialism, and here's why. Socialism is totally secular and is predicated on atheism. That is a fact. Our faith in Jesus Christ is built on the Word of God, the revelation of Scripture, and the belief that God exists. We believe in the coming resurrection of Christ, and with that faith comes freedom to live an abundant life that is founded on liberty."

It is important that America needs to reaffirm that truth and faith "In God We Trust" to bring about the restorations for millions of broken relationships, and healings for millions of people with broken hearts, pains, sickness and sins. It is time to reaffirm again that America is "The Nation Under God" to shine His light and will in this nations. It is time to acknowledge that "God Bless America" and God does.

It is just a short statement, yet "In God We Trust" is the power behind the many great records made by President Trump and his administration in his first term and more records to come. It is just a short statement, yet "In God We Trust" is the moral behind the many policies made by President Trump and his administration to bring about moral transformation and restoration of morality

It is just a short statement, yet "In God We Trust" is the character behind the miraculous transformation of imperfect people like President Trump to bring about social and moral transformation of America. It is just a short statement, yet "In God We Trust" is the backbone behind all the courageous and strong decisions and moves of President Trump's Administration to stop the atheistic agendas.

Yes, President Trump is not perfect and he can never be perfect. Yet he acknowledges "Americans do not worship the government but Americans worship God." Yes, President Trump may be unconventional in his ways of talks. Yet he believes "God bless America." Yes, President Trump is still new in his faith, yet he knows that "If we stay devoted to our Creator our best days are yet to come."

He emphasized that "But we know that our families and churches not government officials know best how to create a strong and loving community. We know that parents not bureaucrats know best how to raise children and create a thriving society. And above all else we know this in America we don't worship government we worship God." He reminds Americans that America is "The Nation Under God."

The opponents in Washington "will do everything in their power to try to stop us from this righteous cause, to try to stop all of you. They will lie, they will obstruct, they will spread their hatred and their prejudices but we will not back down from doing what is right. We know that the truth will prevail that God glorious wisdom will shine through and that the good and decent people of this country will get the changes they voted for and that they're so richly deserved."

As President Trump said in his speech at Faith and Freedom Coalition in June 2018, "Faith inspires us to be better, to be stronger, to more caring and giving and more determined to act in selfless and courageous defenses of what is good and what is right." Yes, all Americans need right now is to reaffirm this faith in their lives, in their relationship and their jobs.

President Trump strongly stated during his speech at the 2018 National Day of Prayer that, "we take this step because we know that in solving the many problems and our great challenges, faith is more powerful than government and nothing is more powerful than God." Yes, that is what Americans need to do now is to reaffirm that faith at home, offices, and public places.

As he concluded his speech at Faith and Freedom Coalition, "As long as we have pride in our beliefs, courage in our convictions and faith in our God then we will not fail. And as long as our country remains true to its values, loyal to its citizens and devoted to its creator then our best days are yet to come because we will Make America Great Again"

That is very true. America is great because of her great moral leaders. America is great because of her great people of faith. America is great because of her great moral values taught by the people of faith. America is great because of her trust in the powerful, living and loving God. Keep that precious faith my friends and Make America Great Again and Keep America Great.

CHAPTER 5

THE FREEDOM SPEECH

Freedom! It is just a simple word yet it means so much to billions of people around the world and it means everything to those who are in incarceration and long for Freedom to become a reality. They long for Freedom at the absence of oppression, imprisonment, and suppression. They thirst for Freedom at the state of being inhumanly controlled, brutally restrained and unthinkable enslaved.

Freedom reveals one's philosophy with the freedom to think and to be transparent with what is thought. It reveals one's rhetoric with the freedom to speak and to reveal the truth. It reveals one's will or determination with the freedom to act and to fight for justices. It reveals one's choice with the freedom to believe and to live up to their belief. It reveals one's moral with the freedom to act from their consciences.

True freedom is the desperation cry of millions of people for liberation and deliverance from oppressions in socialist countries and nations where tyranny reigns. Oppression is a short word yet it reveals abuses, cruelties, inhumanities, despotism, ill treatments, brutalities, injustices, pains, sufferings, suppressions, persecutions, tyrannies, imprisonment and murders and many more.

The freedoms of press, of speech, of religions, of pursuing one's happiness and life are very limited in many socialist countries. Those Freedom may just be the memories of the long past. Those freedoms could not even be bought with mountains of gold for everyone in socialist countries. But those freedoms could be available to the people again when the leaders make the decision to do so.

This speech was delivered at a religious freedom conference at the U.S Congress in 2018 with some revisions as it is stated here.

The Bloody Prices For Freedom

Dear Beloved Delegates and Leaders of The Nations,

My father was put in prison for almost two years just because he wanted a better FUTURE for his children and family. Is this the "abnormal" desire of a father? Yet the INJUSTICES deprived him of his grand desire for family and children. Then, children were separated from father and mother, husband was taken away from wife and the siblings were separated. That was just a small cost for Freedom.

My teacher and mentor, Rev. Dr. Paul, was in jail for all kinds of suffering and humiliation for more than 10 years just because he wanted to see the Hopeless to see Hope and the Sinners to become the Saints in the salvation of the Lord Jesus Christ. Is this not a noble desire to bring HOPE to the Hopeless? Yet the cruelty kept him incarcerated and millions of people remained in hopeless situations

My dear Joseph was imprisoned and in a labor camp for 20 years at two counts just because he was a rightist and a servant of the Almighty God. Is this how we want to spend our prime time? Joseph had no FREEDOM to pursue his dream but was forced to suffer the worse treatment conditions and to suffer the separation, the loss of his dear daughter and the scattering of his own children to different families.

My friend and co-leader, Rev. David, was sentenced and was behind the heartless bars for more than 10 years just because he wanted to see PEACE and PROSPERITY for his own family and the families of millions. He wanted to see Justices restored for the Montanards. Instead of PEACE, JUSTICE and PROSPERITY, he and his family suffered PAIN, OPPRESSION and POVERTY.

My youth was spent in fugitive for exactly 20 years now at the threats of incarceration and the risk of my own safety in one socialist country. Then, I was persecuted, threatened, interrogated and later deported and separated from my family by another socialist country. I wanted to see Bondage people be Set Free, the Victims to become Victors, and the Oppressed to be the Overcomers.

Today is also the precious birthday of my dear wife and yet, due to the inhumanity of the authorities, I have not been able to celebrate this happy day with my wife and children for two times now. How many more times or years do I have to be separated from my loved ones and how long should I celebrate the birthdays of my wife and my two children just by looking at this emotionless phones?

Today many of us are being deported to live in other countries that are far away from family members, relatives and dear friends. Why? INJUSTICES and CRUELTIES are still rampant in our homeland.

Today many of us are forced to live in new places that we did not really plan to live, adapt and adopt to new cultures, learn new languages that we are still struggling to comprehend. Why? FREEDOMS are still not available in our homeland.

Today, many of us have opted to run for our lives to other nations in search of brighter futures, equal opportunities and better living conditions Why? PROSPERITIES and EQUALITIES are only applicable to certain groups of people.

Today, many of us are not even allowed to go back to the places of our childhood, homes of our own, countries of our birth, spend time with our loved ones, or enjoy the foods we love. WHY? You know well the many answers to these WHYs of mine.

Who or what can repay the absence, care and love of a father, mother or loved ones that a family is supposed to have but is derived of? Nothing could repay the lost care, love, and protection except the presence and the reunion of the loved ones.

Who could compensate for the humiliation and sufferings that our families encountered during those long and terrible periods? Nothing can do except at least having the PEACE of mind that our sacrifices may bring better changes for the new generations.

Who could replace the loss of a father, the loss of a mother or the loss of children that we love dearly? Nothing could replace that loss but JUSTICE and the Reunion of families who are now facing the similar situations that we faced before.

Who could return our lost youth, our lost dreams, and our lost opportunities for better lives? Nothing could return those but the FREEDOM of those who are under suppression and of the generations to pursue their dreams, opportunities and futures.

I am not here today to condemn any leader, any regime, or any nation for the inhumane Treatments and terrible Sufferings. I am here to ask you to return PEACE to our homes, our communities and our nation.

I am not here today to seek revenge on any leader, any regime, or any nation for the great Inequalities and the horrible Deaths of people in the millions. I am here to ask you for Equal Opportunities for everyone and not just a special group of people.

I am not here today to seek the overthrow of any leader, any regime or any country for the terrible Oppressions and unacceptable Injustices. I am here to ask you to give FREEDOM to our families, individuals, and common people.

I am not here today to blame any leader, any regime or any country for the unbearable Injustices and unbearable Humiliations. I am here to call you to carry out JUSTICES to our loved ones and everyone.

I am also here to ask, do you really want to be separated from your family just like what you did to us and the pains we did go through and are still going through? If your answer is NO, and I am sure that you do not want that to happen to you and your loved ones, please, let those who have been separated for so long be united and let PEACE now be brought back to them.

I am also here to ask, do you really want injustices to happen to you and your family like what you did to us and the sufferings we went through and are still going through? If your answer is NO, and I am sure that you do not want that to happen to you and your loved ones, please bring back JUSTICES to those who have been suffering with injustices.

I am also here to ask, do you want terrible incarceration to accompany you like what you did to us and the humiliations we did go through and are still going through? If your answer is NO, and I am sure that you do not want that to happen to you and your loved ones, please give back FREEDOM and EQUAL OPPORTUNITIES to those who are wrongly incarcerated.

Let us together bring PEACE, JUSTICE, FREEDOM, PROSPERITY and EQUALITY back to every home, village, city, province and nation. We can do that with the help of God the Almighty and "let justice roll down like waters and righteousness like an ever-flowing stream. May God bless America! May God bless socialist nations and May God bless nations of the World! Thank You

The Loss of Freedom

That was my speech and it still remains an empty and meaningless speech if the socialist governments and leaders did not take quick actions to now release thousands of the victims who were wrongly accused and are still in incarceration like Bishop John was. He was a highly respected leader not only for his dedication to God and his life of integrity but also for his commitment to God and sacrifice for God.

Bishop John was serving God and he was the vice president of a seminary. Out of the blue, the policemen came one day. They were not there to tell him how free he was or what freedoms he had but they handcuffed him and took him away. He thought he would have been fine and would be released soon. Yet his loss of freedom took him to an unknown and unsure future. He was incarcerated for 30 years.

Nobody knew that how long that he would be incarcerated but he himself knew very well that he was there to die. He received "special treatment" as the member of water prison. During the day he worked hard in the labor camp and he went through the night by standing inside the water. It was still a mystery that how could he survive that horrible water prison for a long time.

Indeed, it must be a miracle from God that his legs were not swollen by the long period in the water. The water was dirty and the bacteria could enter his body through the scratches or the open wounds on his legs. The bacteria could eat up his flesh and could cause the unbearable pains and sufferings. How could he survive the cold wintertime in that icy water? He was the only lone survivor of the water prison.

Yes, his freedom was 30 long years in loneliness, hard labor, pains, maltreatment, hunger, tortures, freezing, humiliation, desperation, frustration, and sickness and so many more. His **Freedom of Speech** was completely silenced in those long years of being re-educated by socialists. Every wrong word he made was recorded and used against him and to add more years for his re-education and hard labors.

His **Freedom of Press** was far from him in the prison cell and all he could experience was their Freedom to Press him to pieces. Who dared publicize his pitiful stories anyway? Does anyone dare in socialist countries? His **Freedom for Information** was totally cut off. He wanted to know the whereabouts of his parents or his loved ones but prayer was his only way to connect to his loved ones in spirit.

His **Freedom of Travel** was confined to the four cold and motionless prison walls with freezing water where he stood and slept from nights to weeks and from weeks to months and years. How many times in those years did he wished and wished thousands of times that he could be Freed from those emotionless walls though these walls were his only faithful supporters and listeners during his anguishes.

His **Freedom for Pursuing Happiness** was dying every day and every time the prison doors closed, closing down his happiness with his family members and friends. It closed down his happiness to love and to be loved, and his happiness to search for truth and to pursue his dream. Even his simple happiness to just walk around and to smell the flowers was also closed down as an impossible wish.

His **Freedom of Religion** was only available in his long, travail and endless nights and that Freedom was available and silent in his thought only. His **Freedom of Expression** was completely lost and he was forced to recite the socialist ideology that says Freedom but he was not Free at all. His **Freedom of having a Fair Trial** was not fair at all or else he would not have faced the loss of his Freedom for years.

His **Freedom for further Education** was inaccessible and could never be realized except the constant repeats and re-education of the mind by the socialists to force him to reject what he truly believed and to accept the socialist ideology that destroyed him. His **Freedom for Equality** in this socialist country and ideology for Equality was indeed the horrible inequality. He was equally treated like animals.

Was he a Murderer that he had to face 30 years of punishment? Nope.
Was he a Terrorist that he had to face 30 years of tortures? Nope.
Was he a Freedom Fighter that he had to face 30 years of bondages? Nope.
Was he a Betrayer of the country that he had to face 30 years of humiliation?
Was he a Spy that he had to face 30 years of being checked?

It was none of those reasons. He was God's servant and he had no real Freedom of Religion in his socialist country as the socialists said. While he was behind the bars and the real world, he worked hard during the days in the labor fields. He was re-educated at night and he stood and slept in water in the prison late at nights. The bacteria in the water could invade his open wounds and torture him to death.

Yet he miraculously survived through prayers and by faith in God throughout those 30 horrible, long and merciless years. If it had not been for his faith in God, he could have died frustrated like many prisoners did. If it had not been for his trust in God, he could have died depressed like many prisoners did. If it had not been for his hope in God, he could have died by many suicidal attempts like many prisoners did.

Does he receive any **due compensation** for those 30 years of imprisonment? If he was wrongly charged and imprisoned like that in the U.S., he could receive millions of U.S. dollars to at least compensate for his loss of freedom, the physical exploitations of the labor camp, the wasting years of his life, the violations of his rights, and the emotional struggles. All he got was to be released from prison.

The Cries for Freedom

This is the true face of socialism and the injustices are still happening right now as you read this book for the many freedom fighters, human right activists, religious workers and so many innocent people. Now that you are already informed about the true face of socialism, you will understand that the freedoms and rights you have in America are very precious. Please do not take your freedom for granted.

We risk many lives including our own and our family members to tell you the truth that you would hardly hear and see from mainstream media. We risk the freedoms of many loved ones to let you know truth from deception so that millions of you will not be trapped in the concentration camp or the labor camps of the socialist governments so that you may enjoy your Freedom and be blessings to nations.

You don't need to take that risk in your free world and you don't need to take that risk in the future. All you need to do is to take your Rights, your Freedoms, your Faith and your votes to make sure that godly leaders will be in charge of the U.S. or your nations so that justice would flow. All you need is to take your Freedom to vote for your Freedom, and for the Freedom that we, the socialist victims already lost.

Americans are so blessed and they already have great freedom and rights. Do not fall into the trap and nice words of socialism and you would loose your great freedom and practice limited freedom as described and discussed in the **12 Commandments of Socialism**. More than ever before, this is the time that Americans must be united together to protect America and Americans from socialism.

America and Americans are now facing the critical time when the American communists, the socialists, the anarchists, the terrorists, the betrayals of the U.S., the leftwing democrats, the liberals, the leftists, the radicals and the mobs are all working together to destroy Americans and American communities, American cultures and American values, American freedom and American rights.

They have been causing disorders and lawlessness. They have been vandalizing streets and attacking people. They have been setting homes and communities on fire. They have been dividing the peoples, races and America. They have been destroying businesses and the economy. They have been planning for the radicals and the socialists to take over the United States.

They are increasing child abuse and elder abuse. They are promoting gang violence and lootings. They are encouraging sex trafficking and human trafficking. They are promoting sexual assault and raping. They are approving vices and murders. They are opening to drug dealings and drug addictions. They are welcoming all the ungodliness, unrighteousness, vices and abominations.

American patriots and believers could not just sit and watch the U.S. to be divided and destroyed, and Americans hurt and murdered. It is time for Americans to protect their nation, their faith, their rights and their freedom. Your decision today to support President Trump, Vice President Mike Pence, the Republican candidates and the conservative leaders would save America and Americans from:

The Destruction of the Left
The Oppression of the Socialists
The Tyrannies of the Radicals
The Reign of the Regimes
The Violence of the Extreme Racists

The Loss of Precious Freedom
The Violations of Human Rights
The Incarceration of the Innocent People
The Persecutions of Religious People
The Sufferings of the Civil War

The Wicked Ways
The Rampant Lawlessness
The Ungodly Immoralities
The Horrible Destructions
The Unnecessary Deaths and Pains

This is the time that American patriots and Americans believers must take a stand for their faith to protect their religious freedom. This is the high time for Americans to take actions against the violent mobs and the extreme rioters. This is the significant time for Americans to put back laws and orders. This is the historic time for Americans to save this prosperous nation from destructions.

Wherever the United States of America faced the crisis, wars or turbulences, the people always prayed and called on the name of the Lord Jesus Christ. When the people come together to call on the name of the Lord Jesus Christ, the deliverance from God would come and peace would reign. It is the critical time for Americans and people of the nations to call upon God for His protection and blessings.

God is always faithful to His promises and God never fails His people. "For everyone who calls on the name of the Lord will be saved" (Romans 3:13).

The unity of American believers and churches to protect their faith, their nations and their lives during this critical time would also spring forth a great movement of a powerful spiritual revival and awakening in the U.S. Do not miss the powerful touch of God upon the U.S. and Americans when the Body of Christ is coming together in Unity, Missions and Revival in His name.

CHAPTER 6

NOT FREE YET

Joseph was put in prison and labor camp for 20 years simply because he was a rightist and a Christian who did nothing against the socialist government, or the socialist leaders, or the people. He committed no violations of laws, no wrong doings, and no crimes. He survived with all the sufferings, discriminations, tough weather conditions, humiliations and hard labors behind the bars.

Whenever I met him, I tried to convince him to share about his life, his experiences and his struggles in prison and labor camps, as I believed that his stories would challenge many young generations like me. Yet, he mostly tried to avoid talking about it and I could see the pains and the sadness on his face whenever he was asked to think about his painful pasts and unhappy experiences.

He was free from the four cold prison walls but his mind is not totally freed from those walls yet. He was free from the hard works of the labor camps but his hands are not free from the scars of the past. He was free from the sights of sufferings but his eyes are not freed yet from the humiliations. He was free from the lengthy lectures of reeducation, but his ears are not free from the sounds of tortures.

These are also the unforgettable experiences and the nightmares of the million victims who went through the oppressions of the socialist regimes or tyrannies. They want to forget the pasts but the pasts keep haunting their lives. They want to burry their negative thought but the repeated nightmares keep torturing their minds. For years they still could not sleep well. For years, they could not find peace.

The recent rise of socialism in America through the presidential campaigns of Sen. Bernie Sanders in 2106 and 2020 is tearing apart the thought-to-be-healed wounds and stirring up the pains of the struggling lives of millions of socialist victims who run away from socialist countries for lives and they are now still living here in the United States of America. The rise of socialism reopens their ugly scars.

In fact, not many Americans and these victims of socialist nations could imagine that one day socialism would survive in this land of freedom and one day socialism would become so popular in America as it is right now. They could not even imagine that one day Americans who once defended for the victims of the socialist regime, would embrace socialism and would allow socialism to take over the U.S.

Memories of The Past

Millions of the socialist victims and their children could not forget the lies and the lists of deception of the hypocritical socialist leaders and socialism. They could not forget the madness and the mocking of the furious socialists. They could not forget the injustices and the imprisonments by the heartless socialists. They could not forget the raping and the robbing of the greedy socialists.

How could they forget the sadness and the sufferings in the socialist countries? How could they forget the poverties and the pains? How could they forget the loneliness and the lamentations? How could they forget the melancholies and the man-made havocs? How could they forget the humiliations and the hurts? How could they forget the bombards and the bandits of socialism?

They could not forget the blades and the bloods. They could not forget the escapes of life and death and the eating of human fleshes to survive. They could not forget the pains and the persecutions in the emotionless prisons. They could not forget the many risks and the rivers of tough life that they went through. They could not forget the tortures they bore and the tombs of their loved ones.

How could they forget when they are the first generation victims of the socialist regimes and they are still alive? How could they forget when their properties and lands were taken away from them leaving them wandering? How could they forget when their friends were shot down in front of them? How could they forget when their lives were even almost taken away by the inhumane socialists?

They were having a great time with their wonderful family members and suddenly they were separated for years and hundred thousands of them could never have a chance to see their family members again. How could they forget? They were having a great job and suddenly they were put into the labor camps and prisons and millions of them could never see freedoms again. How could they forget?

My mother often told me so many scary stories of killing and murdering by the socialists, which were taken place at her hometown especially during the time I was penning these words. She said in her scary expressions, "Whenever I remember my hometown I could not forget the many fears and deaths caused by the socialists. They are very cruel and they killed so many people in those days."

Her relative whom she called uncle Peter was a wealthy man and a business owner. At the threat of the socialists, he immediately took his family members and precious jewelries and gold on a truck and drove away. They were leaving their hometown, their business, their homes, and many other properties. They thought that they could find a safer place for him and the family members.

Yet they were stopped by the socialists on the way and they cut open the throat of uncle Peter in front of the family members. Blood was pouring out and uncle Peter was stretching out his hands for help at the helplessness of the family members. All the family members could do was to plead for his death body and brought his body home for a proper burial so that his spirit could be comforted.

Upon hearing that my mother and the relatives went immediately to his home and she could see dry blood was all over his body and his throat was cut open. His eyes were still open to tell the people that, "You would be the next target of the socialist." Do you think that the family could ever forget what they witnesses by their own eyes at the death of a husband, a father, a son, an uncle, and a relative?

Until The Grave

It is not just about the unforgettable memories and it is not just about the negative experiences that they went through. It is not just about the un-forgiveness of the pasts and it is not just about the many losses. It is the emotional struggles that they have to deal with every day. It is the mental tortures that they have to encounter every night. It is the haunting nightmares that they have to see in every dream.

Those painful moments are gone but still kept alive in their minds. Those horrible scenes are the pasts but still felt strongly in their emotions. Those abusive experiences are hidden but burning in their hearts. The victims thought that could forgive and forget, yet those pains, hurts, abuses and losses have turned into hatred, prejudices and they just could not even realize that.

The millions of the socialist victims and their children could not forgive and forget the socialists and could never accept socialism because their open wounds were too wide to be knitted and their hurts were too deep to be restored. The millions of the socialist victims and their children could not forgive and forget the socialists because their hearts were already broken into thousand pieces.

They could not forget and forgive because the socialists never say a word of apology to them until now. They could not forget and forgive because the socialists never show even a bit of regret at what they did until now. They could not forget and forgive because the socialists never return justices to them until now. They could not forget and forgive because the socialists never return their properties until now.

They could not forgive and forget because the socialists are still mistreating and making the hopeless people to suffer. They could not forgive and forget because the socialists are still oppressing and overpowering the poor and powerless people. They could not forgive and forget because more victims are still sufferings and running away from the suppressions and the tyrannies of the socialists.

I happened to talk with many victims of the socialist nations and I asked them, "Why don't you go back to visit the country because you are now American citizens?" Most of them dared not go back out of fears. I explained to them that, "You are now American citizen, the socialists cannot do any harm to you." But once someone was already beaten by a snake, it is hard to convince them that snakes would not bite.

Many victims always think that the socialist leaders pretend to welcome them to go back the countries and once they are there in the socialist country, they would be captured by the socialist and they would be imprisoned for years just as the socialist leaders did to hundred thousands of people before. Millions of the victims were deceived the socialists before and they don't want to be deceived again.

They said, "as long as the socialist leaders still reign the country, we would not go back until their deaths." It is not that they don't miss their hometown, their people who are still in the socialist countries, it is just that they have no securities and trusts in the promises of the socialists as they already experienced and they already knew so well the lies and the deceptions of the socialist leaders.

The Continuous Nightmares

The million victims of socialism and socialist nations have been enjoying the many precious freedoms and rights in America for the last few decades. These are the freedoms and the rights that millions of people in the socialist nations could never dream of. They were able to follow their dreams in this nation. They are free to pursuit their lives and happiness and to exercise their human rights and freedoms.

Suddenly, the lives of these victims are not at peace again. They are troubled at so many news about socialism on the media. They are surprised at the fast changes. The nightmare of socialism in their lives is not over yet and it is now at their doorsteps. They can't bear to see socialism to take over America, the great land of freedom for more than 330 million peoples and these people would be at odds soon.

When Sen. Bernie Sanders praised the former president of Cuba, Fidel Castro, a wage of reaction immediately arose against him because former Cubans who fled to America knew better the reality of the education, healthcare and equality and poverty in Cuba. As the result, he lost the supports of so many former Cubans. He would face the same rejections by most of the former victims of socialist nations.

Reina Howard, a former citizen from El Salvador who came to the U.S "in the late 1980s during a time of severe political turmoil and attacks from the Communists guerrillas to the population and financial targets that would devastate the economy," said, "I am so passionate against agendas that pretend to care for the poor but enslave entire nations" reported Brenda Krueger Huffman.

While millions of the former socialist victims are struggling and are being reminded of their painful pasts at the rise of socialism, millions of Americans are exciting at that prospect. Millions of American millennials are still very innocent and even so happy to embrace the great promises of socialism. They are as passionate and hopeful as the millions of the young guards in the socialist countries before.

These young guards were so passionate with the new ideology and were fascinated at the prospect of a prosperous nation where everyone was equal and there would be no longer sufferings economically. They were taught and were so indoctrinated with the idealistic ideology of socialism that they gave up their education and spending their times to advocate and to spread the greatness of socialism.

As they were young and passionate, they were willing to go to the countryside and remote areas to spread the great ideology of socialism and the plans of the country leaders. Little did they know that they would soon become the instruments of hatred, destructions and even murdering by the glorious promises and powerful grips of the socialist leaders! The evil acts that haunted the rest of their lives.

They went to every house to check if there were people who went against the political party and the political leaders and if they stored literatures that were forbidden by the socialist leaders. They searched everywhere and they would drag the people that they suspected to be counter-revolutionaries and reported them to the authorities or even beat them to dead as great warnings to others.

They were so happy to hear from the leaders that they were the history makers. They were the agents of changes and were the hope of the future. They were the people who made the nation great. They were the people who were the watchdogs of the nation and they really were. They were admired and they were praised for all the searches and discoveries of rebels among the neighbors and their friends.

These young guards did not even spare their teachers, their family members, their relatives and even their parents. They persecuted all those dear people, accused them for the things they did not do, tortured them for the thoughts they did not think, criticize them at the words they never spoke, imprisoned them for the crimes they never knew, and killed them for the acts they never committed.

They accused people's thoughts wrongly in the great name of the socialist ideology. They confiscated people's wealth greedily in the lovely name of the egalitarianism. They took away people's freedom cruelly in the nice name of loyalty to the power. They destroyed human rights in the cute name of submission to the leaders. They killed people's lives inhumanely in the good name of the socialist party.

The beautiful promises of equality brought about wider gaps of inequalities. The wonderful promises of prosperity came with widespread poverties. The great promises of happiness turned into pandemic sufferings. The great handshakes of the comrades assured the insecurities of their lives. The passionate embraces of the neighbors could be the warning sign, "You will be the next criminal to be judged."

Life was hades on earth to the common people and heaven for the socialist leaders. Fears, insecurities and nightmares were filled their sleeps because no one and even the young guards could feel secure and could say for sure that they were saved.

Their passions and innocence were well manipulated by the socialist leaders that these young guards committed all crimes and evils they could never thought of. Their energies and curiosities were well caught in the great prospect of a powerful future that these young guards broke every norm and trust of the social values and relationships that they did not even sense. But their consciences were still at work.

Just like the story of Alexander, the son of a powerful and high-ranking socialist leader, his future seemed to be great until his father showed his disagreement to the top leaders of the country. His family was purged and punished and his father was imprisoned and tortured, and his sister died as the result of the persecution. He also suffered with discriminations, humiliations and physical attacks.

He must do something in order to receive the pardons of the socialist leaders and to make a difference for his life. When his father was brought before the public to be criticized and humiliated due to his betrayal to the political party and leaders, he also joined others to torture his father. He kicked his father in the presence of many people to show his loyalty to the party and to denounce his father.

His kicks were kind enough to break three ribs of his father. Was he ashamed at what he did to his father? Was he guilty at his great acts? Was he tortured for hurting his father physically, mentally and emotionally? Only he knew about. His father said, "your cruelty will make you a big leader in the future." His father's words were true and he became one of the powerful leaders of the country later.

At the moment, his identity and story could not be publicly revealed yet, and history would let you know his name in due time. It seemed that he was powerful and yet he was counting days of his downfalls and painful endings. But one thing people could say for sure was he could never teach his daughter to be filial to parents and he could never became a great model to the generations about filial piety to parents.

She or just call her Guilt, was a very active member of the young guard. Guilt dreamed of the day she could be promoted to the leadership. But she must have accomplishment or achievement to be recognized by the socialist leaders. Guilt thought of the popular way that many young guards often did, and then she accused and reported her parents to the authorities as counter-revolutionary people

Her parents were punished and were put in the prison and labor camps to suffer the hard labors and to be reeducated. They were taken away and she could never see them again. As time passed she could no longer bear the guilt and the shameful things that she did to her parents. She could never forget the shocking looks and puzzled eyes of her parents when she accused them in front of the leaders.

She could not bear the fact that her parents did not scold her or blame her for what she did. She could not forget their love and their care for her and her loneliness and pains now. Her conscience squeezed her and her mind tortured her and her emotions gripped her heart. She could not forgive the pitiful looks and the heavy hearts of her parents the day they took away by her, her team and her leaders.

She was not peaceful to think of her parents who were in the hard labor camps. She could not stop thinking about their sufferings and her wrong acts so she went to the leaders and confessed what she did. They did not believe her words and how could they believe the words of the ones who even betrayed the parents. Her parents never came back and she became crazy because of her guilt, pains and thoughts.

These stories revealed the cruelties and evils that are evident in the lives of the socialist leaders and socialist nations. In order for them to gain power, they must be heartless and emotionless to others even to their parents. If they could beat, denounce, destroy and kill even their own parents and their close ones, would they spare the common people who are their steps to position, power and prosperity?

When the leaders of the country are evil, cruel, heartless and immoral, what would be happen to the people in that country? When they only care for their party, position and power, what do you expect the country would be? At least 40 former socialist countries could tell the same answers: corruption, abuses of power, suppression, imprisonments, limited freedoms, limited human rights and murders.

Socialism and the socialists could turn the most innocent people to become the most ignorant people and the moral people to become the immoral ones. They could turn the elegant people to become the evil ones, and happy people to become the hopeless ones. Socialism and the socialists could turn kind persons to become killers and friends to become foes. They could turn a prosperous country to a poor country.

Yet many young American socialists and millennials today are so impressed with the many great promises of the socialist leaders. They are challenged by Sen. Bernie Sanders, the leftwing leaders the socialist leaders and the socialist organizations to knock at every door of American homes and apartments to convince Americans to buy in their plans and to vote for Sen. Bernie Sanders.

That great ideology or socialism is now turning thousands of the millennials from law-abided citizens to lawlessness suspects. It turns kind people into violent people. It turns hard working people into looters. It turns great-minded people into mobs. It turns peaceful people into terrorists. It turns contributors into destroyers of the countries. It turns innocent people to criminals.

That great socialist ideology opens greater opportunities for hatred to be expressed, violence to be manifested, and divisions to be manipulated. It also opens to the abuses of racism, power and lawlessness for the political purposes. It is for sure to lead to suppressions, pains and injustices if Americans and patriots are not going to protect their precious rights and freedoms that they have been enjoying for so long.

History of the many socialist nations is repeated again in the innocent U.S soil. Today, many American millennials are following the same regretful and remorseful paths of those million young guards in socialist nations. They are just naïve as the former millions of young guards who only see the immediate solutions for their needs but they do not see the ultimate intentions of the socialists yet.

We hope that more Americans would read these books of ours: **The 12 Commandments of Socialism** or **The Boat of Destiny**, and share these books to others. These books would help Americans realize the socialist promises are just the baits given so that the socialist leaders could take over America and they could carry out the socialist plans here in America.

Our children often travelled with us for mission trips since they were still very young. One of the things that our children were very good at was to help us detect the "tail." The "tail" means the following of the authorities that loved to follow us everywhere we went. They were not really afraid of the policemen then because they thought that was fun, as their capable dad would cut their "tails" soon.

So every time we went out, our children would keep looking around if there was suspected cars or strange people who were following us. If they found something fishy, they would whisper, "Dad, the policemen are behind or there is a car following us." At home they would not say anything about the churches or the ministries because an implanted chip somewhere in the house could record everything.

I did not need to spend a lot of time to train them to be cautious at what they should say at home and to detect the "tail" when we went out. They learned that quickly as they grew up in that tense environment. But that was just fun for them. Then, they witnessed the frequent visits of the policemen and heard the many calls that the authorities called me for "tea times" as the persecutions became serious and tough.

My wife and I did not tell our children about the persecutions but they got scared at the frequent visits of the authorities. At the beginning, they often opened the doors if there was any knocking. As time went by, they dared not open the doors because they did not want to see those serious faces and the serious talks that made them scared. They could sense something serious as our prayer increased on protections.

One day, they saw about 40 policemen came and surrounded our church from the inside and outside of the building. They saw the policemen ordered church members to sit down as they searched the place and confiscated things. Our sons saw by their own eyes the first time in their lives that so many church members were arrested and interrogated while others tried to escape.

And they saw by their own eyes for the first that I was surrounded by so many policemen and the security people as these people forced and took me away in their hopelessness and at the loss of their shouts. They even tried to protect me from the pushes of the policemen but it was of no prevails. They run after me until I was pushed into a van and was driven away leaving them in confusion and fears.

I could understand those hopeless feelings and desperations of my son because I also witnessed by my own eyes the arrest of my father for the sake of freedom and the future of the children. I could understand their fears as years earlier my father and I walked through the scaring night to escape the arrest of the socialists. I also knew that those sights would never be forgotten in their memories ever.

Then I was deported out of the country, my wife and our children were "invited" to stay back in the country. The condition was if I did stop all the mission works including church planting, Bible School training, leadership training, missionary training, church planter and missionary sending, mission mobilization, mission conferences, charity works... then we could be united again.

I was forced to wander the world without knowing where should I go and how the future would be. I once wandered the new world when I escaped a socialist country due to religious persecution in 1998. I was on exile for many years and it was still ok because I was still single then. Then I started my life and ministry all over again in another socialist country and now 20 years later, I was forced to leave home again.

This time it was really hard because I am no longer a single man. I have my wonderful wife and precious children. Though life is not easy to start again in a new world but at least I am in a free world but it is tough for them back home. They face with all the struggles and needs that a single mother and children of a single mother would go through and plus so many worries, uncertainties and fears.

Just like my mother did when my father was put behind the bars, my wife was both the father and mother to the children. She was the bread earner for the family. She was the spiritual leader and counselor to many young pastors and leaders in our ministry. She had enough burdens, and yet she still had the daily fear and worries of my security, my living and my many needs and of her own struggles.

One day, the policemen and the fire department staff came to the school and our children were so scared and nervous at these officials. They thought that these officials came to arrest them in front of their many friends as they did to their father. The worse moments came when these officials came to their classes and stayed there for a whole period; my children were not even dare to look at the officials.

These officials came to demonstrate and to teach the children how to prevent fire and emergent circumstances but my children thought these people came to arrest them. The fears and the anxieties in their hearts and minds could not be removed immediately because they could not forget the experiences of their father's arrest not because of doing any bad things but because of preaching the Gospel.

They could not forget the unhappy things in their eyes, in thoughts, in feelings. And those feelings are still there anytime they hear the door knocking or the presence of any policemen who happened to pass by. In the same way, the socialist victims still have those nightmares and fears that are not far from them now. The socialist leaders still watch over their victims from home regardless of where they are.

Even Senator and socialist Bernie Sanders could not win the 2020 presidential election, America and Americans and millions of victims of socialism and socialist leaders are not yet free from the threats of socialism. AOC and the DSA will continue to lead American millennials to run for the future presidential elections soon unless American millennials understand the true issues of socialism.

Now, the socialists and the leftwing leaders manipulate the young people and their innocence to make that political and cultural revolution through recent riots. That revolution was once the nightmare and horror of hundred millions of people. They have been educating and indoctrinating the minds of the young generations with their ideology for decades and it is not easy to make a great shift in people's mind.

The Tough Tasks of Reeducation

Marion Smith, the executive director of the Victims of Communism Memorial Foundation in Washington D.C. said, "when we don't educate our youngest generations about the historical truth of 100 million victims murdered at the hands of communist regimes over the past century, we shouldn't be surprised at their willingness to embrace Marxist ideas."

This is very true but the task is a lot easier to say than it is to be done. The task of reeducation the young generations is tough and enormous. It needs the concert of effort of the society to make the reeducation possible. It needs the many supports of the government, schools, media and families. It also requires time and the responses of the young generations. Yet it is never be late to start with even small steps.

Firstly, Americans would find this a tough and imbalanced battle when the mainstream media is still largely dominated and influenced by the leftists and the liberals. The conservative and alternative media are basically the only channels where Americans may hear the truth. The leftists and the liberals are now trying to dominate these channels with their massive information.

The mainstream media is still doing better jobs in leading their readers and viewers to the promising future of socialism. They are good at selling their ideas and ideology to their followers and the audiences. The mainstream media and their leaders know how to integrate their socialist ideology into the political events and with the needs of American to see their dreams and desires to soon come to pass

The millennials are indeed the victims of the mainstream media "programed" by the Democrats without knowing the consequences of that deception. Little do they know the decision for socialism has brought so many nations into tyrannies! That was the decision that has caused the sufferings and tragedies of millions of people. That was the decision that has brought the death of millions of innocent people.

President Trump is wise in using both the conservative and alternative media. He criticized a lot about the lies of mainstream media and hoping that they would talk the truth in most of his presidential campaigns. Of course mainstream media also always fought him back at his every word. Yet, through his countless tweets, he reached out to the wider audiences, which the mainstream media limits him to.

This is not possible in socialist countries. When a socialist president spoke at a certain event whether it is big or small, the media would cover his speech and the newspapers would sum up his or her message. It is a great honor for any media to do so and they all have to make the best presentation of his or her speech. There are only praises about the speech and there is absolutely no negative response at all.

Media is the face of the political party so media is not supposed to make the face of the political party to be messy and ugly. Media is the best friend of socialism so media is not supposed to make its friend upset and unhappy. Media is the powerful weapon of the political leaders so it is not suppose to attack and destroy its leader. Media is also the double-edged sword if it is not used properly.

In socialist countries, any channels, any websites, and any media that go against the will of the socialist ideology and governments, the government would block them all. The mainstream media only communicate the message of socialism. Thus, it is difficult and even impossible for someone to share other ideologies through mainstream media as it is tightly and strictly controlled by the government.

The only possible media where people can still communicate is through alternative media. Yet the government still strictly monitors and controls the operation and the content of alternative media. The operation and control of American mainstream media by the Democrats and the liberals are very much the same way the socialists do to their media. Birds of the same feathers are flocking together now.

In socialist countries, people who like and share the messages, information and videos that are against the socialist government, leaders and socialism would be punished severely. They are not seen as human rights fighters but betrayers, counter-revolutionaries, spies, and liars. They are the dangerous people who spread wrong and bad ideologies and they should be punished.

Secondly, the task to reeducate the millennials and American also faces fierce battle in educational institutions when most of the public education is still largely taught, dominated and influenced by the liberals and the leftists. Value education and conservative topics sound boring to the students, yet progressive values and socialist benefits are touching their every needs and excitement.

It is hard to bring about changes to the many prejudices and strong reaction to the conservatives. Many American millennials were indoctrinated with the thought that the conservative values and policies would not work and are outdated. To them, the conservatives are always against the new ideas and scientific development. Thus, the millennials do not even care to listen to ideas shared by the conservatives.

David Nammo further explained the rise of socialism, "It is obvious where such thinking abounds and continues to spread: in our colleges and universities. The ideologies of professors and educators have proven stronger than facts: The "benefits" of socialism and Communism are taught from the Ivy League to the local community college. A generation has been taught a lie, and they now believe it."

Most of people in Barna's poll were liberals: "three fourths support same-sex marriage; seven our of ten advocate legalized abortion; a majority want socialism to replace capitalism; and nearly one our of five claim to be LGBT... This oddity does, however, reflect how the ideological Left consistently appropriates language and imputes new meaning to terms that are known and popular" reported David Nammo

As the result, millions of millennials and Americans are still uninformed, unalarmed, and uneducated about the poverty, oppressions, pains in socialist countries. They seem to know little about the stories of millions of refugees who run for their lives from socialist countries. Dr. Jack

Graham explained the reason that accounted for the attitudes of the millennials toward socialism in the following words.

Dr. Jack Graham explained, "Those under 30 years of age have not seen the devastating effects of Soviet-style repressive governments under socialism. It is the big bad brother, communism. We're past the Cold War now, and a generation has arisen that either hasn't been taught history, doesn't read or understand it, or doesn't care. They are listening to their liberal teachers, professors and politicians; and what they have been told sounds good. It appears compassionate and living. But is it? I can say emphatically that it is not."

In socialist countries, education is strictly controlled by the government. The socialists know very well that education is the way to control the heart, mind and obedience of the people. Though there are private educational institutions but they are mostly international schools and the school fees are to expensive for common people to dream of the chances to be a student at these schools.

Thirdly, it is hard to reeducate the millennials when pastors, leaders and religious workers of churches and faith-based educational institutions or organizations do not want to get engaged in political talks or political topics. This was because of the earlier constraints of the Johnson Amendment. The task is still possible when leaders and Christians take actions as America has a large number of Christians.

Now that pastors and leaders of faith can freely talk about politics, they may develop more materials and trainings to educate about the issues of progressive values and socialism and how Christians may reach out to others. Christian educators and Christians in general also need to be challenged to be more active in teaching and preaching the Gospel and sharing the issues of socialism to people around them.

Pastors of middle-size churches and especially mega-churches did not often talk about politics and their favorite political leaders because of the diversity of the members in the congregations. If the pastors and leaders are not careful the church could be split. Even President Trump is very pro-life and this is very biblical yet pastors of big churches may hesitate to talk about his pro-life policy.

Let us pray that God would give them the wisdom to change the situation. The outcome would be enormous when the Body of Christ is active in preaching the Gospel and sharing the issues of progressive values and socialism. Recently, the preaching of Dr. Jack Gram about communism is a great example that pastors and leaders of churches and organizations may learn from.

We pray that this book would serve as the springboard for the reeducation of church members, the millennials and the general public about the true face of socialism. This book would serve as significant reminders of the real threats, deceptions, limited freedoms and abusive power of socialism. This book would give many practical insights to the operations of socialism and socialists.

Total Freedom?

If the above stories and the discussion could not explain to you enough the reality of socialism yet, I hope this story may do that well. When my dear Joseph was put into prison because he was a Christian and because he was a rightist, the two counts that were considered as the most serious crimes in those days, the whole family was discriminated and no one even the relative members wanted to get close to them.

If the local people helped the families of the severe criminal like Joseph, they may also be charged with a crime. Thus, people kept distance from Joseph's wife and criticizing her and her children to show their loyalty to the socialist government. It was wintertime and they had no food left and the hunger was so bad that his wife must feed the children with grasses and snow.

She knocked the many doors of the neighbors for help but every door kept closed. She knew that the children could not survive for that long so she quickly asked the relatives to take care of the children, they took the boys away but no one wanted to take away the daughters and she gave away one daughter to a stranger who wanted to adopt the daughter and promised to provide the needs of her innocent daughter.

Her heart was so painful to do so but she had no choice or else her daughter could not make it. She still had one daughter left and the daughter was getting weaker as the days past. She was also weak and exhausted as well but she did not want her daughter to die. So she carried her dying daughter in her arms and knocked every door again, and hoping that they could give something.

She knelt down in front of some homes and cried, "Please help and please give something so that my daughter could survive. The child is innocent." Yes, the heartfelt cries of a mother could not touch the fearful hearts of the people toward socialism and the socialist leaders. The dying child did not open or even move the cruel and emotionless hearts of the socialist leaders.

Do not expect the socialists to have mercy on you when they disliked you. Do not wish that they would spare your wealth and you. Do not hope that they would help you in your desperate moments. Do not dream that they would distribute equal wealth to people. Do not even think that they would eliminate the inequality. They are only good at making promises for their own gains and delivering the havocs.

Yes, the socialist leaders are good at giving people equal poverty. They are great at providing people equal miseries. They are excellent in supplying people equal oppressions. They are super good at sending people equal injustices. They are experts in making people with equal limited freedoms. They are generous in giving people equal limited human rights.

That story of Joseph and his family is just an example of the million deaths caused by the ruthless socialists. Millions of people died because of poverty. Millions of people died because of hard labors. Hundred thousands of people died in prisons and detention centers. Half a million people died as they escaped from the socialist nations and regimes. Do you think that they could forget and forgive the socialists?

At the moment, they could hardly stop thinking about their painful experiences because socialism is very close to them. They may be happy to hear President Trump said, "Tonight, we renew our resolve that America will never be a socialist country." It maybe ok if President Trump win the second term but how about the next candidate and the next socialist like freshman Rep. Alexandria Ocasio-Cortez?

Graham Vyse said in 2018, America saw "the rebirth of the American socialist movement after generations in retreat… "This is a movement, not a moment," says Gonzales." "This is going to take time, and we plant seeds every time we engage a new volunteer to knock doors for the first time… to achieve concrete change in our communities." What seeds could they plant at the doors of the socialist victims?

Thousands of the socialist victims and their families escaped from one socialist country to another country and they did not know that the second country also became a socialist country later and they run again to the U.S. and free countries to escape the socialist regimes. I also run away from one socialist country for live and then I was deported by another socialist country before coming to the U.S.A.

The victims run their lives to escape socialism and socialism still chased after them. What would be the next country that these victims and Americans could run to in a near future? If America were taken over by socialism, please do not forget to take us with you or inform us which country should we run to together because we would be broken into thousand pieces by the socialists because we wrote this book.

CHAPTER 7

FREE FROM THE BURNING FIRES

Whether it is the socialist countries that offer limited freedom and free world like the U.S that offer many freedoms, there are certain things that people of the world could not be free from. Regardless of how powerful the nations are, there is no system, government, country or leader in this world could release people of the nations from the fearful fires of the spiritual attacks and oppressions.

It was about 2600 years ago in Babylon and the modern day Iraq, the powerful king Nebuchadnezzar made an image of gold and set it up on the plain of Dura in the province of Babylon. Then, he called his governors, magistrates and all provincial officials to come together to dedicate and to worship the golden image that king Nebuchadnezzar set up according to Daniel 3.

"Then the herald loudly proclaimed, "Nations and peoples of every language, this is what you are commanded to do: As soon as you hear the sound of the horn, flute, zither, lyre, harp, pipe and all kinds of music, you must fall down and worship the image of god that King Nebuchadnezzar has set up. Whoever does not fall down and worship will immediately be thrown into a blazing furnace" (Daniel 3:4-8).

Then the astrologers reported to king Nebuchadnezzar that Shadrach, Meshach and Abednego did not bow down at the command of the king. King Nebuchadnezzar was furious upon hearing that and he ordered these three friends of Daniel to come and telling them, "But if you do not worship it, you will be thrown immediately into a blazing furnace. Then what god will be able to rescue you from my hand?" (3:15)

"Shadrach, Meshach and Abednego replied to him, "King Nebuchadnezzar, we do not need to defend ourselves before you in this matter. If we are thrown into the blazing furnace, the God we serve is able to deliver us from it, and he will deliver us from Your Majesty's hand. But even if he does not, we want you to know, Your Majesty, that we will not serve your gods or worship the image of gold you have set up."

King Nebuchadnezzar was furious again at their disobedience and the king ordered the furnace to be heated seven times hotter than usual. Then he commanded the strongest soldiers to tie up the three rebels and throw them into the blazing furnace. The furnace was so hot that the flames of fire even killed the strongest soldiers who threw these three friends of Daniel into the furnaces.

Suddenly, "King Nebuchadnezzar leaped to his feet in amazement and asked his advisers, "Weren't there three men that we tied up and threw into the fire?... He said, "Look! I see four men walking around in the fire, unbound and unharmed, and the fourth looks like a son of the gods." Nebuchadnezzar then shouted, "Shadrach, Meshach and Abednego, servants of the Most High God, come out! Come here!"

"So Shadrach, Meshach and Abednego came out of the fire, and the satraps, prefects, governors and royal advisers crowded around them. They saw that the fire had not harmed their bodies, nor was a hair of their heads singed; their robes were not scorched, and there was no smell of fire on them." They were completely fine and king Nebuchadnezzar said in amazement:

"Praise be to the God of Shadrach, Meshach and Abednego, who has sent his angel and rescued his servants! They trusted in him and defied the king's command and were willing to give up their lives rather than serve or worship any god except their own God. Therefore I decree that the people of any nation or language who say anything against the God of Shadrach, Meshach and Abednego be cut into pieces and their houses be turned into piles of rubble, for no other god can save in this way."

Shadrach, Meshach and Abednego were not only saved and freed from the blazing furnace miraculously but they earned the respect from the King Nebuchadnezzar and the people. The king also appointed them in high positions and greatly used them in the province of Babylon. King Nebuchadnezzar also recognized that only God could save them and could do so.

This story revealed the important truth of life that human beings are opened to many attacks. People could be attacked by unfriendly friends or enemies and they could be vulnerable to the tricks and the ruthless attacks of rivals or the cruel leaders. There are enemies whom we know and whom we do not know, whom we may see and whom may not see and they are there to put fires or attacks on us.

The fires represent the attacks, tricks, traps that our rivals set up to go against you and I. The fires could be the hidden plans and evil schemes of our business partners or rivals who want to destroy us so that they could take over our positions, our homes, our shares, our businesses or our wealth and even our life. They could be the false accusations and schemes that aim at destroying our reputations, and names.

There are also invisible enemies that are attacking our lives and people do not often see or recognize though there are times people could feel their presence. The devil sends spiritual attacks and oppressions over people. While people may be unharmed by or may overcome the attacks of rivals, but it is impossible for people to stand against the spiritual attacks without the protection of the Almighty God.

Free From The Fires of The Enemies

The background of the story revealed the fact that the astrologers and the enemies of Shadrach, Meshach and Abednego tried to plot against them. Their enemies knew that Daniel and his three friends would not bow down at the golden image so they asked king Nebuchadnezzar to make a decree that allowed the enemies to kill anyone who did not bow down at the golden image.

The enemies plotted against them and wanted to destroy the three friends because they were jealous of these three administrators. These friends were from the royal family and were the nobble people. They were "young men without any physical defect, handsome, showing aptitude for every kind of learning, well informed, quick to understand, and qualified to serve in the king's palace" (Daniel 1:3-4).

"To these four young men God gave knowledge and understanding of all kinds of literature and learning. And Daniel could understand visions and dreams of all kinds... In every matter of wisdom and understanding about which the king questioned them, he found them ten times better than all the magicians and enchanters in his whole kingdom" (Daniel 1:17, 20).

They were placed in high positions, respected and favored by the king. Even King Nebuchadnezzar fell prostrate before Daniel and paid him honor for the wisdom and the gift he had from God and for the God Daniel worshiped. The king said to Daniel, "Surely your God is the God of gods and the Lord of kings and a revealer of mysteries, for you were able to reveal this mystery" (Daniel 2:46-47).

"Then the king placed Daniel in a high position and lavished many gifts on him. He made him ruler over the entire province of Babylon and placed him in charge of all its wise men. Moreover, at Daniel's request the king appointed Shadrach, Meshach and Abednego administrators over the province of Babylon, while Daniel himself remained at the royal court" (Daniel 2:48-49).

The enemies wanted to take the three friends down from the positions so that they could corrupt and enjoyed their evil lives. These three administrators were so righteous and upright that they prevented the enemies from abuses of powers, crimes, illegal gains for wealth and corruption. The three friends were not willing to compromise to the offers the enemies for evil.

The enemies also felt uneasy with the holy lifestyle of these three friends. The excellent moral lives of the three friends made them feel guilty at the evil things that they did. The consciences of the enemies kept reminding them about the godly lives of these three friends and these three friends did not defy their lives with any evil thing that was not pleasing in God's sight.

The enemies were not happy because they were unmatched to and they could not compete with Daniel and his three friends and administrators. They were jealous because these free friends are promoted and used by the king in high positions. The positions that these three friends had may block the promotions and the benefits of the enemies so the three friends must be get rid off as soon as possible.

You may say, "I am a kind person and I don't have any enemy or unfriendly friend." It is common to think that we may have no unfriendly friends or enemies but you may wrong someone unintentionally and they wanted to revenge on you. You may be deceived by wicked people at their will and you are being attacked. You may be the victims of incurable diseases that you did not even know earlier.

You may be the victims of the cultic groups and you are depressed. You may be the victims of your family members due to conflicts over lands or properties. You may be the preys of your colleagues or business partners and they want to get your businesses or your positions. You may be wrongly accused for a crime or you may be charged with a certain crime when you are innocent.

You may be trapped for sex trade even by your best friends for money sakes. You may be the victims of gangsters for drug dealings. You may be the victims of your peer pressures for murdering someone. You may be the victims of terrorist groups and activities. You may be the victims of the drunk driver and you are paralyzed on your bed for the rest of your lives. Your disability may be the result of a heart attack.

Singer Archie Williams shared his painful and touch story of the wrong legal charge against him on America's Got Talent. The misery and the shame were poured upon Archie when he was suspected of raping a thirty-year old woman on December 9, 1982. Though there were three people who witnessed that Archie was at home during the rape took place but injustice still fell upon him

He was incarcerated because he had no economic ability to defend himself and to fight against the state for the wrong charge. He was charged for the crime that he never did. He was put in prison for 37 years for someone's crimes, wickedness and evil pleasures. He said that he was tried and tested in prison as "days turn into weeks, into months, into years, and into decades. And it is like nightmare."

His dream, his prime, his youth, his passion, his energy were buried in prison for those 37 years. He had to bear all the guilt, shames, loneliness, rejections, humiliations, pains, and the loss of his freedom and his many rights of a free person for 37 years. He could only live and survive those years with hope for freedom, justice and with nightmares of course. That fire of wrong charge devastated his life.

Archie was innocent but he was charged because someone needed to be charged for the crime. Daniel and his three friends were good people but their integrity blocked their enemies the opportunities to accumulate wealth under tables. They loved their God but their devotion to their God was a big offense to people who followed other gods. Their high positions were big obstacles for the great future of their enemies.

Just as Daniel, Shadrach, Meshach and Abednego were attacked because they did not bow down and worship the idol as they were told, you were also attacked by the many fires of other people because you do not bow down or follow their corrupted plan, their unreasonable requests, and their threats. Your rivals set fires at you because you don't compromise your integrity, convictions, beliefs or consciences.

Wilson is used to be a leader of street fighters. His group members and he often fought with other groups to claim their territories. They also got money from protecting businesses and helping business owners to get money from their debtors. He often spent his night at various bars and casinos almost every night for businesses or for enjoying himself.

For people who feared no God and no sins like him, he would soon become a top leader in the mafia world as he was young, powerful and arrogant and he was a fearless fighter. He thought that he could enjoy his life and his status as a leader with money, power and luxurious life. But life always took a surprised turn and Wilson did not know that he was targeted and framed for a deadly attack.

One day, his wife got involved in a fight at a bar and he immediately entered the fight to defend his wife and his people. But he was so drunk on that day so he was beaten up badly. His head was hit open by many bottles of wines and he fell on the floor consciously. His opponents run away quickly as they thought that he was dead. He was brought to the emergency and he was in a coma for a long time.

Nobody thought that he could survive because he was horribly attacked by the other gang members who were not less cruel than he was. But miraculously and surprisingly he awoke from coma though his head was damaged badly at the hard hits. His brain was also damaged for the rest of his life at the diagnosis and analyses of medical experts although he was alive.

His wife and daughter also left him when he needed them most. He also lost his ability to work, he lost his memories, and he lost almost everything except his life. He became homeless and wandered on the street. He was so desperate and he wanted to end his life. He put oil all over his body and burnt himself many times but he was rescued. He wanted to die but he could not even die.

Years later a Christian brought him to church and the believers prayed for him. Miracle took place and God healed him and his mind was slowly restored. Then he found out from his gang members that his wife betrayed him because he was a big threat to other groups due to his aggressive expansion of the territories and they wanted him dead. She made him drunk so he could not fight on that day.

Whether you are a good person or not a good person, a rich or a poor person, you are all vulnerable to the attacks of the unfriendly friends or enemies. Even though many people tried to protect them with the securities systems and arms, yet they were still robbed, attacked and harmed. You may possibly be Free from the Fires of the Enemies but how about the Fires of the Flesh?

Free From The Fires of The Flesh

The Bible teaches us that, "The acts of the flesh are obvious: sexual immorality, impurity and debauchery; idolatry and witchcraft; hatred, discord, jealousy, fits of rage, selfish ambition, dissensions, factions and envy; drunkenness, orgies, and the like. I warn you, as I did before, that those who live like this will not inherit the kingdom of God" (Galatians 5:19-21).

Let us briefly paraphrase these sentences to see the obvious consequences of the fleshy acts. Sexual immorality leads to unfaithfulness and broken marriages. Impurity and debauchery brings about incurable diseases and sicknesses. Idolatry and witchcraft make people superstitious and fearful of the underworld. Hatred is the causes of many cancers, tragedies and crimes.

Discord leads to disagreement and disunity. Jealousy is deadly with evil plans and thoughts of destroying others. Fits of rage are the causes of murdering and imprisonment. Selfish ambition leads to the abuses of power and injustices. Dissensions are the causes of division and conflicts. Drunkenness leads to loss of control and health damages. Orgies lead to addictions and bondages.

▶ As the result, many people are now the HIV victims
▶ As the result, many people are now the victims of broken families
▶ As the result, many people are now the victims of drugs
▶ As the result, many people are now the victims of violence
▶ As the result, many people are now the victims of witchcraft

▶ As the result, many are now the victims of incurable sicknesses and diseases.
▶ As the result, many are now in sufferings and incarceration
▶ As the result, many are now regretting and wailing for what they did and do.
▶ As the result, many are now in the dying bed and wishing for another chance
▶ As the result, many are now in debts and dangers

The fires of the flesh then refer to the many works of the flesh and the negative consequences coming from the exercises of those works of the flesh. Those works of the flesh are against the godly ways. Those who followed the works of the flesh would produce bad consequences of disunity, disorder, destructions, and deaths and they will not receive the eternal life in heaven but eternal punishment in hell.

BE FREE OR NOT BE FREE

Living in the flesh is to live a life that is not pleasing God. It is a sinful and a rebellious life against God. The Bible also teaches that the true seriousness of sin can only begin to be understood when it is seen in terms of a rebellious relationship against God and rejecting attitude to God himself. People do not want their sins to be reckoned and they opposed God who condemns those sins.

Sin is a revolt and rebellion against God. It is man asserting his will against God's will. They say there is no need for God. Man is God himself. Sin is to deny the true God and to accept the worship of the man-made god and idols and objects of creation. They say the sun, the moon, and the star are their gods. They even blaspheme to say that man came from monkeys and a by-product of evolution.

Sin means defying God and fighting against God. Sin means rejecting God and refusing to live for the glory of God. The rebellious people curse God and they choose live in lust, greed, and corruption. They choose to reject God's call to forgive one another, to love one another, to edify one another, to help one another, and to protect one another.

You may say again, "I am a good man, I do no wrong to anyone and I live according to my conscience." Thank God that you are a good man and you are trying to do good things. Yet being a good man does not mean that you are not sinful or free from sins. The Bible says that if anyone says he has no sin, he is deceiving himself and the truth is not in him. All have sinned and missed God's marks for a holy life.

We are all sinners in many ways. The Bible says that even anger or lying is a sin, looking at someone lustfully is a sin, indulging ourselves in game, drug, alcohol, sex is also a sin, knowing what is good and do not do is a sin before God, destroying our bodies is also a sin, and knowing someone's corruption and do nothing about that is a sin before the Lord

The Bible says that knowing someone is in need and do nothing about that is a sin before the Lord, abortion of unborn babies is a sin, premarital sex is a sin, homosexual is a sin, raping is a sin, masturbation is a sin, unnatural sex is a sin, unfaithfulness to your spouse is a sin, thinking yourself has no sin is already a sin before God, and rejecting God as your Creator and Savior is also a sin.

Have you found yourself so addicted in pornography that you could not even control yourself from looking at, kissing and licking those porn pictures?

Have you indulged in sex too much that you cannot control yourself but to imitate the sexual acts that you watch from porn movies?

Have you found yourself driven by sexual needs so badly that you even want to release it on the animals?

Have you found yourself dreaming and engaging in adulterous thoughts when you look at a man or a woman?

Are the lusts of your eyes are burning so strong in your heart and mind that you could ever overcome the strong fire inside of you?

Are you in a rage that you disregard everything and you want to do everything bad things that your thought is leading you?

Those are not the natural desires as you thought, those are the perverted influences and the evil drives of your flesh for things that you even found yourself disgusting but you could not control it any way. This is because your mind, your will and your emotions are under the leading and control of your flesh, desires, the evil influences of this world, sins and the control of the spiritual power to be discussed later.

A few years ago, millions of people were shocked when a recorded video about a sexual exchange that went viral on social media. The few couples involved were the government officials. They found bored to have sexes with their own spouses so they discussed and agreed that they would exchange their spouses with the spouses of their friends for sex to find new feeling and experiences.

The man was almost impotent with his wife yet he became as strong as bull with someone's wife. The wife had no feeling for sex with her husband yet she screamed in satisfaction with someone's husband. One might wonder how was it possible for them to have such a shameful idea and how could the wives and the husband bear to allow the spouse to be used by others? They are not the lone people led by the flesh.

Many people today are driven by the fleshly desires, the immoral lifestyle, and unrestrained freedom that they could not control and overcome themselves but to go to KTV, club bars, strip show or prostitute home for pleasures. Others look for services to rent "a wife" or a "husband." Red Zone districts are not only for men but also for women, and of course for people with unidentified sexes and homosexuals.

Others find themselves at the deadly excitement of car racing, high in drug, lost in scary music, crazy in fighting, or one nightstand with their idols. They brought sicknesses, deaths to themselves and others. There are also so many people were driven by material things, fames and positions that they are willing to sell their bodies, dignities, their integrity, and their souls in order to attend those things

Hundred thousands of families were broken, bankrupted, and destroyed due to the consequences of gambling addiction. Casinos sent their workers to look for wealthy people and they offered these wealthy people with free high-class vacation packages at the casinos with free luxurious hotel, free air tickets with business class, free foods and free credits for gambling. It sounds good to be free but it is not free.

Out of curiosity and fun and joy of the games, many got caught into gambling. The more they lost, the more they wanted to play to get back their losses. Then they were in debt at the many big losses. Then they were arrested and threatened so they had to contact their family members to sell houses, businesses, or factories to pay the debts. Many went bankrupted. Others could not take it and killed themselves.

How about the fire of furious angers? Anger is a double-edged swords, it may help one to release the emotions and pressures, yet when it is wrongly used it may totally destroy someone's life and his or her life. Whether it is the unnatural desires for pleasures or it is one's curiosity for new things, or the cravings for powers, positions, and material things, the fires of the flesh all leave negative consequences.

As the result, you are now the victim of your excitement in gambling
As the result, you are now the victim of the broken relationship
As the result, you found yourself pregnant and going for abortion
As the result, you engage in conflicts to fight and hurt others and yourselves
As the result, you cause someone to die in the high of drugs and you are drugged.

As the result, you are being killed or kill someone
As the result, you end up in prison and serve the life prison
As the result, you destroy your marriage due to unfaithfulness
As the result, you are caught in pains and loneliness due to broken relationships
As the result, you are caught in crimes, guilt and shames

"But the fruit of the Spirit is love, joy, peace, forbearance, kindness, goodness, faithfulness, gentleness and self-control. Against such things there is no law. Those who belong to Christ Jesus have crucified the flesh with its passions and desires. Since we live by the Spirit, let us keep in step with the Spirit. Let us not become conceited, provoking and envying each other" (Galatians 5:22-26).

Those are the precious words that God wants you and I to take to heart seriously. The only way that you could be free from the fires of the flesh is to crucify the flesh with its passions and desires when you are in the Lord Jesus Christ. He would transform your life and you would soon discover that your life starts to bear the fruits of the Spirit of love, joy, peace, forbearance, kindness, goodness...

Then the fruits of the flesh such as sexual immorality, impurity and debauchery; idolatry and witchcraft; hatred, discord, jealousy, fits of rage, selfish ambition, dissensions, factions and envy; drunkenness, orgies, addictions, abortions and many more would be cut off from your life. Praying that you would enjoy your great journey with the Lord Jesus Christ. Are there any more Fires that people face?

Free from the Fires of the Merciless Devils

In 2018, a friend of mine and I talked to a client of my friend as we noticed that something was not right with this client and he was so weary. He started sharing his painful story and he really poured out his heart as I asked, "Why are you looking so tired and sad?" Just a few months ago his wife suddenly got mad and she beat their only child and she smashed the child's head on the wall.

The child died and she went crazy and she acted so strange. The authorities came and inspected the cases and his wife was arrested. The medical report said that his wife had mental problems and this was the cause of her weird actions to kill their child. Medical doctors, researchers and scientists are great, but many of them may not see or believe the spiritual forces behind the act of killing like it is in this case.

I asked the client if his wife had the strange behaviors such as she just sat at a corner of the house and talked to herself, or she heard strange voices, or she saw black shadow or she just sat a place, starred and pointed fingers at a wall or something before the incident took place. He responded that those were the things that puzzled him for a long time about his wife but he did not know why did that happen to her.

I talked to him about some potential causes that could lead people to such weird behaviors such as idol worship, eyewitness of horrible death, involvement in magic, vow making to the spirits in exchange for something, haunted houses, addiction to violent or ghost movies and others. When I talked about ghost movies, the client said, "I think ghost movies may be the cause."

He said that his wife liked violent and ghost movies. He did not like it but he just accompanied her from time to time to watch those movies. His wife really enjoyed the horrible scenes. Sometimes she was scared and sometimes she laughed hysterically. Then she imitated those acts and he tried to stop her from watching ghost movie but it was too late because she was already possessed by the spirits.

People may not realize that there are spiritual forces and evil spirits that are working. The spirits are not only able to influence one's behaviors and to attack people but they are powerful enough to control people's mind. This is called demon-possession. It usually begins with curiosity and fun with games, movies, or magic. Then it comes to a new level of addiction.

The devil uses the addictions and talks to the addicted people through the violent contents, plots and pictures that they are watching and playing. When people are addicted, you find them talk and respond to the games and movies but they did not realize that the devil is talking to them in many ways. As time passes, those addicted people start to lock themselves in the room and they don't talk much to people.

But they talk a lot to the invisible world and the visible images and content. Then their behaviors suddenly changed and their talks also changed. They act according to what they see in the games or movies, in their imagination. People thought that these people have hallucinations but actually these people are in the spiritual world. They cut themselves and they talk to the wall and to object.

They start to have many weird behaviors as the lady who was possessed and killed her daughter in the story above. In most cases, people and doctors would say that these people have mental issues and they need medication and rest. Though they are under medication but they are still "abnormal." Yes, there are many people with mental issues, but many of these people may be under spiritual bondage.

Science may not have answer to the spiritual world because it is beyond their scope but the Bible explains clearly that the jobs of the devils are to steal, to kill and to destroy? "Your enemy the devil prowls around like a roaring lion looking for someone to devour" (I Peter 5:8). The devil is your real enemy and it looks for the opportunities to come into your life and to take control over you and your life.

The devil is going to steal your joy and happiness
The devil is going to steal your humility and good morals
The devil is going to steal your opportunities to know God and His salvation

It is going to kill your passion and your dream for God
It is going to kill your trust and faith in God
It is going to kill your soul in the lake fires

It is going to destroy your happiness and your marriage
It is going to destroy your health and your home.
It is going to destroy your life and future in sins or prison

It is going to lure you into suicides and deadly practices
It is going to inflict diseases and sicknesses upon you
It is going to control your thoughts and movements
It is going to torture your mind and your body
It is going to give you more temptations and traps to bind you

You may say, "Mr. Evangelist, I don't worship idols or provoke evil spirits, I don't think that the evil spirits would controlled me." Many of you may not hear about this topic before and others may not believe in the existence of the spiritual world and the devils. You may just take this opportunity to learn something new first whether you agree or disagree, believe or not believe.

It is recommendable that you don't worship idols or engaging in magic and witchcrafts. You should not have anything to do with psychic readings, tarots, palm readings, fortunetelling, calling the death or spirits... Yet, even you don't have direct contact with the idols or evil spirits but that does not mean you would not come into contacts with them or would they spare you because you don't worship them.

There are many ways that the evil spirits could attack people or to take control over you. Sometime you accidentally hit an object on the road that is possessed by the evil spirits then the evil spirits come into your life. Sometimes you accidentally touched or purchased an object that is possessed by the spirits, then you are haunted and tortured by the spirits.

Sometime you accidentally picked up an object where a dead spirit lives and then you begin to act weirdly. Sometimes you are swimming in places that there were people drowned to deaths, then you find yourselves thinking of committing suicides. Sometimes you accidentally go to an area where the spirits are worshipped by people, then you start to feel something that disturbs you.

Sometimes you accidentally ate certain foods that were offered to idols and spirits but you did not know and then you begin to hear strange sounds and voices. Sometimes you played black magic for funs, and then you see many black shadows appearing in front of you or in your dream. Sometimes you accidently purchased a house where someone was killed, and then your nightmares begin.

Those are just some cases that you may accidentally encounter and you did not even know that those things are affecting you. The evil people and the witchdoctors today are setting up many spiritual traps so that you would fall into their control. Please also take look around you when people of so many religions have brought their idols and spirits, charms to cast spells to people who are unfriendly or unkind to them.

One day a cousin of mine picked up a precious ring in her garden and she kept it for herself. Soon after that her husband noticed dramatic changes in her behavior. She used to be a very obedient wife and listening to her husband always. Her husband was an atheist and he forced her to give up her Christian faith and she did listen to her husband to give up her faith to follow him.

But now her attitudes were changed, she began to scold her husband. She became violent to him and she was extremely strong physically. Violence and incredible strength are the usual signs of people who are demon-possessed because the spirits are working inside demon-possessed people. She did not really sleep at night but sat at corner and talking to herself or someone who was invisible.

Soon, she did not allow her husband to touch her and she even hit him whenever he came close to her. Then she chased him out of their bedroom and she began to act violently and many times she threw things at her husband. Her husband called the father-in law who was a pastor for help and he described the situation and the strange behaviors of his wife to the father-in law.

The father-in law immediately knew what was going on and he told the son-in law that his wife was demon-possessed and he asked the son-in law to accept Jesus and to pray for the deliverance of his wife and telling him to take his wife to the church. But his son-in law refused to accept Jesus and did not believe in the spiritual world or that his wife was demon-possessed.

As time pass, the son-in law could not bear any longer with the terrible situations of his family and the weird behaviors of his wife that caused him and children sleepless nights so he just sent his wife to the church for deliverance prayer though he still refused to accept God. When his wife was brought near to the church, she refused to come in as she said, "This is the house of God, I don't want to go there.'

During one of the delivering sessions, another cousin of mine, a church coworker and I prayed for my cousin who was demon-possessed. We prayed for God's protection upon us and we proclaimed in the name of Jesus to bind the evil spirit and casted it out of her body. We could see clearly the spiritual battle to take place as the evil spirit fought back because it did not want to go out of her body.

The evil spirit began to manifest through grinding of her teeth, biting her tongue or shaking her head repeatedly. The evil spirit also shouted and shook her body. The devil kept on saying, "No, I will not go out of her. She is mine. She is mine." Her eyes turned red and the devil closed her mouth so that she would not say it loud or repeat the phrase, "In the Name of Jesus."

We asked the evil spirit, "Where do you come from and how do you get in her body?" The devil said, "I love her. I want her but that man captured her heart and she married him. So I was broken hearted and I went to join the army." The devil also said that before the man went to join the army, he went to take a look at my cousin again and he wanted to talk to her for the last time.

But he was shy to talk to her and he dared not give the ring to her so he just left the ring in her garden and hopefully she could pick it up somehow. We continued to ask the evil spirit, "Where is the man now?" The devil said, "He was killed." Then we again commanded the devil to go out of her and the spirit shook her body but it did not want to go out of her yet because she was dear to the evil spirit.

As we prayed, we also asked the fire of the Holy Spirit to burn the evil spirit. The spirit shouted, "So hot, so hot. I will go out. I will go out." We asked, "Where will you go?" The spirit said, "I will go to the temple to eat some fruits and I will come back soon." We commanded the spirit to go out and that it was not allowed to come back into her body again because it had no right to come back again.

At that moment, the spirit suddenly said, "Oh, I will go back and I will go to that fat man inside the room." Suddenly, the husband of my cousin who was praying with me at that time, run out from his room as he shouted, "I believe, I believe." He run to us and said, "I want to accept Jesus. I want to accept Jesus. Pray for me now." We were so surprised and shocked at that and we did not know what really happened.

Of course we were so glad to pray for him and dedicate him to the Lord as we had been praying hard for the salvation of his soul for so long but he always objected us and anyone who shared the Gospel to him before. This cousin-in-law of mine was an atheist and he always persecuted my cousin for believing in God and serving God. My cousin shed a lot of tears in many prayers for him get to know the Lord Jesus.

Many pastors and family also shared the Gospel to him but he just disregard whatever the things they said. On that day, when we brought the cousin who was demon-possessed to his house and prayed for the deliverance, he was inside of his room. He thought that all of us were superstitious and crazy. He talked to himself that the cousin had mental problem so we should send her to mental hospital.

As we prayed he even mocked at us in his head and just laughed. But out of curiosity he just listened to our conversations with the evil spirit, and he said to himself, "These people are crazy. I don't believe that people are possessed by demons or evil spirits and what can the evil spirit do to me." At the moment when he said that, the evil spirit said that it would enter the fat man who was sitting inside the room.

This was the reason why my cousin-in-law suddenly run out of his room and dedicating his life to God. Now he understood that the evil spirits were real and they could possess his life just like the other cousin of mine. How could a mental person know that he was inside the room? How could a mental person know that he was fat without seeing him? How could the mental person know his thought and his mocks?

How could a mental person know that he did not believe when he just spoke to himself? How could a mental person know how to respond to him exactly the moment he thought the evil spirits could not do anything to him? This was not a coincident. How was it possible for a mental person to answer at the command in the name of Jesus? The only possible conclusion was God and the spirits were real.

He wanted to accept God because he now knew that God had the power to cast out the demons and the evil spirits in His name. He wanted to believe God because he was now scared of being possessed and tortured by the devil. He now knew that how scary and miserable it was for someone to be controlled by the devil that he or she could loose the consciousness. He did not want to be like that cousin.

Please bear in mind that the power of darkness is not just waiting for people to fall into their schemes but it is also working actively to get people under their control. People who know that the existence of the spiritual power is real and they only know to look for witchdoctors, psychics and spiritual healers to pray for their deliverances from the attacks of the evil spirits and peace would come back to them.

People did not know that even the witchdoctors are powerful but people could never be freed totally from the control of the evil spirits. The witchdoctors may help people to appease the evil spirits that are less powerful than the powerful evil spirits that they are worshiping. That is how the spiritual world is operated. The witchdoctors are still under the control of the evil spirits that they are worshipping.

Thus people could never save themselves from the curses of witchdoctors
Thus people could never save themselves from the spells of witchdoctors
Thus people could never save themselves from the spiritual oppressions
Thus people could never save themselves from the terrible nightmares
Thus people could never save themselves from the devil's hand

But they are under fears and superstitions at the power of the darkness
But they are under spiritual bondages and oppressions of the evil spirits
But they are under curses and spells of the witchdoctors
But they are under the tortures and nightmares of the devils
But they are under the control and deception of demons

Maybe you have heard about the haunted houses and even you do not believe in the spiritual world or the existence of the evil spirits but you can hardly deny the fears or hair-standing moments when you heard about the stories of the haunted house. You maybe among the many people who did not believe the haunted house and you want to sleep in the haunted house to prove that there was not ghost as others did.

Yet, these people could not help but run out of the haunted houses in the middle of the night because they were scared to death at the manifestations of the devils. Yes, the witchdoctors may come and help the owner to appease the spirits if the evil spirits that the witchdoctors are more powerful than the evil spirits dwelling in that haunted house, but the evil spirits are still there and more powerful spirits come in.

Then the owner must offer so many foods to the evil spirits and money to the witchdoctors so that the evil spirits would not disturb them, but the evil spirits are still there and they would continue to cause you more troubles.

A lady came to me and my coworkers one day and she asked how to overcome the evil spirit as she heard others about the deliverance ministry that we did. She said that her house was haunted by the devils and she could not stay there at her house. She could not do anything else but to run away from that house because it was horrible and she was terrified at the presence of the evil spirits.

Some years ago she bought a house from an old woman and she was so happy because she could purchase the house at a cheap price. She was also happy because the owner gave her all the expensive and nice furniture in the house for free. The owner said that she was old and she was now alone so she did not need many things and she already had all things she needed at her new place.

After some renovation, the new owner moved into her new house. The first few weeks seemed to be fine yet she felt there was something strange in the house. She felt as if someone was lying down besides her and touching her when she slept. Sometimes she was awaken by some the sounds of spoons hitting the rice bowl or the sound of a bowl falling on the floor and broken, or noises in the kitchen.

She woke up and she went to the kitchen to check but everything was fine. She often heard the knocking sound on the door in the night. She went out to see but no one was there knocking at the door. As an atheist, she did not believe about the spirits and she was not afraid of the spirits before. But now she felt nervous and she was even scared when she heard those noises or sounds again.

So she called her boyfriend to come and stayed with her. While they were sleeping, their bed was moving around and was shaken violently as if the spirits were getting very upset. Her boyfriend was so scared and just run away and he did not want to come and stay there anymore. But where could she go? Then she looked for the previous owner and she asked what was going on in the house.

The old lady told her the truth that her husband died inside the house. After knowing the truth she went back home and she offered foods to the spirits hoping that they would find new place and would not disturb her any longer. But the same things happened, and she could feel the presence of the spirits when she slept. Out of her desperation she shouted and talked to the death spirit one night.

She said, "I am not your wife, why don't you go to your wife. I bought this home and this house does not belong to you anymore. Please go to your wife and do not disturb me." At the advise of her friends, she went to the temple the next day to ask the monks to help her. The monk gave her a dog and she had to pay a lot of money for that special dog and she thought that her troubles would be gone soon.

This dog would bark whenever the spirits came and the dog did bark in the night but that was all the dog could do. It could only bark but it had no power to drive the spirits away. Every time the dog barked, she got scared and more worried. She asked her friends to come and stayed with her but they were already frightened at the many scary things that she told them so they dare not come.

She looked for one witchdoctor to another at the advise of people and it cost her a lot of money but she still felt the presence of the spiritual power. One day, when she was taking a bath, she suddenly saw a face of an Asian man appearing on the wall of her bathroom. She thought it was the coincidence that the face was formed by the water or the vapor of the hot water.

She was scared of course but she took courage to wipe that face out and thinking that everything would be ok. But then the face appeared again and she thought that she was thinking too much and that was why she saw that face again. So she wiped that face out again and then she saw the face appeared again. At that moment she screamed and quickly run out of the bathroom and out of that house.

Since that day, she never dared to go back to her house. She tried to sell that house but her haunted house was now known to people in her city so no one dared to buy that house. She was quite a courageous lady I would say to live in that house for so long. She was also blessed because she was not possessed by the devil yet. If she were to stay in that house a bit longer, she would be in a worse condition.

Just like many of you, she was an atheist and she did not believe in the existence and power of the spiritual world but now she did. She was not afraid of the spirits and now she was. She did not believe that the evil spirits could attack her or do anything harm to her, but now she went through shocking and terrifying experiences. She thought she could overcome the darkness power but she must run for life now.

You might now be curious to ask what would happen to her and her house after she came to know the Lord Jesus Christ. If she believed in God before, she might not go through those horrible experiences even she purchased the haunted house. She could experience the victory and the defeat of the evil spirits at the name of the Lord Jesus Christ. Yes, at that name of Jesus, the evil spirits would run away.

Because there is power in the Name of Jesus
Because there is restoration in the Name of Jesus
Because there is deliverance in the Name of Jesus
Because there is breakthrough in the Name of Jesus
Because there is victory in the Name of Jesus and that is the sure promise of God.

The good news for you is that you can overcome the power of the evil spirits when you are protected by God. God also give you the power to defeat the evil spirits in His name. When you don't have God as your Savior, you are under the oppressions and possessions of the devils but when God is the Lord and Savior of your life, the devils and the evil spirits must obey your commands in the name of the Lord Jesus.

The name of Jesus has power and that is real because His name is above all names, "that at the name of Jesus every knee should bow, in heaven and on earth and under earth, and every tongue confess that Jesus Christ is Lord, to the glory of God the Father." At the name of Jesus, the devils could not stand but to flee and God allows you and I to use His name to command and devils must obey.

There is also another fire that you and I could not escape without the power of God and His assurance. You and I could be free from the Fire of Hell when we are accepted by God and when He wrote our names in the Book of Life. Why don't you come to God just as we do and asking God for your name to be written in the Book of Life so that you could experience the eternal life that only God could give.

Free From The Burning Fire of Hell

Just like people could never be freed from the fires of the devils, no one could ever be Free from the Burning Fire of Hell without God. There is hope that you may avoid from the Fires of the unfriendly friends or the enemies. There might be the possibility that that you could get out of the Fires of the Flesh. There might be chances that you may be exempted from the Fires of the Merciless Devils.

But there is no way and no remedy that you could escape from the the lake of fires without Christ. The Bible says that the wage of sin is death, the eternal death that everyone must face soon or later. Please be reminded of a very important truth that no one can escape the eternal death and no religion or leader can help you escape the eternal punishment when his or her sins are not forgiven.

The Bible says that, "do not be afraid of those who kill the body but cannot kill the soul. Rather, be afraid of the One who can destroy both soul and body in hell" (Matthew 10:28 and Luke 12:4-5). "If your right hand causes you to stumble, cut it off and throw away. It is better for you to lose one part of your body than for your whole body to go into hell" (Matthew 5:30).

There is good news for you and that your sins could be forgiven by God so that you would face the eternal death but have the eternal life. Your sins would be washed away in the blood of the Lord Jesus Christ if you recognize your sins and confess your sins as God promised that, "If we confess our sins, he is faithful and just and will forgive us our sins and purify us from all unrighteousness" (I John 1:9).

Some of you may say, "Mr. Writer, what you write is great, but my religion, my culture and my atheist teachers teach me that I am not a sinner. I may have mistakes but that is not a sin. I may do something wrong but that is not a sin." Thank you for your insightful thought. Many people tried hard to explain away from sins so that they may not live in guilt and shames but they could not escape from it.

- ▸ Do you think that stealing, robbing and destroying others are just mistakes?
- ▸ Do you think that lying, hurting and deceiving others are just mistakes?
- ▸ Do you think that adultery, unfaithfulness, and deceiving are just mistakes?
- ▸ Do you think that fornication, incest, and sexual maniac are just mistakes?
- ▸ Do you think that enmities, strife, and jealousy are just mistakes?

- ▸ Do you think that murdering and killing people are just mistakes?
- ▸ Do you think forcing and hurting others for personal gains are just mistakes?
- ▸ Do you think that drug smuggling and money laundering are just mistakes?
- ▸ Do you think that human massacre and chemical weapons are just mistakes?
- ▸ Do you think abortion and violence are just mistakes?

I believe that now you will not think those things are just mistakes but human intentions. They are sins and they are committed by the willful and evil thoughts and desires. I believe that now you agree with me that people have sinned and fall short of the glory of God. I believe that now you will recognize that you have also committed many of those sins in your life. The destination for sinners is hell.

Hell is not a product of imagination or man-made product but it is real. Hell is the place for evildoers and the people who rejected the salvation offered by the Lord Jesus Christ "For God so loves the world that he gave his one and only Son, that whoever believes in him shall not perish but have eternal life" (John 3:16). Evildoers and ungodly people are to suffer and face the wrath of God in hell.

Hell is not a place for vacation and then you may go back as you please but it is a place of no return. It is the designated place for those who say that they don't need God and they are God. Hell is not a club bar where you could dance and enjoy but hell is a place of suffering and burning with fires and pains. Hell is the place for those who rejected the grace and love of God.

Hell is place of eternal punishment. It is the place where your whole body is thrown into the fiery lake of fire of burning sulfur (Rev. 19:20). If the blazing furnace of king Nebuchadnezzar was seven times hotter than usual, then hell is even 1000 times hotter than the blazing furnace of king Nebuchadnezzar. The furnace of the king would burn people to death but hell would burn people alive in pain and horror

Hell is not a place for fun but it is a place of condemnation and full of tears and agonies as the Bible says. It is the place for people that the Bible says, "You snakes! You brood of vipers! How will you escape being condemned to hell? (Matthew 23:33). "They will be punished with everlasting destruction and shut out from the presence of the Lord and from the glory of his might" (II Thessalonians 1:9).

You may say, "I am not afraid at your scaring message about hell." This is not to threaten you. This is to let you know about the reality of hell and to warn you about the real consequences of the fire of your enemies and of your flesh. This is not to scare you, but this is to tell you the truth about the fires of the devils and that the fires of hell is not just scary, but it is really horrible and it is real.

This message about hell is not a fairy tale, it is the biblical truth, and "Anyone whose name was not found written in the book of life was thrown in the lake of hell" (Rev. 20:15). Hell is the place "for the cowardly, the faithless, the detestable, as for murderers, the sexually immoral, sorcerers, idolaters, and all liars, their portion will be in the lake that burns with fire and sulfur, which is the second death" (Rev. 21:8).

Hell is the place that people rejected God to be thrown into the blazing furnace or the fiery lake of burning sulfur where there will be weeping and gnashing of teeth. You do not have to wait for that day to come and you may choose to be in a better place called heaven after life on earth. Heaven is the place for eternal life where there is no more pains or tears. It is the place for people who are redeemed.

You may ask, "My religion taught me that Jesus is only a good man. He is only a prophet. He is not God so how can he saves me from hell?" The Lord Jesus Christ is no doubt a good man and a great prophet but the Lord Jesus is not just a good man and a great prophet. He is the King of kings and the Lord of lords, and he is God. That is why even the devils are afraid of Him and listened to His command.

Can any prophet have the power to forgive people's sins? Only God can
Can any prophet be born without sins? Only God has no sin
Can any prophet have the power to cast out demons in his name? Only God can.
Can any prophet have the power over death? Only God can
Can any prophet could say, "I am the Way, the Truth, and the Life." Only God can.

Can any prophet save you from the death of sins? Only God can
Can any prophet save you from the punishment of eternal death? Only God can
Can any prophet save you from the lake of fires? Only God can
Can any prophet save you from the oppressions of the devils? Only God can
Can any prophet save you from the sufferings in hell? Only God can

No one died on the cross to save you and I except the Lord Jesus.
No friend lived a sinless life to save you and I except the Lord Jesus.
No one took our sins on our behalf except the Lord Jesus.
No leader could purchase our lives from the control of devils except the Lord Jesus

No scientist could resurrect us from death except the Lord Jesus.

No theory could set us free from sins except the Lord Jesus.
No technology could offer you and I the eternal life except the Lord Jesus.
No ideology could set us free from addictions except the Lord Jesus.
No philosophy could wash away your sin and my sin except the Lord Jesus.
No religion could redeem us from the eternal punishment except the Lord Jesus.

Only one powerful name could save you from sins and His name is Jesus
Only one beautiful name could transform your life and His name is Jesus
Only one amazing name could heal you from all sicknesses and His name is Jesus
Only one incredible name could deliver you from the devils and His name is Jesus
Only one glorious name could give you eternal life and His name is Jesus.

Free By The Fire of The Holy Spirit

Do not wait any longer. As the Bible says, "Today if you hear His voice, do not harden your hearts as you did in the rebellion" (Hebrew 3:15). Just obey and open your mouth and call upon His Name. What is keeping you from praying and calling on His name now? Do not hesitate any longer, your freedom is just a step away and your deliverance is just at hand at your call.

▶ He will pull you out of the drowning sea of drunkenness and losses
▶ He will pull you out of the nightmare storms in pit of hell and home violence
▶ He will pull you out of the tsunami in drug addictions and terrible abuses
▶ He will pull you out of the evil waves in party life and corruptions
▶ He will pull you out of the painful storms in broken relationship and homes

- He will pull you out of the sinking sands of marriages and brokenness
- He will pull you out of the dark clouds of despairs and disappointments
- He will pull you out of the raging waters of agonizing soul and spirit
- He will pull you out of the flaming fires of sexual desires and lusts
- He will pull you out of the electric shocks of unfaithfulness and betrayals

- He will deliver you from oppressions or any forms of tortures
- He will grant you the desires of your hearts and your dreams
- He will heal your wounds and your hurts
- He will heal your sickness and your diseases tonight
- He will set us free today because His Truth will set us free.

God will save our body, soul and spirit. We will be saved from our broken relationships. We will be saved from our hurtful emotions. We will be saved from our sinful minds. We will be saved from the terrible nightmares and the generational curses. We will be saved from the spells of the witchdoctors and the attacks of the darkness power. We will be saved from the eternal death.

When we call on His name, salvation is at our doorstep. Salvation is a promise and an assurance from God for you and I. Salvation is a free offer and a precious gift from God for you and I. It is a mercy and a grace from God for you and I. His promise is "If we confess our sins, He is faithful and just and will forgive us our sins and purify us from all unrighteousness" (I John 1:9). He will save us

- From our terrible sins and evil deceptions.
- From eternal punishments and death in hell
- From every curses and incurable sickness
- From terrible violence and abuses
- From every bondage and addictions.
- **Can your religion and your knowledge save you from those things? No. Only the Name of Jesus does**

- ▶ From the horrible oppression and attacks of the devils
- ▶ From the generation curses and spells of witchdoctors
- ▶ From your emotional depression and unforgiveness.
- ▶ From the terrible nightmares and fears.
- ▶ From the wraths and eternal punishment of God
- ▶ **Can your political party and your wisdom save you from those things? No. Only the Name of Jesus does.**

The sad news for you and I is that no one except the Lord Jesus Christ is willing to die on the cross on the behalf of your sins and mines. No friend except the Lord Jesus Christ lives a sinless life to save you and I from our sins. No one except the Lord Jesus Christ would take your sins and mines upon him. No philosophy or ideology except the Lord Jesus Christ who washed away our sins.

No religion except the Lord Jesus Christ who redeemed you and I from the punishment of eternal death. No political or religious leader except Jesus who purchased our lives from the control of the devils. No technology except the Lord Jesus Christ can offer you and I the eternal life. Only his name can save us and that is the beautiful name, the powerful name, and the glorious name of Jesus Christ.

The Lord Jesus is here to bring transformations for your communities and your lives. He is here to bless you, your family and your country. When Jesus is here miracles will take place. When Jesus is here your lives will be transformed. When Jesus is here there is a releasing of His unlimited power to save and to heal and deliver. When Jesus is here your lives will never be the same. You got to believe that.

There is another good news for you is that you could be filled with the Fire of the Holy Spirit. That is the spiritual power, regeneration, transformation and anointing from God that you would receive when you are coming to him, and searching for God and the gift of the Holy Spirit that God promises to give to His children. The fire of the Holy Spirit would empower you and I for witnessing about God.

When we are filled with that fire of the Holy Spirit, the supernatural power of God would be manifested in us and you would experience that supernatural power to break your addictions and your evil control. You would have the power to cast out demons that you were under bondages you had no power upon before. That power is manifested in you to bring healing and miracles to you and others.

When we are filled with the fire of the Holy Spirit, we could feel the joy and the freedom that we could never experience before when we were still under the shackles of devil. We would be edified, encouraged and filled with passion for God and others. When we are touched by and filled with the fire of the Holy Spirit we would see many great things happening in front of us.

The fire of the Holy Spirit will burn away all filthiness
The fire of the Holy Spirit will burn away all uncleanliness
The fire of the Holy Spirit will burn away all unhealthy desires

The fire of the Holy Spirit will empower you to overcome the fires of the enemies
The fire of the Holy Spirit will empower you to overcome the fires of the flesh
The fire of the Holy Spirit will empower you to overcome the fires of the devils

The fire of the Holy Spirit will surround you and protect you
The fire of the Holy Spirit will edify you and anoint you
The fire of the Holy Spirit will sanctify you and make you whole.

Please do not forget to seek God for that fire of the Holy Spirit. Your life would never be the same and you would experience the fact that you could demonstrate the Gospel with the power of the Holy Spirit just as the apostles, the disciples and many great men and women who walked and are walking in the demonstrations of the supernatural power to bring salvation, breakthroughs, healings and deliverance.

Prayer of Dedication and Confession

The Bible says, "If we confess our sins, he is faithful and just and will forgive us our sins and purify us from all unrighteousness" (I John 1:9). "If you declare with your mouth, "Jesus is Lord," and believe in your heart that God raised him from the dead, you will be saved" (Romans 10:9). Yes, you will be saved by calling on His name, confessing your sins and receiving him into your life as your Lord and Savior.

If you are willing to rededicate your life to Him or if you willing to accept Him as your Lord and Savior, kindly pray this prayer of confession and declaration. This prayer is only a basic

Dear Lord Jesus Christ,

I thank you for your love and your promises of salvation. I understand now that you were born of the Virgin Mary to this world to seek and save a lost like me. I know that you died on the cross as a ransom for my sins and my life. You were buried and you rose again from death to life to give me the power to live and overcome sins and her temptations. You ascended to heaven to prepare a place of eternity for me.

You will come back again to reign and to bring the final judgment to the world and I will reign with you as your child. I recognize that I am a sinner and I need your forgiveness of my sins and my pasts. I am willing to follow you and learn more about you from your words. I am willing to open my heart and accept you as my Lord and my Savior for the rest of my life. Please transform my life according to your words.

In the Name of Jesus, I ask the blood of Jesus to cover me and cleanse me from all of my sins and the original sins. In the Name of Jesus, I break every curse away from my life and my family. In the Name of Jesus, I break every sickness and diseases away from my body and my home. In the Name of Jesus, I ask for your protection and blessings over my life and my family.

Thank you Lord Jesus for dying on the cross to redeem my life. Thank you Lord Jesus for your resurrection power. Thank you Lord Jesus for the everlasting life. I dedicate my life and my family into your hand. May your grace and goodness follow me all the days of my life! May your will and your plan be done in my life! May your protection and abundant blessings be upon me and my family!

Thank you Lord. I pray this in the Name of Jesus. Amen.

Millions of Americans Must Come Together For This

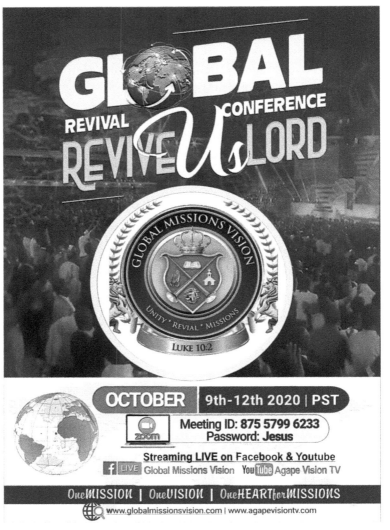

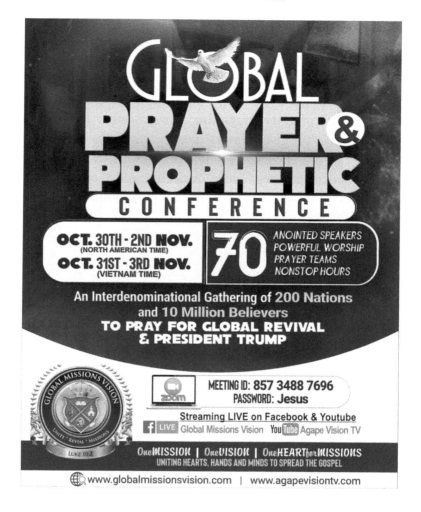

We Are Called For Such A Time As This:

Connecting 1 Million Believers To Pray For The Global Unity, Missions and Revival, Vision 20% and President Trump and Vice President Mike Pence, America and The 2020 Presidential Election

Three-Month-Challenge: For Global Believers To Pray, To Connect, To Serve and To Be On Fire For God. Will You Take The Challenge?

Global Missions Vision Is Called To Bring The Global Body Of Christ To Come Together In Prayer, Repentance, Unity, Missions and Revival

To Prepare for the Global Revival and Mission Movement. October 9-12 Global Revival Conference and October 30-November 2nd Global Prayer and Prophetic Conference aims at connecting 1 million believers to pray together for America and Americans.

The global Body of Christ will also come together through zoom conference to pray for global revival and to pray for nations that have been affected by coronavirus. Millions of believers would specifically pray the President Trump will be reelected and God would bring American believers and churches together for a powerful time of renewal and revival.

America and American believers are just a step away from the losses of the religious freedom, precious rights, great morals, godly values and freedom if the left, the radicals and the socialists were to take over the U.S. Their radical, ungodly and dangerous ideologies would soon turn America to another Venezuela if the left, the radicals and the socialists were to take over the U.S.

Then, millions of people would run for lives to seek asylum in other countries just as millions of victims have been running away from their socialist countries and tyrannies to the U.S. and to make the U.S. a new home and a new county. It is the critical time that American believers need to realize the coming destruction and to come together to support President Trump and to protect America from the wicked plans of the ungodly leaders.

The Global Body of Christ would accomplish this goal when each of the pastors, leaders and believers is willing to give a hand to connect believers and churches by forming one of the following supporting teams? The time is short and we need prompt actions from each of you. Are you willing to partner with Global Missions Vision to form the supporting group through social media?

100 Mission Supporting Teams: Any leader or believer is called to form a supporting group on the social media and invite 30-300 friends for the group to pray. Will you be willing to open 1 supporting group?

Supporting Team 1:   30- 300 Gideon
Supporting Team 2-100:   30-300 Gideon

100 Prayer Teams: Any believer, prayer warrior or leader may form a prayer group on the social media and invite 30-300 friends and believers to the group. GMV will have Zoom accounts available for prayer warriors who are willing to form a prayer team and arranging team members to take turn to intercede for the global revival and America on Zoom.

Prayer Team 1:   30-300 Gideon
Prayer Team 2-100:   30-300 Gideon

100 Church Supporting Teams: Any pastor or leader or small group leader may form a church supporting team by inviting his or church members into this group on the social media, and pray for the global revival, missions and the local church.

Church Supporting Team 1:   30-300 Gideon
Church Supporting Team 2-100: 30-300 Gideon

100 Supporting Nations: Any pastor or leader from countries of the world may form a group of pastors, leaders, ministry team leaders and believers for their nations and encourage leaders and believers to pray for the global revival. Praying that every American church would mobilize their church members to pray for America in this critical time.

National Team 1:   30-300 Gideon
National Team 2-100:   30-300 Gideon

100 Supporting Departments: Any person is called to form a supporting group of friends from your companies or departments such as educator group, lawyer group, children ministry group, youth group… to pray for the global revival. Praying that members of various departments would pray for America in this critical time.

Department 1:   30-300 Gideon
Department 2-100:   30-300 Gideon

Kindly let us know if you are willing to start a supporting team, a prayer team, a national team, a department team or a church supporting team so we can be connected and pray together. That is how we can mobilize church members from every sector around the world to pray and to take actions for missions. But this approach only works if you are taking action to form a supporting group.

Basically, supporting teams and members would do the intercessory; they also encourage group members to send out flyers, videos, information of the events to friends. Supporting members also invite friends to attend their churches or ministries. Group leaders may also challenge group members to participate in church's missions or ministries.

It is only about 100 days away from the 2020 Presidential Election in the U.S. It is impossible for 1 person or 1 church to mobilize 1 million believers to be connected and pray together. But with the great supports of the global Body of Christ, we can make it together and it is you and your networks could make the number of 100 groups to 1000 groups and even more when we are trusting God and standing together for such a time as this.

Please contact GMV, if you are willing to start a supporting group: nationsrevivals@yahoo.com

Please Make Sure That You Would Post This Message On Your Social Media, Share The Message and Send The Message To Every Friends and Believers. Your Brave Actions Today Would First Save America and Million Americans and Would Bring About A Great Revival That We Had Never Seen That Before. Please let us know if You Are Called To Pray Together With Global Missions Vision and To Trust God To Make This Vision To Come To Pass. Amen

The 3-Month-Challenge Begins Now. Will You Take The Challenge Now?

One Vision, One Mission and One Heart For Missions
Uniting Hearts, Hands and Minds To Bring
The Gospel Back To Jerusalem

The Promise: if my people, who are called by my name, will humble themselves and pray and seek my face and turn from their wicked ways, then I will hear from heaven, and I will forgive their sin and will heal their land (II Chronicles 7:14)

Theme:	Revive Us Lord! (Global Revival Conference)
What:	Revival USA!
Time:	October 9-12, 2020 (70 Nonstop Hours)
	(Friday @10am till 12 Noon of Monday, PST)
Through:	Zoom Meeting ID: 817 4071 8671 (Password: vpf)

Theme:	We Are Your People
What:	Global Prayer and Prophetic Conference
Time:	Oct. 30, 31, Nov. 1-2, 2020 (70 Nonstop Hours)
	(Friday @10am till 12 Noon of Monday)
Through:	Zoom Meeting ID: 826 3850 4362 (Password: Jesus)

The Vision of Global Missions Vision is to connect churches around the world for the global revival and to mobilize the Body of Christ for world missions. This needs not only the global Body of Christ to come together for Unity but also for Missions and Revival. Global Missions Vision partners with national churches to carry out crusades, evangelistic events and mission mobilization.

Global Missions Vision also partners with nations and regions of the world to carry out Vision 20% with the local churches in the region so that there will be an increase of 20% of the population in their villages, cities, counties, provinces, states and nations to come to know the Lord Jesus Christ as their Lord and Savior. That is the long term plan.

For 2020, millions of believers around the world need to come together to pray for nations and millions of families that have been affected by coronavirus, the economic crisis, unemployment, disasters, violence… We pray that God would bring healing and restoration. At the same time let the global Body of Christ also prays that millions of people would open their hearts to receive the Lord Jesus Christ as their Lord and Savior through this trouble time.

Importantly, millions of believers also need to come together to pray for America from the destructions of the leftist and liberal, radical, atheist and ungodly leaders, so that God continuities to bless this nations to even send more missionaries to nations to accomplish the Great Commission in partnership with nations of the world. This is also the call for American believers to come back to God and confirm their faith in God.

So the September Global Worship and Revival Congress, October Global Revival Conference (October 9-12) and November Global Prayer and Prophetic Conference (Oct. 30-Nov.2, 2020) aims at connecting a million believers to pray for President Trump, Vice President Mike Pence and of course America and Americans and that there would be a great revival in America when American believers are coming together in Unity, Missions and Revival.

These events present 60-70 nonstop hours of God's word, praise and worship, prayers, repentance and calling out to the Lord for His mercy and touch at His promise, "if my people, who are called by my name, will humble themselves and pray and seek my face and turn from their wicked ways, then I will hear from heaven, and I will forgive their sin and will heal their land." (II Chronicles 7:14)

These events will be interpreted and operated in 10-15 major languages or more of the world depending on the availability of interpreters. Each language needs 30-50 interpreters, will you serve to make your languages available to your people. Each even presents more than 300 powerful speakers in many languages, 100 praise and worship teams, 100 prayer teams, 100 dance teams from 100 nations.

GMV needs 3,000-30,000 supporting members to pray for the event, connect GMV to pastors, worship teams, prayer teams, dance teams, media teams... Members of the supporting teams also send information, flyers, videos, interviews of these events to millions of people and inviting them to pray together for the global revival and America 2020. Will you form a supporting team with 30 members through a social media to do this?

In order to mobilize 195 nations of believers to pray together for Unity, Missions and Revival of the nations, GMV also needs coordinators of each country. The coordinators would volunteer themselves to invite pastors, leaders, prayer warriors and believers in a group so that we can mobilize more people to pray together to break down the misunderstanding and division walls between denominations, churches and believers. Will you be willing to serve as one of the national or regional coordinators?

Will you, your churches and your ministry teams be willing to connect, partner, serve and pray together for the said purposes. You may encourage your church to pray for these events. You may send information, flyers and videos of the events to your members. You may form supporting groups so the members would help share information of the event to their friends and social media.

You may invite your church members to join the event and pray together with millions of believers around the world for the global revival and especially America this year. You may help GMV to invite World Revivalists, Generals of Faith and Mega-Church Pastors to be our Speakers. You may be GMV coordinators to organize the events. You and your teams may serve to lead worship, prayer. We need hundreds of interpreters for 10-15 languages and we really need you

You may also make financial contribution so that GMV would have sufficient to make preparation to organize these world changing events by God's Grace and Blessings. Kindly let us know your involvement by sending the areas of ministries that you or your church, your team, your organizations are going to serve to this email: Nationsrevivals@ yahoo.com

www.agapevisiontv.com
www.globalmissionsvision.com
www.chinaforworldmissions.org

For Generous Support and Partnership, Please Send Your Check Payable To China For World Missions
Address: 16027 Brookhurst St. Suite I-642. Fountain Valley. CA92708

Global Missions Vision:
Address: 16027 Brookhurst St. Suite I-642. Fountain Valley. CA92708

Please Keep In Touch With Global Missions Vision

After this prayer of Confession and Declaration, please take your time to visit any Evangelical Churches or Pentecostal Churches nearby in your area. If you have any questions about the churches or you need guidance to find a church in your area, kindly contact us and we will love to assist you in any way possible.

Please send us a note about your decision to recommit or dedicate your life to the Lord Jesus Christ so we can rejoice with you and pray with you and for you and your family. Welcome to the Kingdom of God and welcome to your new life in the Lord Jesus Christ. We rejoice with you and "In the same way, I tell you, there is rejoicing in the presence of the angels of God over one sinner who repents" (Luke 15:10).

Congratulations on our new life in Christ. "Therefore if anyone is in Christ, he is a new creation. The old has passed away. Behold, the new has come" (II Corinthians 5:17). Thank you very much for your response to the message and thank you for contacting us at: Email: nationsrevivals@yahoo.com

Coming Books

Thanks a lot for your generous and continuous support for the books. If these books have really helped you in anyway, please help make these books available to your family members, friends, neighbors, colleagues, business partners and others.

The 12 Commandments of Socialism: Socialist Promises

The Boat of Destiny: Socialist Victims

Unbeatable: The Great Record Achievements
of President Donald J. Trump

Be Free Or Not To Be Free: Socialist Freedom

The Kills of Socialism

Thanks a lot for your blessings and partnership. Global Missions Vision and China For World Missions are blessed to partner with you and your organizations.

For More Information, Please Contact Us at
Email: Nationsrevivals@yahoo.com

www.agapevisiontv.com
www.globalmissionsvision.com
www.chinaforworldmissions.org

APPENDIX: GLOBAL MISSIONS VISION AND VISION 20%

GLOBAL MISSIONS VISION AND MISSIONS TO GOSPEL-RESTRICTED NATIONS

Global Missions Vision (GMV) is an inter-denomination mission organization and faith-based ministry and GMV is blessed to partner with you and your church or organizations to bring the Gospels to the nations. For two decades, our ministry has been reaching out to Gospel-restricted nations through the following ministries:

Bible Schools and Seminaries
Charity Works: Livelihood project, Clean Water (Well), Food and Gift Distributions, and Wheel Chair Outreach…
Christian Literature Distributions and Church Planting Training
Evangelistic Crusades and Financial Support to Church Planters
Leadership Training and Mission Conference
Missionary Training and Missionary Sending
Pastoral Training and Revival Conference
Short-Term Mission Trips and TV Ministry
Vocational Training: English, Music, Media Training, Handicrafts…

Each of us has different callings and giftings. GMV is pleased and blessed to have you come to conduct different trainings and seminars, partner for charity projects, and organize events as you are called to do. You are most welcome to partner with GMV by providing financial support or joining GMV fund raising teams.

For Ministry Involvement and Partnership, Please Contact Joshua
Email: nationsrevivals@yahoo.com

For Joining Fund Raising Team, Please Contact Tiffany
Email: nationsrevivals@yahoo.com

For Joining Our Media Team, Please Contact Christine
Email: nationsrevivals@yahoo.com

For Sending Your Financial Support, Please Contact Henry

Please Make Your Check Payable to: Global Missions Vision
Address: 16027 Brookhurst St, Suite I-642, Fountain Valley, CA 92708

For More Information Please See Our Websites

www.agapevisiontv.com   www.globalmissionsvision.com
www.chinaforworldmissions.org   Email: nationsrevivals@yahoo.com

Missions Partnership and Financial Support

Global Missions Vision and China For World Missions are also looking for mission partners and generous donors to stand with us and to accomplish Vision 20%.

I was brought for a "tea time" when they caught me at a new church. The persecutions had been intense and widespread in the land. My co-workers and I also faced tough times with the local authorities due to the martyrdom of the two mission workers. They were very serious when I met the authorities from various departments such as national defense, terrorist defense, national security, policemen, and religious affairs.

I would share their stories of martyrdom when the time comes. The authorities told me that they had been warning me many times in many years to stop the mission works but I did not listen. This time they would deport me out of the country and they would not let my family leave if I were not going to stop the mission works. This was not the first time they told me so, and every time, God gave me different words to respond to them.

I told them, "Do you prefer to monitor 1 person or do you want to monitor 100 persons, or 1000 persons or more?" They said, "Dr. (my name), what do you mean?" I said, "For years, you have been monitoring me. You can call me anytime you want, and you may come to my home any time you need. Whenever you arrange a meeting, I always follow your request. You know where I go and what I do."

"If I am still here, you can still monitor me but if I am not here anymore, I will be travelling and challenging churches to support 1000 mission workers, 10,000 mission workers, then you would not just be monitoring 1 person like me but many people. I think you would prefer to monitor only one person instead of many people". I was even surprised at what I said. They stared at me angrily because of what I said but I just kept smiling and praying.

They did not say directly anything about their choice of monitoring one or more person. They just told me the story of a businessman who owned a factory with a few hundred workers. That businessman also planted churches and they met him and warned him many times to stop the church services. Whenever they found and closed his church, he would open the church in a new place as my coworkers and I often did.

So they arrested him and as the result his factory was closed and he lost his business. And that was their direct answer of what they planned to do to my ministry and me. I also had about 200 full-time co-workers including staff, teachers, trainers, church planters and many volunteers to do church planting, mission mobilizations, various trainings, charities, evangelistic trips, mission and leadership conferences, crusades...

The authorities knew well that I planned to reach up to 300, then 600 and 1000 full-time co-workers and the goal is 10,000 to carry out Vision 20% and that there would be 20% of the population coming to know the Lord Jesus Christ as their Lord and Savior. They knew that if they did not take quick actions, my ministry and the mission networks would be able to accomplish the goal and the vision.

So they wanted to close down the operations and they have been working too hard to stop the ministries. Yet, the works of men can never prevail against the works of God. Though there are up and down moments, God has always been faithful to provide needs and expand His Kingdom. Global Missions Vision and China For World Missions is looking for generous donors so that the ministries could carry out Vision 20% and would be able to support: **2000 church planters in Gospel-restricted nations.**

Will You, Your Organization or Church Support 1 Church Planters or More with $50 or $100 or $200 per month and per Church Planter for a period of 3 years?

The strengths of Global Missions Vision (GMV) are in missions-orientation and partnership. GMV has been partnering with various ministries as an inter-denominational organization to pioneer more than 500 house churches in Gospel-restricted countries through supporting Church Planters. GMV has been training more than 700 young co-workers through Bible Schools.

GMV also trained more than 4000 leaders through its Seminary, Leadership and Mission Training Centers. GMV also organized many evangelistic trips and mission conferences in many nations of the world. GMV is also called to organize Evangelistic Crusades in many African nations, Myanmar, Pakistan, Thailand and others. By the grace of God, the ministries of GMV are still growing in the midst of severe persecutions.

Global Missions Vision and China For World Missions are looking for speakers and trainers to minister to pastors, leaders and brethren in Gospel-restricted countries. Please send email to nationsrevivals@ yahoo.com

Let us partner and pray together so that the Gospel-restricted nations would also reach their Vision 20% soon. They need your generous support to see the Gospel preached, lives touched, souls saved, and churches planted across the land.

For Donations and Partnership, Please Make Your Check Payable To And Send To:
China For World Missions
Address: 16027 Brookhurst St. Suite I-642. Fountain Valley. CA92708

Global Missions Vision.
Address: 16027 Brookhurst St. Suite I-642. Fountain Valley. CA92708

For More Information, Please Contact and Check Out Websites
Email: nationsrevivals@yahoo.com   www.globalmissionsvision.com
www.chinaforworldmissions.org   www.agapevisiontv.com

Vision 20% and The Global Worship and Revival Conference

September 2021

Ask Me, and I Will Make The Nations Your Inheritance,
the Ends of the Earth Your Possession (Psalm 2:8)

Will You Not Revive Us Again,
that Your People May Rejoice In You? (Psalm 85:6)

Lord, We Ask You For The Vision 20%

Vision 20% Is The Call To The Body of Christ To Come Together:
In Prayer, Intercessory and Spiritual Warfare.
In Repentance, Confession and Declaration.
In Unity, Missions and Revival.
In Mission, Charity & Demonstrative Power of The Holy Spirit.

So That There Will Be An Increase of 20% of The Population In Our Villages, Districts, Counties, Cities and Nations To Come To Know The Lord Jesus As Lord and Savior.

I pray that Vision 20% would bring about the great move and the great awakening of God for this generation and that your churches, organizations, individuals and you would partner with GMV for the Unity, Missions and Revival of the Global Body of Christ. It was not my plan to be here in California, yet God has His plan and purpose to send a powerful revival here in California and this nation for His glory.

I am called to prepare for that great and powerful coming and the last outpouring of the Holy Spirit from this nation to the nations. Please pray and partner with my ministry and I, so that, together, we can accomplish the great things that God has in store for us here, and, praying that I will be faithful to commit my life to the realization of Vision 20%. Thank God for the healing, unity and revival for the many places I travelled to.

Now is the time for the Body of Christ to come together in prayer and repentance. Now is the great time for the Body of Christ to come together in unity and missions. Now is the high time for the Body of Christ to come together in boldness and in the empowerment of the Holy Spirit. Now is the significant time for the Body of Christ to come together in preaching and demonstration of His supernatural power.

Now is the historic time for the Body of Christ to come together in the great harvest of souls and the revival of the nations. It is not about our tasks, our talents or our territories, but, it is all about His Kingdom. It is not about our deeds, our dreams, or our denominations, but, it is all about His Power. It is not about our plans, our purposes, our passions, or our projects, but, it is all about His Call.

A couple was put into prison because they were very brave to talk about God and because they were not willing to deny their faith in God. The man was placed behind bars in male prison and his wife was placed in incarceration in a female prison. The two prisons were just steps away from each other. Every morning the wife and her husband could see each other from short distance as they went to work in the fields.

Every morning, the wife would shout calling her husband, "Old man, are you ready to go to heaven?" The husband was also quick in his response, "Old woman, have you prepared well to go to heaven?" Whether the day was rainy or sunny, they would repeat the same question and the same answer, "Yes, I am ready." The jailors stopped them from doing so and the authorities beat them for doing so.

Yet, they never gave up. Many times the prison guards threatened to shoot them dead with their guns at hands. Yet the couple never showed little fear of death. They told the prison guards, "I cannot commit suicide because that is a sin. Please execute me so that I can become a martyr and go to heaven soon. I am not of this world. Please send me to heaven." The prison guards gave up and saluted them.

The courage of this faithful couple and their faith in God and thousands of stories like that have been a great encouragement to many other Christians to stand firm in faith and to overcome their tough persecutions. It was with this determination, passion and desire to live for God that the Gospel is preached everywhere in the socialist nations. Millions of souls are saved and the Kingdom of God expanded.

I pray that their stories, their courage and their sacrifices would encourage you and I and churches to confirm our identity and our missions in Christ, again. Also, we must become more active to live out our faith and our callings regardless of the pains, challenges, failures, circumstances and obstacles or even death. Let us ask God together for His healings, deliverances, restorations, strengths and anointing.

As the Apostle Paul said, "Who shall separate us from the love of Christ? Shall trouble or hardship or persecution or famine or nakedness or danger or sword? [36]As it is written: For your sake we face death all day long; we are considered as sheep to be slaughtered. [37]No, in all these things we are more than conquerors through him who loved us. [38]For I am convinced that neither death nor life, neither angels nor demons, neither the present nor the future, nor any powers, [39]neither height nor depth, nor anything else in all creation, will be able to separate us from the love of God that is in Christ Jesus our Lord." (Romans 8:35-39)

We Ask Specifically That:

Each Believer be Active In Outreach.
Each Family Glorifies God in their Community.
Each Church Department Is Mobilized For Missions.
Each Church Supports 1 Missionary or More.
Each Church Sends 1 Team or More for Missions.

Each City Operates 1 Inter-Church House of Prayer or More.
Each City Conducts 1 Revival Meeting or More.
Each City Provides 20 Prayer Warriors or More.
Each State Organizes The Annual Worship and Revival Congress.
Each Nation Is Active In World Missions.

We Ask Further Lord That You Would Bring These Following Gideons To Come Together for Vision 20% and Global Worship and Revival Congress 2020:

300 Pastors, Leaders.
300 Ministry Team Leaders.
300 Prayer Warriors for Houses of Prayers.
300 Members for Worship, Dance, Banner Teams.
300 Speakers for Vision TV.
300 Financial Sponsors.
300 Volunteers to Serve.
300 Christian Business Men and Women.
300 Politicians and Government Officers.
300 Medical Doctors and Nurses.
300 Charity and Missions Organizations.
300 Educators and Teachers.
300 Christian Artists and Singers.
And Others

If You Are Willing To Be One Of Those Gideon, Please Send Your Information (Name, Areas of Ministry or Works, Telephone Number and you Web page, if available) to: nationsrevivals@yahoo.com so we could be connected and pray together and take action together for Vision 20% and the revivals of the nations for His glory.

Rev. Dr. J.D. and Global Missions Vision are calling you and your ministry to be part of the different Gideon ministry groups to pray and to prepare for the coming great revival, as our great God is about to do so. Praying that you would come together at the 2nd Global Worship and Revival Conference 2020 and with one voice, one mind, one heart and one mission, we pray for the great revival to come.

You are invited to partner with Global Missions Vision and China For World Missions according to your callings and giftings. Kindly see the ministry opportunities in the coming pages and get involved in preaching, teaching, visiting, encouraging, praying, or supporting financially. The ministry opportunities are available in Asia, Africa and now North America and soon in South America.

We Also Ask for the Redemption of the 7 Mountains

Arts and Entertainment	(Through Inter-Cultural Shows).
Business	(Through Global Expo).
Education	(Through Educational Forum).
Family	(Through Family and Health Care).
Government	(Through Leadership Summit).
Media	(Through Media Forum).
Religion	(Through Charity and Mission Festival).

For the last three years, GMV has been in partnership with different ministries and partners to organize International Summer Fair in July 2018 at Westminster Mall, California and Global Expo 2019 in September 2019 at Anaheim Convention Center, California. The 1st Global Worship and Revival Congress and Charity & Missions Festival in 2019 was organized at the same time with Global Expo.

The purpose is to encourage Christian leaders and believers from various fields to come together to pray for the Unity, Missions and Revival of the global Body of Christ. It is also to challenge the Body of Christ to reach out to the 7 Mountains or 7 Spheres of Influences and people in those influences. The vision is clear and our experiences and networks are still at beginning stages.

Global Missions Vision invites ministries and organizations to partner with GMV to organize the conferences, cultural shows, forums and festival at the 2nd Global and Worship Revival Conference 2020. Let us partner together to accomplish His-given vision and that churches across the globe would pray, partner and take actions for Vision 20% in their respective villages, counties, cities, and nations.

For more information, please see the website at: www.GlocalExpo.org or send your concerns and partnership to: nationsrevivals@yahoo.com

We Ask for MORE:

That more believers and people would pray more for President Trump and that they would understand how God uses an imperfect person for His perfect plan to revive the U.S. economy and life stability, to bring about religious freedom and revival, and to protect Christians from persecutions, to restore morality, and to destroy atheists' anti-Christ agendas.

Thousands of pastors, leaders, ministry team leaders and worshippers and people from nations of the world would come together at the 2nd Global Worship and Revival Congress 2020 to Pray For The Great Awakening, To Take Actions for Missions, and To Exalt His Glorious Name. This is the call for the global Body of Christ to come together for Repentance, Unity, Missions and Revival.

3nd Global Worship & Revival Congress
September 23-26, 2021 (In Planning)
VIP Free Tickets for Pastors & Leaders.

Kindly Send Your Name, Church,
Position and Contact Number to
Nationsrevivals@yahoo.com

For General Free Tickets and Information
Please Contact: Nationsrevivals@yahoo.com

Don't Forget To Register Your Business Booth For 2021 Global Expo or Charity and Mission Booths for Global Charity and Missions Festival Which Are Taking Place at the Same Time and Venue of Global Worship & Revival Congress 2021.

And Be Ready For:

Powerful God-Encountered Moments.
Supernatural Demonstration of The Power of The Holy Spirit.
Powerful Prayer, Praise and Worship.
Anointed Healing Evangelists and Powerful Speakers.
Great Teams from the Nations and Famous Artists, Singers, Celebrities.
Global Events: Expo, Health, Charity and Missions Festival...

Sponsors For Book Publication and
Christian Literature Distribution

Through the years, Global Missions Vision has been raising funds to provide Christian libraries to churches and underground Bible Schools, Bible School textbooks to leaders, and students in underground Bible Schools, and Christian literatures to different groups of people. GMV is looking forward to partnering with you and your organizations so that GMV continues to provide the many needs of Christian literatures.

Global Missions Vision is also looking for generous financial donors and partners to make the following new books available into the hands of millions of people so that at least Americans would be aware of the truth of socialism and its rise in this land of freedom. GMV plans to have many of the books translated and published in various languages and to distribute these free books whenever funds are available to share the Gospels through current topics. People need God to walk with them through good and tough times.

The 12 Commandments of Socialism: Socialist Promises

The Boat of Destiny: Socialist Victims

Be Free Or Not Be Free: Socialist Freedom

Unbeatable: The Record Achievements of President Donald J. Trump.

The Kills of Socialism

Please Make Your Check Payable To:

Global Missions Vision
Address: 16027 Brookhurst St. Suite I-642. Fountain Valley. CA92708

For More Information Please See Our Websites

www.agapevisiontv.com
www.globalmissionsvision.com
www.chinaforworldmissions.org

Kindly send your feedbacks or recommendations to: nationsrevivals@
yahoo.com

Speaking Appointments With Authors

Dr. A. Y. was a former university professor who was called to preach the Gospels to the nations as a Healing Evangelist. He is an anointed speaker for revival, leadership and mission conferences. He is also the organizer and speaker of many crusades, leadership, missions and revival conference. He is the Founder and President underground Seminary, Missions organization, and Vision TV Ministry.

Dr. A. Y. is glad to be a guest speaker at your churches and conferences to inspire and challenge the Body of Christ for missions and ministries. Please contact Dr. A. Y. to make arrangements for his speaking schedule and appointment at: nationsrevivals@yahoo.com

Dr. S. Y. is a university professor who is gifted with prophetic words. She is called to bring His healing and restoration to families and challenging precious women and families to develop a strong and daily family devotion. God uses her stories of persecutions to inspire many people towards faith, prayer life, holiness, missions and revival. She is known for her dedication and love to God and peoples' inner beauty, fire and passion for God's Kingdom.

Dr. S. Y. is also blessed to be your guest speaker at your churches, missions and women conferences to share her many experiences of ministry and life in Gospel-restricted countries. Please contact Dr. S. F. to make arrangements for her speaking schedule and appointment at: nationsrevivals@yahoo.com

ADOPTING CHURCH PLANTERS AND VISION 20%

The heart of Global Missions Vision is Vision 20% which calls for the many prayers and mission partnership so that there would be 20% or more of the population in socialist countries to come to know the Lord Jesus Christ as their Lord and Savior, GMV is looking for each of 2000 individuals, or churches, or organizations or businesses that is willing to support 1 church planter in the socialist nations.

By God's grace, in the last two decades, GMV has been able to train thousands of leaders, mission workers, church planters. Through the generous supports of GMV partners, more than 500 home churches were planted in Gospel-restricted countries in partnership with the local churches and various denominations.

Would You Support 1 Church Planter of the 2000 Church Planters?
Would You Connect GMV To 1 Donor or
Church To Support 1 Church Planter?

These church planters would reach out to the millions of the lost souls, pioneering thousands of churches, building up houses of prayer, organizing evangelistic events, sending out evangelistic teams, connecting churches, leaders and believers to pray and to take actions for Unity, Missions and Revivals, and being used by God to bring about soul saving, life changes and social transformation for His glory.

For Ministry Involvement and Partnership, Please Contact Joshua
Email: nationsrevivals@yahoo.com
For Joining Fund Raising Team, Please Contact Tiffany
Email: nationsrevivals@yahoo.com
For Joining Our Media Team, Please Contact Christine
Email: nationsrevivals@yahoo.com

For Sending Your Financial Support, Please Contact Henry
Email: nationsrevivals@yahoo.com

Please Make Your Check Payable to:
China For World Missions
Address: 16027 Brookhurst St. Suite I-642. Fountain Valley. CA92708
Global Missions Vision
Address: 16027 Brookhurst St. Suite I-642. Fountain Valley. CA 92708

For More Information, Please Contact and Check Out Websites
Email: nationsrevivals@yahoo.com
www.globalmissionsvision.com
www.chinaforworldmissions.org
www.agapevisiontv.com

PARTNERSHIP FOR CHARITY WORKS

Global Missions Vision also invites you, your churches, businesses or organizations to partner with GMV to reach out people and communities through social works. For Charity Works, GMV has been doing the following works:

1. Wheelchair Outreach: Providing wheelchair to disable people. We also invite their family members to come when we distribute the gift so we can get to know them and share the Gospel at the same time. Usually we can preach publicly and the team members also pray for people.

2. Clean Water: There are so many places in great needs of water. There are places that the local people must walk a long distance to fetch water. We have various ways to help the local people depending on the situations. There are places that we help them dig a well or thrill a well. There are places that we have to pup water from the river to the communities. Thus, we need to buy a water pump, build a water stellar, connecting water pipes from the river to water stellar. We may also provide the local people with water tank so they could fetch water from the newly build water stellar in their community and store water in the water tank at their home.

3. Scholarship: Providing scholarships to children that have excellent academic achievement from poor families so we could encourage the children to keep on studying and preparing them a better future

4. Vocational Training Center: so far we can only teach English, Music, Media, or teaching people how to do handcrafts so they can have better chances for better works.

5. Love Gift Distributions: This is given in various forms such as food distributions, school items to students, clothes and daily-usage items, urgent cashes for families in need, motorbikes for pastors or church planters…. Love gifts are distributed to orphanages, elderly homes, families, schools...

6. Livelihood Projects: helping the needy people with start-up plan of 200 USD so they could support themselves. We do not give cash to the needy. Depending on the needs of people, we provide them chicks, ducklings, baby goats, piglets, rabbits, small fishes and then 3-6 month foods for these live stocks or animals. Other families may do farming or gardening so we can provide them seeds and fertilizer and they could do the jobs by themselves. This project has been transforming more than a thousand lives so far.

7. Gospel Bridges: There are many remote places where children and people must cross through rivers or bamboo sticks over the hill in order to go to schools or markets and it is dangerous for people and lives were lost because of the situations. We are now working on this project so we can bless the people and their communities and sharing His love to people

8. Daycare Centers: GMV also opened three daycare centers for children from 2 years-old to 6 years-old and after-class care for students as their parents could not come back home early due to the works. At our daycare centers, children and students are taught to pray, worship, read the Bible, develop godly characters.

May the Lord bless us so that we could invite more people and team to go to minister and bless needy people across our land! May God use everyone of us to reach out to people and to glorify God in all we are doing to bring the Good News and salvation to the people. Amen.

For Donations and Partnership, Please Make Your Check Payable to:

China For World Missions
Address: 16027 Brookhurst St. Suite I-642. Fountain Valley. CA92708

Global Missions Vision
Address: 16027 Brookhurst St. Suite I-642. Fountain Valley. CA 92708

For More Information, Please Contact and Check Out Websites
Email: nationsrevivals@yahoo.com

www.globalmissionsvision.com
www.chinaforworldmissions.org
www.agapevisiontv.com

UPCOMING AND ANNUAL EVENTS

Through Zoom Meeting ID: 793 812 3439 (Password: Jesus)

Weekly:	Friday Prayer, Worship, Healing and Testimonies @7pm, PST
January:	Global Intercessory Conference & Pray-For Vietnam Conference
February:	Global Children Conference
March:	Global Leadership and Pastoral Conference
April:	Vision Talent Contest
May:	Asia Missions and Revival Conference
June:	Global Marriage Conference
July 24-25:	Send Out Conference or Global Missions Conference
August:	Global Charity and Mission Festival
Sept. 4-6:	Global Worship and Revival Conference

Oct. 9-12:	Global Revival Conference
Oct. 30, 31 &	Global Prayer and Prophetic Conference
Nov. 1-2:	
Dec. 4-5:	Global Youth Conference

GMV is calling for various ministry teams such as Praise and Worship Teams, Prayer and Intercessory Teams, Dance Teams, Drama Teams, Choirs, Artists and Singers, Media Teams Business and Professional Teams to serve, to partner and co-organize the events to mobilize churches and the global body of Christ to come together in Unity, Prayer, Missions and Revival.

For Donation and Partnership, Please Make Your Check Payable to:

China For World Missions
Address: 16027 Brookhurst St. Suite I-642. Fountain Valley. CA92708

Global Missions Vision
Address: 16027 Brookhurst St. Suite I-642. Fountain Valley. CA 92708

For More Information, Please Contact and Check Out Websites
Email: nationsrevivals@yahoo.com   www.globalmissionsvision.com
www.chinaforworldmissions.org   www.agapevisiontv.com

**Please Follow Us On Our Websites and Media
Channels, Would You Please Connect and Subscribe
Our YouTube and Facebook Channels**

Chinese Vision TV:	Mandarin YouTube and Facebook Channels
Vision TV:	English YouTube and Facebook Channels
Viet Vision TV:	Vietnamese YouTube and Facebook Channel

SOURCES

Aleem, Zeeshan. "Bernie Sanders Says the U.S. Could Learn a Lot From Scandinavia. Here's Why He's Right." Mic, https://www.mic.com/articles/117334/bernie-sanders-says-the-u-s-could-learn-a-lot-from-scandinavia-here-s-why-he-s-right

All Scriptures are taken from the Holy Bible, New International Version®, NIV® Copyright ©1973, 1978, 1984, 2011 by Biblica, Inc.

Alonso-Zaldivar, Ricardo. "$10,345 Per Person: U.S. Health Care." PBS, NewsHour Productions LLC., 13 July 2016, https://www.pbs.org/newshour/health/new-peak-us-health-care-spending-10345-per-person

Amadeo, Kimberly. "FY 2020 Federal Budget: Trump's Budget Request." The Balance, Dotdash Publishing Family, 28 February 2020, https://www.thebalance.com/fy-2020-federal-budget-summary-of-revenue-and-spending-4797868

Amadeo, Kimberly. "The Rising Cost of Health Care By Year and Its Causes." The Balance, Dotdash Publishing Family, 28 February 2020, https://www.thebalance.com/causes-of-rising-healthcare-costs-4064878

Amir. "Top 5 Countries with the Highest Total Number of Abortions in the World." Country Ranker, Country Ranker, 9 July 2014, http://www.countryranker.com/top-5-countries-with-the-highest-total-number-of-abortions-in-the-world/

Answers. "Why Do The Scandinavian Countries Have High Taxes? Answers, Answers, https://www.answers.com/Q/Why_do_the_Scandinavian_countries_have_high_taxes

Ashworth, Will. "7 Reasons Americans Should Embrace Socialism." InvestorPlace, InvestorPlace Media, LLC., 3 April 2019, https:// investorplace.com/2019/04/7-reasons-americans-should-embrace-socialism/

"Back To School Statistics." IES-NCES, National Center for Education Statistics, https://nces.ed.gov/fastfacts/display.asp?id=372

Bader, Hans. "Fidel Castro Did Not Give Cuba Literacy or Better Healthcare." *Intellectual Takeout*, Intellectual Takeout, 25 February 2020, https://www.intellectualtakeout.org/article/fidel-castro-did-not-give-cuba-literacy-or-better-healthcare?fbclid=IwAR2h6oLQa_9TbNc--xYaXrPXSoxxjRUTTtYdA3YxOg-vLsL480U_i7KwlYM

Bailey, Megan. "Is There Christian Persecution in America? Beliefnet, Beliefnet, Inc., https://www.beliefnet.com/news/is-there-christian-persecution-in-america.aspx

Barrett, James. "How Many Muslim Immigrants Has Obama Admitted? Here's What Congress Just Learned." *The daily Wire*, The Daily Wire, 20 June 2016, https://www.dailywire.com/news/how-many-muslim-immigrants-has-obama-admitted-james-barrett

BBC News. "Top 10 Countries With The Highest Crime Rates." BBC News, BBC News, http://www.bbcnewshub.com/top-10-countries-with-the-highest-crime-rates/

Benko, Ralph. "Bernie Sanders And The Resurgence of Socialist Sentiment In America." *Forbes*, Forbes Media, LLC., 15 December 2017, https://www.forbes.com/sites/ralphbenko/2017/12/15/bernie-sanders-and-the-resurgence-of-socialist-sentiment-in-america/#2fcb8f0c32bd

Blumberg, Yoni. "Here's The Real Reason Health Care Costs So Much More In The U.S." *CNBC*, CNBC LLC, 3 September 2018, https://www.cnbc.com/2018/03/22/the-real-reason-medical-care-costs-so-much-more-in-the-us.html

Bowden, Ebony. "Democratic Debate: Bernie Sanders Won't Back Down on Support of Castro, Cuba." New York Post, NYP Holdings, Inc., 25 February 2020, https://nypost.com/2020/02/25/democratic-debate-bernie-sanders-wont-back-down-on-support-of-castro-

Briney, Amanda. "Countries of Scandinavia." ThoughtCo., ThoughtCo., 10 December 2019, https://www.thoughtco.com/countries-of-scandinavia-1434588

Bolyard, Paula. "Christians Beware: Biden Declares His #1 Priority Will Be The Anti-Christian LGBTQ 'Equality Act'", PJ Media, PJ Media, 3 June 2019, https://pjmedia.com/faith/biden-declares-his-1-priority-will-be-the-anti-christian-lgbtq-equality-act/?fbclid=IwAR2xhQPVjJM3Ox rnwrXLW2rUC_FlCv2i8QpRqcBjXTBn-TruBWRB238B_EI

Campbell, Todd. "The Average American Spends This Much On Healthcare Every Year—Do You?" The Motley Fool, The Motley Fool, 15 March 2015, https://www.fool.com/investing/general/2015/03/15/the-average-american-spends-this-much-on-healthcar.aspx

CBN News. "Fire for Praying: High School Coach Gets Day in Court." CBN News, CBN News, 13 June 2017, https://www1.cbn.com/cbnnews/us/2017/june/fired-for-praying-high-school-coach-gets-day-in-court

CDC. "Health Expenditures." CDC, Centers for Disease Control and Prevention, 20 January 2017, https://www.cdc.gov/nchs/fastats/health-expenditures.htm

Chasmar, Jessica. "Black Lives Matter Chicago organizer says looting is 'reparations': 'Business have insurance." The Washington Times, The Washington Times, 11 August 2020, https://www.washingtontimes.com/news/2020/aug/11/ariel-atkins-blm-chicago-organizer-says-looting-is/

Clark, Heather. "State-Level Bills to Outlaw Abortion, Criminalize as Murder Growing Nationwide." Christian News, Christian News Network, 9 February 2019, https://christiannews.net/2019/02/09/state-level-bills-to-outlaw-abortion-criminalize-as-murder-growing-nationwide/

CMS. "National Health Expenditures 2017 Highlights." *CMS.gov*, Centers for Medicare & Medicaid Services, https://www.cms.gov/ Research-Statistics-Data-and-Systems/Statistics-Trends-and-Reports/ NationalHealthExpendData/Downloads/highlights.pdf

Christian Good In Society. "Good Things Christians Have Done In Society." Christian Good In Society, Christian Good In Society, https:// christiangoodinsociety.blogspot.com

Cohen, David S. "How Trump Is Trying To Effectively Ban Abortion." RollingStone, RollingStone, LLC., 18 May 2018, https:// www.rollingstone.com/politics/politics-features/how-trump- is-trying-to-effectively-ban-abortion-630436/

Collins, Chuck. "We Should Take A Lesson From The Nordic Countries on Inequality." *Institute For Policy Studies*, Institute For Policy Studies, 18 July 2016, https://ips-dc.org/take-lesson-nordic-countries-inequality/

Cooper, Ryan. "Bernie Sanders Wants the U.S. to be Like Norway. Is That Even Possible?" *The Week*, The Week Publications Inc., 6 August 2015, https:// theweek.com/articles/570205/bernie-sanders-wants-more-like-norway- that-even-possible

Countries Now. "Top 10 Countries With Highest Crime Rate in the World." *Countries Now*, Countries Now, https://www.whichcountry.co/ top-10-countries-with-highest-crime-rate-in-the-world/

Christianity. Com. "What Was The Mayflower Compact? It's Meaning and Significance." *Christianity.com*, Christianity.com, https://www. christianity.com/church/church-history/timeline/1601-1700/the- magnificent-mayflower-compact-11630074.html

Dickson, Caitlin and Wilson, Christopher. "After Sanders's Praise for Castro, Cuban-Americans Like Him Even Less." Yahoo News, Yahoo, 24 February 2020, https://www.yahoo.com/news/after-sanders-praise- for-castro-cuban-americans-like-him-even-less-195233809.html

Dmitry, Baxter. "Chicago Mayor Orders Residents Not to Use Guns to Defend Themselves During Violent Riots." *News Punch*, The People's Voice, Inc., 8 June 2020, https://newspunch.com/ chicago-mayor-orders-residents-not-use-guns-defend-themselves- during-violent-riots/?fbclid=IwAR2wTmUCJBoEY7kjlQqFal7l cTs8-CKB4A5ALXVhzYW2cuRzkOCzO-glVPU

Dobson, James. "Dr. Dobson's August Newsletter." *Dr. James Dobson's Family Talk*, James Dobson Family Institute, August 2019, https:// drjamesdobson.org/news/commentaries/archives/2019-newsletters/ august-newsletter-2019

Dorfman, Jeffrey. "Sorry Bernie Bros But Nordic Countries Are Not Socialist." *Forbes*, Forbes Media LLC., 8 July 2018, https://www.forbes. com/sites/jeffreydorfman/2018/07/08/sorry-bernie-bros-but-nordic- countries-are-not-socialist/#1ba2e50b74ad

Dorman, Sam. "Bernie Sanders Seen In Unearthed 1986 Video Recalling Excitement Over Castro's Revolution in Cuba." Fox News, Fox News Network, LLC., 24 April 2020, https://www.foxnews.com/ politics/bernie-sanders-unearthed-video-recalling-excitement-castro- revolution-cuba

Editorial Staff. "America's Schools Began With Christian Education." *The Mandate*, 22 April 2008, The Forerunner, http://www.forerunner. com/mandate/X0056_Americas_Schools.html

Emery, David. "A History of the 'War on Christmas.'" *Snopes*, Snopes Media Group Inc., 29 November 2017, https://www.snopes.com/ news/2017/11/29/the-war-on-christmas/

Emmons, Libby. "Watch: BLM protestors crash church service, assault worshippers." *The Post Millennial*, The Post Millennial, 6 July 2020, https://thepostmillennial.com/watch-blm-protestors-storm-church- service-assault-worshippers?fbclid=IwAR0pF92KmwQKYJRYt3p9JT Hlg-hn2teq3q62frv6YlCo2r3BY9K8DfDYmRA

"Environmental Performance Index." Wikipedia, Wikimedia Foundation Inc., https://en.wikipedia.org/wiki/Environmental_Performance_Index

Evans, Mike. "Donald Trump: Good for Israel." *The Jerusalem Post*, Jpost Inc., 23 June 2019, https://www.jpost.com/Opinion/Donald-Trump-Good-for-Israel-593416

Fact Check. "Fact Check: Are The Scandinavian Countries Socialist?" *Right Wing*, Right Wing, https://www.rightwing.org/fact-check-are-the-scandinavian-countries-socialist/

Faith Facts. "The Impact of Christianity." *Faith Facts*, Faith Facts, http://www.faithfacts.org/christ-and-the-culture/the-impact-of-christianity

GAN Integrity. "China Corruption Report." *GAN Business Anti-Corruption Portal*, GAN Integrity Inc., August 2018, https://www.ganintegrity.com/portal/country-profiles/china/

Gaille, Louise. "18 Advantages and Disadvantages of a Free Market Economy." Vittana, Vittana, https://vittana.org/18-advantages-and-disadvantages-of-a-free-market-economy

Graham, Jack. "What the Bible Teaches about Socialism and Capitalism." *Jack Graham*, Power Point, 4 July 2019, https://resources.jackgraham.org/resource-library/sermons/what-the-bible-teaches-about-socialism-and-capitalism

GFP. "Defense Spending By Country (2020). *GFP*, Global Fire Power, https://www.globalfirepower.com/total-population-by-country.asp

Goldberg, Jonah. "Bernie Sanders' Relationship With Socialism and Communism." *The Baltimore Sun*, The Baltimore Sun, 24 February 2020, https://www.baltimoresun.com/opinion/op-ed/bs-ed-op-0224-jonah-goldberg-sanders-communism-socialism-20200224-3thiotftzvbmnhjw6d2g7t3ho4-story.html

Guandolo, John D. "Islamic Influence in U.S. Schools: Terrorism Taught in Classrooms." *Understanding The Threat*, Understanding The Threat, 27 June 2019, https://www.understandingthethreat.com/terrorists-in-the-classroom/

Guandolo, John D. "U.S. Public Schools Promote Islam." *Understanding The Threat*, Understanding The Threat, 3 December 2019, https://www.understandingthethreat.com/u-s-public-schools-promote-islam/

Hodgson M. Geoffrey. "What The World Can Learn About Equality From The Nordic Model." The Conversation, 30 July 2018, https://theconversation.com/what-the-world-can-learn-about-equality-from-the-nordic-model-99797

Holloway, Carson. "How Christianity Helped Create Our American Democracy." *The Daily Signal*, The Daily Signal, 22 April 2016, https://www.dailysignal.com/2016/04/22/how-christianity-helped-create-our-american-democracy/

Hsieh Esther. "What Universal Child Care Does For Norway." *The Globe and Mail, The Globe and Mail Inc.,* 11 May 2018, https://www.theglobeandmail.com/report-on-business/economy/canada-competes/what-universal-child-care-does-for-norway/article11959366/

Huffman, Brenda Krueger. Business Insider, Insider Inc., 14 August 2012, https://www.businessinsider.com/immigrants-who-escaped-socialist-countries-warn-the-us-2012-8

Investor's Business Daily. "You Can See America's Future Under Socialism, And It Isn't Pretty." Investor's Business Daily, 25 April 2018, https://www.investors.com/politics/editorials/socialism-poverty-democrats-standard-of-living/

Jegede, Abayomi. "Ten Countries with Highest Crime Rate in the World." Trendrr, Trendrr.net, 21 September 2019, https://www.trendrr.net/8838/countries-with-highest-crime-rate-world-statistics/

Jegede, Abayomi. "11 Countries with Highest Rape Crime Rate in the World 2019." *Trendrr*, Trendrr.net, 22 September 2019, https://www.trendrr.net/13049/countries-with-highest-rape-crime-famous-global-statistics/

John. Joseph R. "Obama's Massive Resettlement of 6 Million Muslims to the U.S." Dr. Rich Swier, 2 February 2015, https://drrichswier.com/2015/02/02/obamas-massive-resettlement-6-million-muslims-u-s/

Kamenetz, Anya and Westervelt, Eric. "Fact-Check: Bernie Sanders Promises Free College. Will It Work? *NPR*, NPR, 17 February 2016, https://www.npr.org/sections/ed/2016/02/17/466730455/fact-check-bernie-sanders-promises-free-college-will-it-work

Knoll, Jason L. "The Nordics and the US." Jason L. Knoll, Jason L. Knoll, 17 January 2020, https://jasonlknoll.com/2020/01/17/the-nordics-and-the-us/

Lacono, Corey. "The Myth of Scandinavian Socialism." *Foundation for Economic Education*, Foundation for Economic Education, 25 February 2016, https://fee.org/articles/the-myth-of-scandinavian-socialism/

Lexington Law. "44 Important Welfare Statistics for 2020." *Lexington Law*, Lexington Law, 3 January 2020, https://www.lexingtonlaw.com/blog/finance/welfare-statistics.html

Life Site. "No Christian Persecution in the US? Try Telling That to These Christians." *Life Site*, Life Site News, 21 November 2016, https://www.lifesitenews.com/blogs/if-you-think-christians-arent-being-persecuted-in-the-u.s.-its-because-your

Megahan, Mark. "BLM Release List of Demands for "White People." *Right Wing News Hour*, RightWingNewshour.com, 6 June 2020, https://rightwingnewshour.com/blm-release-list/

Mapes, Terri. "10 Fun Facts About Scandinavia." *Trip Savvy*, Dotdash Publishing Family, 27 December 2018, https://www.tripsavvy.com/fun-facts-about-scandinavia-1626701

Mapes, Terri. "The Difference Between Scandinavian and Nordic." *Trip Savvy*, Dotdash Publishing Family, 15 September 2019, https://www. tripsavvy.com/difference-between-scandinavian-and-nordic-1626695

McDonanald, Kelly. "Scandinavia Isn't A Socialist Paradise." *The Federalist*, The Federalist, 11 August 2015, https://thefederalist. com/2015/08/11/scandinavia-isnt-a-socialist-paradise/

McPhillips, Deidre. "U.S. Among Most Depressed Countries in the World." *U.S. News*, The U.S. News, 14 September 2016, https:// www.usnews.com/news/best-countries/articles/2016-09-14/ the-10-most-depressed-countries

Morgan, Robert J. "Robert Morgan: Trump's National Day of Prayer Declaration Has Deep American Roots." *Fox News*, Fox News Network, LLC, 15 March 2020, https://www.foxnews.com/opinion/trump-national-day-of-prayer-robert-morgan?fbclid=IwAR1GrsUH7xQf-D9q2jAQOdyj5-XT NkuXjzgCGmUqi9AR64jTSOTzVwj9QZE

News Division. "James Dobson Warns Against Socialism Taking Over America." *Pulpit & Pen*, Pulpit & Pen, 5 August 2019, https://pulpitandpen. org/2019/08/05/james-dobson-warns-against-socialism-taking-over-america/?fbclid=IwAR19Eutvyk-CiYKEAgpQPdHW3YrTz-89hSaesH_ VCj-LNjKjf_2cnGYt7IE

O'Leary, Fionnuala. "'Broken Inside' Family of mom, 24, 'shot dead after telling Black Lives Matter protesters "all lives matter" demand justice." The Sun, The Sun. US. Inc., 13 July 2020, https://www.the-sun.com/news/1129315/ family-jessica-doty-whitaker-black-lives-matter-indiana/?utm_ medium=Social&utm_campaign=sunusnewsfacebook&utm_ source=Facebook#Echobox=1594656921

Orr Gabby. "Trump Sets a New GOP Standard in the Abortion Fight." *Politico*, Politico, LLC., 1 January 2020, https://www.politico.com/ news/2020/01/24/march-for-life-trump-abortion-speech-103994

Petkovic, Bojana. "12 Countries with the Highest Rape Crimes Statistics in 2018." Insider Monkey, 10 April 2018, Koala Guide LLC., https://www.insidermonkey.com/blog/12-countries-with-highest-rape-crime-statistics-in-2018-656193/

Religion News Service. "What Is The Johnson Amendment and Why Did Trump Target It?" *The Presbyterian Outlook*, The Presbyterian Outlook, 5 May 2017, https://pres-outlook.org/2017/05/johnson-amendment-trump-target/

Reynolds, Elle. "Grieving Families Of Killed Children Call On 'Black Lives Matter' To Address Community Violence." *The Federalist*, The Federalist, A Wholly Independent Division of FDRLST Media, 6 July 2020, https://thefederalist.com/2020/07/06/grieving-families-of-killed-children-call-on-black-lives-matter-to-address-community-violence/

Shine, Haim. "Trump's Support for Israel Matters." *Solve Israel's Problems*, Solve Israel's Problems, 25 September 2018, https://solveisraelsproblems.com/trumps-support-for-israel-matters/

Tillnett, Emily. "Trump Signs Order to Protect Religious Freedom, Established New White House Faith Initiative." CBS News, CBS Interactive Inc., 3 May 2018, https://www.cbsnews.com/news/trump-observes-national-day-of-prayer-at-white-house-live-stream/?fbclid=IwAR0ECZfCd1LR7hDpwRi_8-CbMsfLQ-oV1NVmq8DwEIWrZEGEZQC5SVXYzZ8

OECD ILibrary. "Health At A Glance 2019." *OECD ILibrary*, OECD, https://www.oecd-ilibrary.org/sites/e88a7402-en/index.html?itemId=/content/component/e88a7402-en

OECD. "Health Spending." OECD, Organization for Economic Co-operation and Development, https://data.oecd.org/healthres/health-spending.htm

OCED. "Health Expenditure and Financing." *OECD.Stat*, OECD, 2 April 2020, https://stats.oecd.org/Index.aspx?ThemeTreeId=9

Pomerleau, Kyle. "How Scandinavian Countries Pay For Their Government Spending." *Tax Foundation*, Tax Foundation, 10 June 2015, https://

taxfoundation.org/how-scandinavian-countries-pay-their-government-spending

Pham, Kevin. "'Socialist' Nordic Countries Are Actually Moving Toward Private Health Care." *The Daily Signal*, The Daily Signal, 13 June 2019, https://www.dailysignal.com/2019/06/13/socialist-nordic-countries-are-actually-moving-toward-private-health-care/

Politico Magazine. "What Would a Socialist America Look Like?" *Politico Magazine*, Politico LLC., 3 September 2018, https://www.politico.com/magazine/story/2018/09/03/what-would-a-socialist-america-look-like-219626

Rambaran, Vandaran. "Bernie Sanders Defends Fidel Castro's Socialist Cuba: "Unfair to Simply Say Everything Is Bad." Fox News, Fox News Network LLC., 24 February 2020, https://www.foxnews.com/politics/bernie-sanders-fidel-castro-cuba-socialist-defense?fbclid=IwAR13_25OR130zjMbe2F7c6IDMcU--S9vFY8nKRHCYYLQuDRtQdIAY1Pu8rU

Rense, Jeff. "The Zion Communist Takeover Of America-45 Declared Goals." *Rense.com*, Rense.com, 24 April 2018, https://rense.com/general32/americ.htm

Reynolds, Elle. "Grieving Families Of Killed Children Call On 'Black Lives Matter' To Address Community Violence." *The Federalist*, The Federalist, A Wholly Independent Division of FDRLST Media, 6 July 2020, https://thefederalist.com/2020/07/06/grieving-families-of-killed-children-call-on-black-lives-matter-to-address-community-violence/

Rothfus, Keith J. "Do Not Repeat The Nightmare of Socialism." Socialism Today, Socialism Today, http://socialismtoday.info/blog/2018/07/18/do-not-repeat-the-nightmare-of-socialism/

Right Wing. "Fact Check: Are The Scandinavian Countries Socialist?" *Right Wing*, Right Wing, https://www.rightwing.org/fact-check-are-the-scandinavian-countries-socialist/

Sanders, Bernie. "Sanders Statement on Venezuela." *Bernie Sanders*, Bernie Sanders, 24 January 2019, https://www.sanders.senate.gov/newsroom/press-releases/sanders-statement-on-venezuela

Sawyer, Bradley and Cox, Cynthia. "How Does Health Spending In The U.S. Compare To Other Countries." *Peterson-KFF, Health System Tracker*, Peterson Center on Health Care, 7 December 2018, https://www.healthsystemtracker.org/chart-collection/health-spending-u-s-compare-countries/#item-start

Schatz, Daniel. "Bernie Sanders' Scandinavian Utopia Is An Illision." Forbes Opinion, Forbes, 18 February 2016, https://www.forbes.com/sites/carrielukas/2019/06/20/calm-down-but-dont-forget-common-sense/#2ce5dafc4575

Schwartz, Elaine. "The Real Facts About Sweden's Wealth Distribution." *Econlife*, Econlife, 11 April 2016, https://econlife.com/2016/04/swedish-wealth-distribution/

Schwartz, Ian. "Seattle City Councilwoman: We Will Not Stop Until We Overthrow Capitalism, Replace It With Socialism." Real Clear Politics, RealClearHoldings, LLC., 7 July 2020, https://www.realclearpolitics.com/video/2020/07/07/seattle_city_councilwoman_we_will_not_stop_until_we_overthrow_capitalism_replace_it_with_socialism.html?fbclid=IwAR2ZB5TaPYGZZWjEYC4Id8iJXnll1MamXxfjDWfa5uZyzFJ5RewDzvoh-zI

Sherman, Amy. "The United States Department of Education has introduced an Islamic indoctrination program for the public schools, called 'Access Islam.'" *PolitiFact*, Poynter Institute, 2 April 2017, https://www.politifact.com/factchecks/2017/apr/05/volusia-county-republican-party/did-us-department-education-introduce-islamic-indo/

Shine, Haim. "Trump's Support for Israel Matters." *Solve Israel's Problems*, Solve Israel's Problems, 25 September 2018, https://solveisraelsproblems.com/trumps-support-for-israel-matters/

Siu, Diamond Naga. "Democratic Socialists of America Scored Wins in the Midterms. What's On Their Agenda?" *NBC News*, NBC Universal, 8 December 2018, https://www.nbcnews.com/politics/politics-news/democratic-socialists-america-scored-wins-midterms-what-s-their-agenda-n941911

Spratt, Vicky. "Is Living In Scandinavia *Really* All That Amazing?" *Grazia*, Bauer Media Group, 20 April 2016, https://graziadaily.co.uk/life/real-life/living-scandinavia-really-amazing/

Sanandaji, Nima. "Scandinavian Unexceptionalism." (2015)

Sherman, Erik. "U.S. Health Care Costs Skyrocketed to $3.65 Trillion in 2018." *Fortune*, Fortune Media IP Limited, 21 February 2019, https://fortune.com/2019/02/21/us-health-care-costs-2/

Staples-Butler, Jack. "The Falsity of the Sanders Venezuela Meme." *Quillette*, Quillette Pty Ltd., 10 March 2018, https://quillette.com/2018/03/10/sanders-venezuela-meme/

Svirsky, Meira. "Pro-Islam Indoctrination in Public Schools?" *Clarion Project*, Clarion Project, 28 August 2017, https://clarionproject.org/pro-islam-indoctrination-public-schools/

Swaraya. "Prosperity In Scandinavia Is Despite Welfare States, Not Because Of Them." *Swarajya*, Swarajya, 2 August 2016, https://swarajyamag.com/economy/prosperity-in-scandinavia-is-not-due-to-welfare-state-but-despite-it

Telzrow, Michael E. "Socialism's Broken Promises." *New American*, The New American, 25 December 2008, https://www.thenewamerican.com/culture/history/item/4687-socialisms-broken-promises

The White House. "Remarks by President Trump in State of the Union Address." White House, The White House, 4 February 2020, https://www.whitehouse.gov/briefings-statements/remarks-president-trump-state-union-address-3/

Trading Economics. "United States GDP." *Trading Economics*, Trading Economics, https://tradingeconomics.com/united-states/gdp

"U.S. College Enrollment Statistics for Public and Private Colleges from 1965 to 2016 and Projections up to 2028." *Statista*, Statista, https://www.statista.com/statistics/183995/us-college-enrollment-and-projections-in-public-and-private-institutions/

U.S. Department of The Treasury. "History of 'In God We Trust.'" *U.S. Department of The Treasury*, U.S Department of The Treasury, https://www.treasury.gov/about/education/Pages/in-god-we-trust.aspx

Valley News Editorial Board. "Close The Gaps: Disparities That Threaten America." *Bernie Sanders*, Bernie Sanders, 5 August 2011, https://www.sanders.senate.gov/newsroom/must-read/close-the-gaps-disparities-that-threaten-america

Vondracek, Christopher. "Trump signs executive order on international religious freedom." *The Washington Times*, The Washington Times, LLC., 2 June 2020, https://www.washingtontimes.com/news/2020/jun/2/donald-trump-signs-executive-order-international-r/

Vyse, Graham. "Democratic Socialists Rack Up Wins In States." *Governing*, Governing, 9 November 2018, https://www.governing.com/topics/politics/gov-ocasio-cortez-tlaib-Democratic-Socialists-state-level.html

Washington, Bushrod. "Federal Court Issues Ruling on Coach Fired for on-Field Prayer." *The Federalist Papers*, The Federalist Papaers, 24 August 2017, https://thefederalistpapers.org/us/breaking-court-issues-ruling-coach-fired-field-prayer

Wax, Trevin. "Kany West, Justin Bieber, and What to Make of Celebrity Conversions." *TGC*, The Gospel Coalition Inc., 23 September 2019, https://www.thegospelcoalition.org/blogs/trevin-wax/kanye-west-justin-bieber-make-celebrity-conversions/

Wellman, Mitchell. "Here's How Much Bernie Sanders' Free College for All Plan Would Cost." *USA Today*, Gannett Satellite Information Network LLC., 17 April 2017, https://www.usatoday.com/story/college/2017/04/17/heres-how-much-bernie-sanders-free-college-for-all-plan-would-cost/37430393/

Wikipedia. "List of Countries By Government Budget." Wikipedia, WikiMedia Foundation, Inc., 3 May 2020, https://en.wikipedia.org/wiki/List_of_countries_by_government_budget

Wikipedia. "Social Ownership." Wikipedia, WikiMedia Foundation Inc., 5 May 2020, https://en.wikipedia.org/wiki/Social_ownership

WND Staff. "Kanye Urges Blacks: Don't Vote Democrat." *WND*, WND, 8 November 2019, https://www.wnd.com/2019/11/kanye-urges-blacks-dont-vote-democrat/?utm_source=Facebook&utm_medium=PostTopSharingButtons&utm_campaign=websitesharing buttons&fbclid=IwAR3e5N04mftZzXtGHA4nzWqRrNGpdXy1 WJVPIIAv9udFUULjselzozWXWwQ

Yale University. "2018 EPI Results." *Environmental Performance Index*, Yale University, https://epi.envirocenter.yale.edu/epi-topline

Zoellner, Danielle. "Five Major Things Trump Has Done To Roll Back Women's Rights." Independent, 6 March 2020, https://www.independent.co.uk/news/world/americas/us-politics/trump-women-international-womens-day-abortion-policies-healthcare-a9380411.html

Lightning Source UK Ltd.
Milton Keynes UK
UKHW021429281120
374253UK00003B/319